THE MECHANIC'S TALE

THE MECHANIC'S TALE
Life in the Pit Lanes of Formula One

STEVE MATCHETT

MBI Publishing
Company

This edition first published in 1999 by MBI Publishing Company, 729 Prospect Avenue,
PO Box 1, Osceola, WI 54020-001 USA

Text © Steve Matchett
Illustrations © Steven Lee/LAT Photographic
Design © Weidenfeld & Nicolson

First published in Great Britain in 1999 by Weidenfeld & Nicolson

The information in this book is true and complete to the best of our knowledge. All
recommendations are made without any guarantee on the part of the author or publisher, who
also disclaim any liability incurred in connection with the use of this date or specific details.

We recognize that some words, model names and designations, for example, mentioned herein are
the property of the trademark holder. We use them for identification purposes only. This is not an
official publication.

MBI Publishing Company books are also available at discounts in bulk quantity for industrial or
sales-promotional use. For details write to Special Sales Manager at Motorbooks International
Wholesalers & Distributors, 729 Prospect Avenue, PO Box 1, Osceola, WI 54020-0001 USA.

Library of Congress Cataloging-in-Publication Data Available.

ISBN 0-7603-0754-7

Printed in the United Kingdom

The quotation on page 9 is taken from *Three Men in a Boat* by Jerome K. Jerome; those on pages
32, 43, 68, 111, 142 and 146 are from 'Jabberwocky' in *Through the Looking-Glass* by Lewis Carroll,
while that on page 170 is from *Through the Looking-Glass* by Lewis Carroll.

Written for

Signor Benetton and Mr Ecclestone

for showing me the world and for giving me a shot at

the Championship. Thank you.

Also dedicated to the memory of

George, Harris and J.

Three faithful travelling companions

'Will it be the same in the future? Will the prized treasures of today always be the cheap trifles of the day before? Will rows of our willow-pattern diner-plates be ranged above the chimney-pieces of the great in the years 2000 and odd?'
Three Men in a Boat – Jerome K. Jerome, 1888

CONTENTS

Acknowledgements

My sincere thanks to my publisher Michael Dover, my editor Marilyn Inglis and to Claire Wedderburn-Maxwell, the in-house editor at Weidenfeld & Nicolson, for making it happen.

Thanks once again to Steven Tee, the photographers and staff of LAT Photographic for their polite and patient assistance during the research and choosing of the pictures.

Many thanks also go to Alistair Watkins of the FIA for allowing me back into the pit-lane; and to Matt Bishop of *F1 Racing*; James Baker of *Autosport* and Jon Gunn of *On Track*, for helping to keep the wolf at bay – and, of course, to Tony Dodgins for making the initial introductions.

Finally, a very special thank you to Sarah Rouche for proof-reading, chicken, guidance, wine, support and for her wonderful resourcefulness in such difficult conditions.

INTRODUCTION

It was 23 May, the eve of the 1998 Grand Prix de Monaco, and I had been invited by a company called Airtrack, Grand Prix travel agents, to give an after-dinner talk in Monaco about the years I spent working as a race mechanic with Michael Schumacher and Benetton Formula, and how we had finally managed to overturn the dominance of McLaren and Williams to win three Formula One World Championships. Indeed, how we had done it was a very good question. How had we done it? For me, Benetton's success in the mid-nineties had been quite magnificent to behold, although our grand accomplishments were destined to be but a few fleeting moments in the grand scheme of things, a few brief seasons of greatness. Then all too swiftly, the spell was broken and we quickly found ourselves back in the real world – back with the also-rans.

Like a thrown stone, we had taken the Formula One pond by surprise and the ripples had rocked the establishment, disturbing the calm order of things – just for a moment – then the waters had settled again after 1994–5. Things were back to normal and McLaren and Williams resumed fighting for first-place honours. After Benetton's brief interruption, normal service has once again been resumed.

The Monte Carlo Hermitage is one of the most luxurious hotels in the world, and there I was, Steve Matchett, motor mechanic, a glass of bright champagne in hand, relaxed and enjoying the splendid terrace garden, and about to have dinner there too. Before 1990 I had never even dreamed of visiting Monaco, let alone the very notion of dining in one of the Principality's most famous hotels; not only that, ten years ago I hadn't so much as laid a finger on a Grand Prix car. Now less than a decade later, I was a published author and an ex-Formula One World Champion mechanic, a one-time winner of the Monaco Grand Prix, arguably the most prestigious race in the world, and the holder of the 1995 Constructors' Championship. Five years ago I couldn't speak a word of French and now I live in France. How odd, the twists and turns of life.

I stood leaning on the garden wall, sipping my wine and watching the world go by on the road below. For the third time in less than thirty minutes the white 246 was stopped by the security guard at the entrance to the car park near the casino. Really, the driver must have suspected another rejection after the first refusal, but he had driven off, circled round and tried again, and now again. This time the parting was far less amicable, the security guard's posture and the fact that he had removed his black shades to talk to the driver made it quite clear that he didn't want to have to tell him again. While this exchange was in progress, the red F40 slipped alongside hardly noticed and into the car park, a discreet beckoning finger from the security guard's friend was all it took. Both cars had seemingly identical, long and blonde passengers on board. I couldn't be certain from where I stood, but I suspected the 246 had failed to pass muster with the doorman because it still sported the original 'Dino' insignia; certainly there weren't any Prancing Horse stickers on the front wings, the addition of which is normally the first sign that the owner wants his car to be recognized for all its worth. 'Look mate, I've told you before, no Fiats in here, not tonight! Now go away!' The doorman wasn't to know, but the Dino was as much a genuine Ferrari as the F40 – the 246 was just blessed with a more subtle and elegant dress sense.

The overnight train from Bordeaux to Nice hadn't been quite as chic as commuting by Ferrari, but it was infinitely more affordable; the girls alone looked like they'd cost a small fortune to keep amused, let alone the insurance and service bills of trying to run an Italian sports car. Ownership was out of my league, not that it bothered me; I had some pleasant memories of working on Enzo's cars. That was enough; besides, I knew how temperamental they could be without having to have one parked in the barn to remind me.

My train wasn't really a sleeper – there was no in-cabin loo or washing facilities, no privacy at all: the cramped, six-berth compartments were fitted with couchettes, just a small bunk, a blanket and pillow. For eight sleepless hours, as the train lurched and rumbled along the eastbound tracks, five of us had stared into the darkness while our room-mate snored and backfired his way through western France and along the dawn coastline of the Côte d'Azur. It had been a bright, early morning when I climbed from the train at Nice and caught the aged and rattling shuttle service to Monaco; but that was hours ago. Now as I stood on the terrace, the sun had tired and the lights on the opposite side of the harbour were much brighter than they had been just five minutes before. The air was still warm, carrying a little salt from the ocean as the breeze rolled inland, up and over the casino and hotels, and onward through the town, until it finally climbed the mountains behind the Principality, circling high overhead, then back out to sea where it would begin its cycle all over again.

The road below the terrace where I stood was busy but surprisingly not jammed with people; I had expected to see many more. Most were ambling up hill to the square; some dressed in shorts and Dekra hats, red and dripping sweat; others dressed in black, tanned and dripping money. But despite the cars and the bustle, the place was calm and the town retained all its composure. There is never any need to rush in Monaco – unless you happen to be working in a hotel kitchen (or the Formula One pit-lane).

I was travelling alone but had arranged to share a hotel room with Tony Dodgins, a Grand Prix journalist I had got to know over the years. We weren't staying in the Monte Carlo Hermitage, however; I suspect a room here would be only marginally more affordable than the Ferrari. We were staying in Beausoleil, an area technically outside Monaco, separated from the Principality's two-square kilometres of multi-billion dollar real-estate by the width of a narrow street. One side belongs to Prince Rainier and the Grimaldi family, while the other side, paved with a multitude of smiling sun tiles, belongs to the distinctly non-Royalist French Republic. If you sit in a bar and dial the café on the opposite side of the road, a distance no greater than a couple of metres, you need to use the international dialling code. It's easier and cheaper to simply shout through the door the way the locals do.

Following a cramped and sleepless night in the couchette, the hot shower at the Hotel Olympia was utter bliss; such a thing had become a rarity to me over the last few months and I was reluctant to get out and dry off. Since moving to France I hadn't yet managed to install a shower in the old farmhouse – I'd been too busy trying to stop the place from falling down to worry about indulgences like showers and hot water. I'd get round to it eventually, perhaps when I had a bit more spare time on my hands. A shower, a shave, a set of posh clothes and I was ready to leave the hotel and depart France, crossing the road to enter Monaco, a country of quite extraordinary wealth and luxury. *Bienvenue à Monte Carlo.*

A waiter took my empty flute and offered me a fresh glass, and as I took a sip of champagne I heard the first engine start and bark into life. From my distant vantage point across the water at the Hermitage, it was impossible to identify which team it belonged to, but I guessed McLaren; over the last couple of years they always seemed to be the quickest at Saturday-night engine changes. Ten minutes later and another team fired up, then another: nice and gentle for a minute or so, to check for leaks, then a succession of swift rifle-like cracks as the transmission shifted up and down the gears, the engine automatically blipping the throttle on down-changes. The heat of early evening was rapidly disappearing into the chill of the night air; I gave a slight, involuntary shudder.

'*Monsieur, s'il vous plait, votre table vous attend*'– a gentle reminder to come and join the others in the dining room, dinner was served. I'd sneaked a look at our menu a little earlier – we were to start the proceedings off with a thick slice of *paté de foie gras* made with fresh Provençal truffles. Delicious! Before turning away I raised my glass towards the chaps beavering away on the opposite side of the harbour and drank a toast to their good health, then it was time for me to go to work as well. I had not planned what I would say when I stood up to address the guests – I thought I would start at the beginning and hope that the rest would just fall into place.

Steve Matchett
Fayolle, November 1998

Chapter one

1988

*An old riddle answered...How to get into F1...Why
I am talking about 1989 now...A proper
apprenticeship...Working with Ferrari...The 288
GTO...Divine intervention at Monza...*

How long is a piece of string? Any ideas? No? Like you I have always been told that there is no answer to this question; the string can be cut to any length and therefore the problem is unsolvable. And for many years I accepted this apparent conclusion too, until late one evening about twenty years ago, as I lay in bed unable to sleep. It was then that the answer to this annoying riddle came to me. A piece of string is twice as long as from the middle to one end. Eureka!

Now the details of how I finally solved this bothersome puzzle may not seem a very relevant way to begin a book about Grand Prix motor racing, but the significance of finally solving such an age-old conundrum has remained with me ever since. And that is merely this: every problem in life has an answer, you just have to be patient and adaptable. Patient and adaptable. Halfway through the summer of 1989, the problem I was facing was how to get a job in Formula One. The main stumbling block, I supposed, was that I didn't have any race experience. At least, that is what I envisaged the problem to be. But as it had proved impossible to receive any sort of reply from the letters of application I had posted, I may have been misreading and over-complicating the situation. It could simply have been the fact that after a cursory reading of my CV, every team manager in the pit-lane had decided I was a total non-starter and completely unsuited to such a career. In moments of uncertainty I have always underestimated the merits of my own worth, and it has taken me years to fully appreciate my own strengths and weaknesses.

Perhaps the next thing that needs explanation is why I'm already discussing the issues of 1989 when this chapter is clearly entitled 1988, and you're probably beginning to feel a bit perplexed. Well, I'm just trying to set the scene. This book is mainly concerned with the years I spent with Benetton working as a race mechanic, and I'm hoping that this opening chapter will give you some idea of the sort of work that any Grand Prix mechanic could have been doing before their big break into the prestigious world of Formula One. Some mechanics work their way through the junior formulae of motor racing, picking up skills and improving their knowledge as they go from team to team, rising from Formula Ford, to F3, up to F3000, and on into Formula One. Other Grand Prix mechanics worked in the road car industry before moving into Formula One, serving apprenticeships, attending college, and learning both traditional and new skills from a solid background in mechanical engineering. I suppose that both of these tracks have their own individual merits, but after talking to many of the current crop of Formula One mechanics in the pit-lane, the majority seem to have arrived via the college and road car route. Perhaps the engineering of a modern Grand Prix car has become too refined, needing a far greater degree of basic technical competence than was required in the past.

. . .

The mechanical experience and qualifications on my CV must have looked fine on paper; I had worked through an indentured City and Guilds apprenticeship – proudly passing the yearly exams with a series of credits and distinctions. I had found, to my own surprise, that absorbing the academic theory associated with the apprenticeship had come with ease. I enjoyed the logical, problem-solving work that a mechanic is faced with, and when I tried combining these two disciplines, I found that learning became a pleasure. I can only speak for myself, but if one wants to learn, then the task is ninety percent accomplished already. If, on the other hand, one is left wondering what the very point of the lesson is – or, even worse, the pupil is forced to stare blindly at lists of meaningless figures or script until they can be repeated verbatim – the act of learning swiftly becomes like trying to sprint through thick mud; mental barriers are erected and the whole process becomes a nightmare.

It was correct practice throughout the duration of any apprenticeship, whether mastering the art of plumbing, barrel-making or mechanical engineering, to start the trainee with a series of simple tasks and then to carefully introduce more complex work as the appropriate techniques were slowly understood and the requisite skills acquired. If the apprenticeship was carried out correctly, it was a costly, time-consuming process and the manager rarely maked a profit out of the trainee until the third or fourth year of employment. Of course, after his training, as the apprentice slowly matured and evolved into a time-served craftsman, the boss started to see the real benefits of his long-term commitment and loyalty to his junior staff. Regrettably, however, this desire and resolve to improve the quality of the workforce is not always present, and some disreputable firms will merely set their 'apprentices' to work carrying out repetitive, unskilled tasks, maximizing any potential income in return for no real training and at as small a wage as it is legally possible to pay. Cheap labour.

I was one of the fortunate ones. My first job at sixteen was with Howlett's of Loughborough in 1977. Terry Howlett, my first employer – and now a great friend – was a stickler for detail. He's an ex-military man and he ran his workshop in the same fashion: neat, clean, a place for everything and everything in its place. 'Matchett, those tappets are still noisy, do them again! They should sound like a well-oiled sewing machine, not a damn Gatling-gun holding off a dawn offensive. And don't over-tighten them either, come and get me when you're happy with them; and smarten yourself up, you look like a refugee from M.A.S.H.' After tax and national insurance had been deducted, my first brown wage packet, handed out with great ceremony on Thursday afternoon, contained £24.83 in cash. I felt like a millionaire! After giving £5 to my parents towards my board, I was left with the rest: books, records, trips to the cinema, a beer in the Pear Tree, new jeans, even £5 in the building society. To be honest, I had trouble spending it all before yet another brown envelope was handed out and off I would go again. If only the passing years hadn't lost to me the secret of enjoying so much financial freedom for under £25 a week!

The jobs I was allowed to undertake in return for these huge wages started small but grew steadily, and as my education progressed so did my desire to learn and find out more. These classic formative years of training were essential in providing the grounding in the basic common sense that would prove, not merely useful, but imperative throughout the duration of my chosen career. One learns to understand the feel of the work, whether something is either right or wrong. It's almost a sixth sense, a sort of inner knowledge that tells you that the work you have done is finished and that the car is safe to leave your hands. It is the knowledge that a nut and bolt are tight, and not merely cross-threaded; it is understanding the feeling, transmitted through the spanner to the hand, that the threads you are working are of the same type, not a mismatch of metric and Imperial sizes. The awareness that a bolt is tightened just right – neither loose nor so tight that the thread is stretching, the material yielding to the point that it appears to be freeing again. An understanding of the difference, felt through the fingers, that a crankshaft is turning freely or that the bearings are fractionally too tight. A difficult concept to put into words, but knowledge of vital importance. A craftsman from any trade will tell the same story. Like the maturation of a fine wine, it is a proficiency that has to be nurtured slowly and with great care. There are no shortcuts.

In the case of Formula One, possessing this natural aptitude marks a clear line between being a trusted mechanic and a walking (stumbling) liability. It is knowing that when he has fitted a front suspension bolt into the chassis bracket, he has also thought to check that the bolt has passed through the wishbone bearing too, for if it hasn't and the car is allowed to leave the garage, the wishbone will work free and fall off! It is thinking to pump the brake pedal after changing the discs and pads; failure to do so will result in the car shunting into the gravel-trap at the first corner as the startled driver presses the pedal straight to the floor. It is being mature enough to listen to sound advise – and being sensible enough to remember it. It is being able to look and study something logically and have the basic mechanical appreciation to understand why something such as an exhaust coupling, has been designed to have a certain amount of free movement, and that to over-tighten it will, quite obviously, cause it to fail on the circuit.

You might think that all of these terribly basic – and, of course, potentially highly dangerous examples – are quite incredible and fall far below the exacting standards expected of any Grand Prix team employee (and I would wholeheartedly agree with you!) but I have witnessed or heard of every single one of them happening. It is a sad fact of life, but just occasionally someone, loaded with go-kart enthusiasm, will be small enough to wriggle through the sieving effect of the interview net and plunge himself into the grown-ups end of the engineering pool, only to find that he is completely out of his depth and floundering for direction while all the time the driver's life is dependent on his very next action. Quite, quite frightening!

All this constant talk of a 'sixth sense', and a 'natural aptitude' for a certain way of life, sounds a bit Yoda-esque – let the feel be with you – but it is most certainly the case that lessons learned in the early years of mastering a profession are almost impossible to pick up in later life. It boils down to this: either you've got it or you haven't. And for the sake of the others around you, if you haven't got it you shouldn't get involved.

. . .

As an apprentice at Howlett's I grew to love the work of a mechanic and the excitement of working on more and more complex machinery spurred me on. I left Howlett's in 1985, a few years after my training was over, and advanced from the routine servicing of Mazda and Vauxhall family saloons to the more accomplished challenges on offer via the lush engineering of the multi-cylinder engines of Ferrari and the advanced electronics of BMW. I was sad to leave Terry – feeling, in a way, that I was deserting him – but he understood my desires and, in fact, he seemed keen for me to go. I like to think that this was because he was seeing the fruits of his years of devotion finally grow up and mature; more likely it was simply because I had been a complete pain for the past six years and he was delighted to see the back of me.

In 1986 I joined Graypaul Motors, the Ferrari dealer for central England, and without doubt, the time I spent there was great fun. One major advantage of working with such a luxurious marque is that the owners are loaded. This meant that, within reason, we could spend as much time as we liked working on their cars, ensuring that the preparation and finished detail was perfect. For example, on a long restoration project all the nuts and bolts would be sent away to be re-plated; the jubilee clips on the radiator hoses would all face the same direction; the wiring harnesses would be secured with the neatness of a work of art; no expense spared. After all, some of these cars – the 250 GTOs and the Le Mans cars of the 1960s – were valued in millions of dollars, and by the time we had completed the job, their value had risen well above the price that the dealership charged its customer for any work.

By working with a Ferrari dealership my own financial worth had increased too, with my offer-of-employment letter stating: 'Your starting hourly rate will be £3.50 for the first three months, rising to £3.70 and finally to £3.96 after a total of six months' service, plus overtime and bonus if applicable.'

Some mechanics would find the detailed work tedious and unnecessary, but I revelled in the chance to delve into the complex engines and work on a multitude of intricate components. I wasn't the quickest of the workforce – I would hate to rush something – but I would never refuse a challenge, and would always volunteer to tackle the more long-winded jobs. This was not out of some crazed obsession, but merely because I saw it all as a great adventure, a playground where the toys were amongst the most desirable in the world and I'd been given permission to play with them for as long as I wanted. I loved the heady, fresh leather interiors of the new 328s and Testarossas. I delighted in the sense of achievement of finely manipulating the four carburettors of a pre-injection 308 to work in unison – at idle, the tiny spits of fuel and the gentle burble from each choke giving lie to the engine's sumptuous reserves of power. To me, the later fuel-injected cars never had the same appeal. Too reliable.

But even after saying that, it was to be a fuel-injected car that finally won my heart. One bright, sunny morning, Martin Keefe, the service manager, announced that we were expecting a 288 GTO to arrive. If I gave it a quick check-over – tyre pressures, oil level etc. – we would, as a favour to the sales department, take it onto the A6 and carry out a full mechanical appraisal of the car's worth by giving it a thorough, comprehensive road test.

Now, rumour has it that when the 288 GTO was launched from Maranello, Italy in 1984, and was driven through the villages surrounding Modena, the locals lined the streets waving and cheering as this great red beast roared past. The release of this first car – production finally stopped at a grand total of thirty-two – was cause for a whole string of major celebrations. The all-conquering GTO of the 1960s had been reborn and its reincarnation was even more beautiful than the original. The Pininfarina-styled body was based – though much improved – on the slender lines they had pencilled seven years earlier for the 308 GTB, and when painted in bright *rossa corsa*, the new car's looks were, quite simply, gorgeous. Underneath the slatted rear cover lay the 2.8 litre V8 engine. Hence the name: 288. Power supply was assisted by two turbochargers – I'm sure that one would have been more than enough – the car capable of producing around 400 horsepower, and was equally capable of being driven through congested city streets at a stately 30 mph too. Everything about the 288 reeked of perfection, and neither before or after that bright day in the early autumn of 1987, as we drove along the A6 putting the car through its paces (just as a favour) have I ever been so besotted by a piece of mechanical engineering.

I had many enjoyable days such as that, but I finally reached the point where I knew the time was right to look for something more. Of course, after working for Ferrari, moving on wasn't easy; but there was one industry that did appeal. I never really had much interest in Formula One before working with Ferrari. Like everyone, I had watched the occasional race on TV and listened to Murray's commentary – with James Hunt, the knowledgeable ex-driver and master of satire, constantly interrupting and correcting him – but I had never really followed it. But then something happened which completely altered my perception of the sport.

Throughout 1988 McLaren International had totally dominated the season, winning fifteen of the sixteen races, with the team's great rivals, Prost and Senna, in a class of their own all year. No other drivers or team seemed able to touch their spectacular form. The only race they lost that year was Monza – and even there Senna was leading until being punted out of the race in a bizarre incident with one of the trailing Williams cars. McLaren was using the powerful and ultra-reliable Honda engine at the time, and all year the team suffered only one engine failure – Prost's car in Monza. With the two McLarens taken out of contention, the way was clear for the Ferraris of Berger and Alboreto to score an unbelievable one-two victory for Ferrari in front of the team's home crowd. The *tifosi* were ecstatic, not merely because of a home win – although that is always cause for celebration in Italy – but mainly because Enzo Ferrari himself had died only days before the event. It was sensational, an unbelievable result. On the face of it, it appeared as if God had arranged for this victory in the Ferrari cathedral of Monza, in honour of the life-long great work of this legend of both competition and road-going sports cars. Throughout the time I worked for his organization I never met Enzo Ferrari, I don't think we even made so much as eye contact, but it pleases me to think that I worked for his company during a period of his life. In its own way that alone is a pleasing memory to hold.

Genuinely moved by what happened that day in Monza, I was left with the thought that if Grand Prix racing is important enough to be subject to divine intervention, then there must be more to this sport than I had given it credit. I began to take a much wider interest. I bought several books on the subject, I now watched all the races on TV, and by reading the weekly Grand Prix news and features in *Autosport* I gradually became more and more fascinated.

Chapter two

1989

A move to BMW...Ferrari and Mansell race in Imola...
Letters in the post...Not a sausage...A trip to
the coast...Confusion in Estoril...In praise of
Oxford...A Benetton history lesson...A phone call to
Onyx...Benetton's win in Japan

At the end of 1988 I took the decision to leave Ferrari, and moved to a main BMW dealership, still working as a mechanic. I wanted to increase my understanding of the latest, state-of-the-art electronics, and while my time with Ferrari had greatly enhanced my knowledge of elegant machinery, it was BMW, in the late eighties, which led the field as far as modern electronics was concerned.

Ferrari may have been using sophisticated multi-valve, four-cam, alloy-cast V8 engines, even in its entry-level equipment, but for its ignition the company seemed happy, for many years, to use a fairly basic system, consisting of one or two sets of points (with the inevitable problems of cracking distributor caps, corroded rotor arms and ever-changing dwell angles, which are associated with such a system no matter which marque they are fitted to). BMW, however, seemed to be pioneers of any electrical advancement, switching from a mechanically controlled ignition to transistorized electronic ignition, and onwards to a full onboard management system as soon as the next advancement was proven.

Porsche, like BMW, was on a similar electrical crusade, and I could have considered a move there but I instantly liked the calm, friendly atmosphere of the BMW dealership I visited; it was close to home, too. A move to Porsche would have meant travelling further. Besides, after working for Ferrari, switching to Porsche would have been too much of a change of allegiance for me to be happy since these two famous marques have been great rivals for many years. I'm aware that in business, people do switch their professional allegiances all the time – the movement of Formula One staff between the different teams is sometimes difficult to keep track of – and I don't state my reluctance to do the same through any form of holier-than-thou piousness; if people feel they can advance themselves by working with a former rival, then all my best wishes go with them. I would just prefer not to do it myself, although I must admit to coming very close to it once, when Stewart Grand Prix was forming, but that comes years after the period I am discussing here.

In January 1989 I started work for Cooper-BMW at their dealership in Rothley near Loughborough, and my initial impressions of the place proved right: it was as calm and friendly a place to work as is possible to imagine. No rush, no panic. Work, chat, have a coffee, have another coffee, finish your conversation and start work again. The cars arrived, the repairs were carried out efficiently, the cars left again. No one complained, no one had reason to; everyone was just happy to be there and every lunch break we had time to drive to the leisure centre and play squash. One afternoon, as we watched the dealership manager gracefully practising his golf swing as he strolled past us, Chris, one of the mechanics, summed it up perfectly: 'You see Steve, in these workshops everyday is the same, everyday is like Christmas Eve. Every single day'. He was right too.

The job also came with the added attraction of another pay rise, and for the first time I was paid a real 'salary' and even asked to sign a proper contract of employment. I'm still not entirely sure what the differences between a wage and a salary are, but when I read through their covering letter and the particulars of the contract I do remember thinking that being paid a salary sounded very grown-up: 'We wish to confirm our offer of employment with this company, as a service technician, at a salary of £9000 per annum, payable monthly in arrears. In addition an anticipated bonus of £2000 p.a.'.

In April another significant Grand Prix event occurred which finally made me decide that working in Formula One would be my next goal. Just into lap four of the 1989 San Marino Grand Prix in Imola, Gerhard Berger – as a result of a front wing failure – crashed the team's Ferrari 640 at Tamburello (the now infamous flat-out and sweeping left-hander, which was to claim Ayrton Senna five years later). The car, full to the brim with fuel, slammed headlong into the wall, and after the car had finally stopped spinning, its ruptured tank burst into flame. Like millions of others around the globe, I was watching the race coverage at home, staring in bewilderment at the pictures of the car on fire with Berger still strapped inside. It was fourteen seconds before the marshals managed to get to the car, and close to half a minute before the flames were put out. The race was stopped to allow the marshals to extract Berger from the wreckage and to move him into the ambulance. Berger, thankfully, received relatively superficial injuries, but the replay of the accident had made it clear that it could have been much worse. The initial speed of impact had been close to 180mph and the resulting colossal shunt had seen most of the car torn to pieces around him.

Nigel Mansell was driving Ferrari's other 640, and as the cameras focused on him walking back down the pit-lane, it was clear that he was terribly concerned about what had happened. Before the race was restarted, it was suggested by some commentators that Mansell would be foolish to continue driving an identical car, and that Ferrari should withdraw from the race. After all, the team had just experienced a most dramatic front wing failure. But as the cameras showed the reformed grid, Mansell was back in the car, ready to go. James Hunt commented that this was unwise and that, surely, he couldn't be in any mood to race. However, he and Ferrari did race, and two decisive thoughts occurred to me about that. First, Mansell is nobody's fool; occasionally he may be a touch theatrical and, certainly, he is a showman, but he is no clown. However, he is, I thought, definitely a man of brave heart. If he is sitting in the car, then that is his decision, and he must be utterly committed to his position within the team. Second, the Ferrari management must have complete confidence in the safety of their car's design and total faith in their mechanics' workmanship. The commitment and confidence shown by both parties was impressive; that they were prepared to restart and race their other 640, not yielding to the enormous pressure put on them by the fact that if another wing failure did occur, it would be in full, public view of the world's watching millions, leaving both Ferrari and Mansell subject to all kinds of criticism. I believed then – and I still believe – that the decisions taken that day were a most impressive demonstration of team effort under very difficult conditions. Of course, if Mansell's wing had failed, their decision to restart the race would have been very difficult to defend. But happily it didn't. I seem to remember that the box gave up after about thirty-odd laps instead.

...

By now I had really been bitten by Grand Prix motor racing. Thinking back, I suppose the one thing that I thought would appeal to me most about working for a Formula One team was that there seemed to be no budget restrictions at all. We all know that Formula One cars are the most exotic automotive machinery in the world, built to the highest standards and specifications. The job seemed to be the perfect next step forward, with even cleaner, more pristine surroundings than a Ferrari or BMW dealership could offer. There would be a multitude of complex assemblies to strip and to build and to understand, with components machined out of the most expensive materials in the world. I would be surrounded by a team of dedicated people, people used to working to the highest standards, people who enjoyed such detailed work too. I would be in my element. Combined with all that, if I ever managed to get on to a race team I would be flown around the world for free, able to attend the races for free; indeed, I would even be paid for the privilege of doing so! That wouldn't be a job, it would be a dream, a permanent round-the-world cruise. All I had to do was to get in on the act and it is at this point, I believe, that the story really begins.

I had written to Williams and heard nothing. I had written to McLaren with precisely the same response. I tried Tyrrell. No reply. I rang Williams and asked if my letter had arrived. Their receptionist advised me to send another letter. A replacement was in the first post the following morning. Two weeks went by. So did four. Nothing. Onyx? Benetton? Lotus? Not a sausage. Patience. It's all about being patient. Someone out there wants me to work for them, they just don't know it yet. If you really want something and are prepared to work for it. I telephoned McLaren and a girl told me that they didn't need anybody at the moment. I asked her if I could talk to the team manager. She hesitated for a moment and then she told me that he wasn't there, and that I should write instead. I told her that I had written. She told me that I would be hearing from someone soon. She didn't venture as to exactly whom I would be hearing from soon. The line disconnected. I sighed.

A week later I rang Benetton. The receptionist advised that it would be prudent to write to the chief mechanic. I informed her that I had written, but that I had addressed my application to the team manager. She said that in that case I should be hearing from someone soon. I asked for the name of the chief mechanic. She said 'Nigel Stepney'. I wrote to Brabham. I didn't really expect a reply but I wrote all the same. I heard nothing.

Then a letter arrived for me. One morning, on the carpet, was a standard, white business envelope. Now there's nothing very outstanding in that fact alone. Everyday, millions of these standard white business envelopes are in constant circulation around the planet; the peoples of the world telling each other that they might have won the latest state-of-the-art cheese-grater made from high-impact resistant injection-moulded plastic. Or that the lucky recipient of the letter has been especially chosen to receive the honour of having the pigment of their credit card changed from blue to gold. So, in the normal course of events, I wouldn't have been so intrigued to be receiving such an envelope, but this envelope was different. The green print indicated that it was from Onyx Grand Prix. A team had finally written back. I was excited!

The letter was from the team manager of Onyx. He said that he had read my CV and that he would be delighted if I could attend his office for an interview. He asked if I could call him and arrange a mutually convenient time. It was a curious feeling, thinking that at last someone had taken my application seriously. Seriously enough to write and invite me to see the inside of their secretive Grand

Prix headquarters. Me! Steve Matchett, road car mechanic, already in pre-interview discussions with a real life Formula One team manager!

As I sat in my mother's tiny upstairs office, staring at the phone, it seemed most unlikely. Had it really happened? I looked at the scrap of paper on which I had scribbled some vague directions and a time. That seemed real enough. Three-thirty, next Wednesday afternoon. The house was silent. My God, what am I thinking of? I don't know the first thing about Formula One cars. What do I say to him? What will he ask me? What questions do I ask him without sounding utterly stupid? I could see the interview happening before me; imagining the questions he would ask. It was terrifying:

'Ah, Mr Matchett, there you are! I didn't think you were coming! The hour of your arrival allows for a whole new set of parameters to be applied to the word late. Anyway, come in, come in. Please, take a seat; let's get started. Now, you don't mention it here in your letter, at least I don't think you do – it took some time for us to decipher the spider-like scrawl – but you do, of course, have previous F1 experience?'

'Err, well to be perfectly honest, no. I really must apologise for my lateness.'

'No matter, no matter. Well, you have at least worked on single-seater race cars before; F3000, or F3s?'

'No. I'm sorry, no, I haven't.'

'Any form of racing?'

'No; err, no, not as such, no, sorry.'

'I see. How about carbon fibre? Ever worked with that? Chassis, brakes, that sort of thing?'

'Err, no. I mean, not actually carbon fibre, no. Glass-fibre I've used a bit; but not really the carbon type of fibre, no.'

'I see, I see. So, let me sum up what we have so far: never worked in F1; never worked in single-seaters, nor, indeed, in any form of motor racing at all, and never worked with carbon before either. Is that about it?'

'Yes; I think that about covers it. I'm sorry. I have set the Weber carbs up on a 308. Oh, and I've changed the cam belts on 512 Boxer and the gearbox and clutch on a 5 Series BM!'

'Goodbye, Mr Matchett. Will you see yourself out, there's a good chap?'

'Engine rebuild on a Testarossa?'

'Goodbye Mr Matchett, and please don't slam the door when you leave.'

...

Despite my fears of appearing completely inadequate, I couldn't have been more wrong. The trip to the Onyx factory was a wonderful experience. I had decided that I would go through with the interview the following week. At least I'd get the chance to look around the factory, perhaps even a glance at the race cars. The factory was on the south coast at Arundel, a stone's throw from Brighton and her famous pier. I would make a day of it: a trip to the seaside, a tour round Onyx, a walk on the prom, a beer in a quayside pub. Why not?

I set off early on Wednesday morning since it was a long drive, nearly five hours. It was hot too, with bright, late summer sunshine all the way. During the journey to the coast I tried to recall all I knew about Onyx (it wasn't much). They were a new young team, set up by a chap called Mike Earle. I hadn't heard of him, to be honest. I later discovered that he was a big name from Formula 3000, who had finally made the giant leap up to Formula One; but as I'd never studied F3000, I didn't know of him. The Onyx cars were pleasantly presented, painted a rich, deep blue, trimmed with pink and white. They were primarily sponsored with money from Marlboro and Moneytron, the latter a company owned by a huge and enigmatic Belgian, Jean-Pierre Van Rossem. At least I'd heard of him, even if I knew nothing of Mike Earle. Jean-Pierre was a financial wizard who had made millions on the stock market. A giant of a man, who by wearing his range of massive, flowing shirts and keeping his long hair in the same liberated style, simply refused to conform to the more traditional dress-codes associated with such wealthy businessmen. He sounded a fun sort of a chap.

I arrived in Arundel in plenty of time, a little after one o'clock. I managed somehow to scramble the directions to the Onyx factory by trying to hastily scribble notes while talking on the phone; I didn't want to appear dim by asking the team manager to repeat everything while I wrote it all down. I thought I'd ask a local and so pulled into a small petrol station. I smiled amiably and inquired of the big, heavy man behind the counter, munching his Mars bar, if he had ever heard of a company called Onyx Grand Prix and if he might possibly have any idea where they were located. The attendant's response rather took me by surprise. Slowly closing the magazine he was reading and calmly laying it on his small wooden desk cluttered with all sorts of papers and chocolate wrappers, he steadily fixed me with rapidly glazing eyes. He started to tremble slightly, his face already glowing a deep, ruby red with some mysterious, though obvious great annoyance. He looked ready to explode. 'For God's sake!' he roared, bits of chocolate sprayed the air, some sticking to his shaggy beard on their way out. I took a step backwards, turning round to see what had given the chap such an odd turn, but could see nothing out of place. Placing both hands on the desk in front of him he breathed deeply, once and then again, raising his eyes to the ceiling. 'Bloody hell!' he bellowed again. 'If I had a quid for every time I've been asked that, I'd be a sodding millionaire! Why don't you lot learn to read a bloody map? I tell you what I'm going to do,' he yelled, staring straight at me again, 'I'm going to stick a map on the sodding door over there,' he gestured with his head to where I had come in, 'and put a big red circle with "you are here and this is Onyx over there" written on it in big, bright red sodding letters. That's what I'm going to do!'

The chap was really rising to his subject now and had started to throw the clutter off his desk, presumably looking for his Ordinance Survey maps. I was a bit worried; his excited onslaught had caught me off guard. I didn't really know what I was supposed to say in response either. I pondered the situation for about half a second and concluded that saying nothing would probably be the most prudent policy to adopt. I quietly backed away and slipped out the door. Best to leave and let him get it all off his chest. I jumped into my old Escort and locked the door; he was still ranting to himself and shaking his head as I cautiously drove off his forecourt. The thing that still confuses me about the whole encounter was trying to figure out exactly who 'you lot' might be referring to.

A few hundred yards down the road the lights changed colour and I pulled up at a zebra-crossing. Two old ladies, both with hats and walking-sticks, were waiting to cross in front of me; one was offering her friend a little paper sweet bag. The green man was lit for them but they were obviously in no hurry to go anywhere. I lowered the window, thinking to ask for directions, but something made me chicken out at the last minute. I slowly put the window up again. The people from around here seemed a mite touchy for some reason, and besides, there were two of them this time. I came across the Onyx factory shortly after: a huge old manor house containing the offices, its outbuildings converted to accommodate the race team. Set in gardens and green lawns it was a most handsome-looking facility. From the car park I could already see the two brightly painted transporters waiting to be loaded for the next Grand Prix; four people, presumably the team's truckies, were hard at work washing the trailers. What a sight! It was worth a five-hour drive just to see the building and the trucks. I walked towards reception with goose-bumps on my arms. Ten years later, recalling these memories and setting them down here, it seems odd, laughable even, that the sight of a couple of race trucks could have brought me out in such goose-bumps of excitement. But they did. I was absolutely thrilled to the core.

Greg Field, the Onyx team manager, collected me from reception and led me through the corridors to his office. A few years later Greg was to join me at Benetton in the role of race team co-ordinator (he had worked at Benetton prior to his Onyx days too). But, on that hot summer's day in 1989, we were total strangers. He, a long-established member of the Formula One fraternity just getting through another day at work, with me being merely another interview for him to conduct. When Greg and I met again at Benetton I reminded him of our initial encounter at Onyx, but he couldn't remember it, yet I can recall every nuance like it took place only yesterday.

The interview went fairly well, I thought. The team was looking to expand its sub-assembly operation, the department where the brakes, uprights and gearboxes, etc. are rebuilt before being handed over to the car crews for the final building onto the chassis. Greg had read my CV and thought that this sub-assembly work would be a good place for someone with no race experience but with a comprehensive background in mechanics to begin a career within Formula One. This made me feel far more at ease; at least there was a chance for someone from outside the world of motor racing to break into this somewhat closed world.

He also asked if I had any 'transverse' gearbox experience, pointing out that this seemed to be the coming trend in transmission design and that mechanics with some practical knowledge of their design might prove useful to the team in the future. Basically, a transverse-designed box moves the shafts and the gear-cluster through 90 degrees, so that in the car they are mounted east-west, as opposed to north-south. The thinking behind this idea was to enable the mass of the ratios and shafts inside the gearbox to move further to the centre of the car. Some designers thought the transverse design was the next big step forward, others didn't. Looking back now, having worked with both the transverse layout and the traditional in-line 'longitudinal' designs (at Benetton we went from longitudinal to transverse and back to longitudinal again), the bottom line is that both systems are good if they are working correctly, and both systems are bad if they aren't. Now, some designers may argue with that brief summary of the merits of each system; but they're wrong to do so. I have seen both systems win races and I have also seen both systems fail to get the car to the end of the pit-lane.

When Greg asked me if I had worked on transverse systems, I told him that Ferrari used transverse gearboxes on all of their rear engine-mounted cars. However, I explained, Ferrari also used transverse engines too. Indeed, the Ferrari transverse engine/gearbox layout was the same in its basic principles to that of an Austin Mini. The only difference was that Austin-Morris had mounted its design in the front, while Ferrari had it fitted in the rear. Formula One designers, on the other hand, were planning to retain their longitudinally mounted V8s, 10s, and 12s, and couple them to a transverse box. This was very different to what I had worked with, requiring the use of two 45-degree bevel gears mating together, which would then allow the drive from the engine to turn through 90 degrees inside the gearbox. (In fact, the later generation of 'mass produced' Ferrari road cars such as the 348, did make use of this design, but they came along after my time.) Greg seemed impressed that even if I hadn't worked on such systems, at least I seemed to understand their operation.

During our conversation that afternoon, Greg told me that before joining Onyx to become the team manager, he had spent many years with Benetton, a time which he had greatly enjoyed, and had only decided to leave because of the offer from Onyx. He had worked with Benetton as the travelling parts co-ordinator, an odd-sounding job title, which basically means issuing and restocking the race trucks with sufficient components to keep the cars in active service throughout a Grand Prix weekend. The job also involves keeping a tally of exactly how many kilometres the numerous components have covered each time they are assigned to a different chassis. Every part on the car has its own serial number, etched on to it if (and only if) it passes the stringent inspection checks after manufacture. This system is universal throughout Formula One. Woe betide any race mechanic who inadvertently fits a component without its own identification number. This means that it has either not yet been inspected or that it has, for whatever reason, failed inspection and shouldn't under any circumstances be in the system. This process of continually tallying the cumulative distance that the individual parts have covered is known as 'lifing' (pronounced life-ing), and is done to ensure they can be removed from the system before they can possibly suffer fatigue failure. For example, if component X is calculated to have a useful life of 1000 kilometres, then it will be scrapped at around 900. Actually, scrapped is not really the correct word; when the components are withdrawn from the race team's use, the remaining kilometres are used up by the test team, and when the part is finally declared 'dead' it will be used to build one of the show cars displayed at annual motor shows and used for promotional work by sponsors.

After the interview I was given a guided tour of the factory. I was shown the race shop where the chassis and the myriad of individual components are finally assembled to become a complete car. Greg also showed me the gearbox shop (and although he was terribly careful not to point out anything specific I managed to see enough to realize that Onyx was already using a transverse gearbox!). I was even shown the layout of the tools and the equipment inside the trucks that the mechanics use when they travel away. I was awe-struck. It was like being a child again, let loose in Santa's workshops. Wherever and whatever I looked at there was something else that grabbed my attention a little further on. I remember thinking how calm and matter-of-fact Greg appeared when he showed me one of the cars' carbon floors leaning against a wall, worn and damaged in a previous race weekend. There was a fist-sized hole in one side. 'Yeah, it's knackered,' he said when he saw me taking an interest in the damage, 'something fell off one of the McLarens, Senna's car. I think it was a skid, or whatever. Anyway, it did enough that it needed changing'.

It was fantastic! Here I was holding a piece of a Grand Prix car, a piece that had a hole in it, a hole made by a skid from Ayrton Senna's McLaren. Ayrton Senna! I was holding a piece of Formula One history in my hand. Of course, when I was working in the pit-lane for a living, the magic of such moments was soon, sadly, lost to me, but at that precise moment, I felt like Carter holding and examining a newly discovered jewel from one of the lost tombs of Egypt.

Then Greg asked me if I knew why I had been invited for an interview. I said that I was delighted that I had been asked but admitted that I had no idea why he had short-listed me. It was the neat presentation of my letter and CV, he explained. Mine was the only one he had received which had been written with such care and then enclosed in a display folder. This, he said, had made me stand out from the rest. It was the only one I had sent out in such a fashion too, the plastic folder just happened to be laying around at home; I hadn't given it a thought since I had posted it off several weeks before. I made a mental note of what he had said. He thanked me for coming and told me he'd be in touch (thanked me!).

I drove the few miles to the coast, walked a while and stood on the prom, thankful that the afternoon breeze carried away a little of the sun's heat. I recalled the interview, what I had seen, the questions I had asked and been asked. I felt as though I'd glimpsed the secrets of another world. I watched gulls hanging above the waves.

> *Long time the manxome foe he sought,*
> *So rested he by the Tumtum tree,*
> *And stood awhile in thought*
>
> ...

Obviously, I heard nothing. To have heard something would have been far too easy. The interview had gone well, Onyx wanted more staff and I wanted to work with Onyx; it would seem, therefore, to have been a relatively simple matter to resolve. A week went by, followed very, very slowly by another one, but there was no response. I always find it difficult to know what to do for the best in these situations. Should I wait a week and then give the company a call, or would such a move appear as though I was pestering and so be a negative factor? Or should I call after a scant few days, to reaffirm my interest in the job and to remind them of who I am? Should I wait two weeks before calling? Is three weeks too long, by which time they've offered the job to someone else, someone keener, someone who bothered to phone two weeks earlier? How time drags when you are waiting for something to happen. My move to BMW had been done and dusted in less than two hours. I met Andrew Weston, the service manager, for coffee at ten o'clock, he showed me the workshops and explained how the service department operated; we chatted about money, and at midday when I left him it was with a verbal agreement that the job was mine, a start date and an assurance that a contract would be in the post to me the same afternoon. It arrived the following day; throughout my time with them I was to discover that such swift efficiency was a BMW trademark.

I decided to think and remain positive. I would wait for a while longer before calling Onyx and, in the meantime, I would reapply to another team as well. For two reasons I decided that Benetton would receive another letter from me. The team was based in Witney, north Oxfordshire, which meant that Benetton was the closest team to home and I'd managed to discover the name of the chief mechanic. This was a bonus, allowing me to write to a real person as opposed to my previous applications which were addressed to either 'Dear Sir' or 'For the attention of the team manager'. He was called Nigel Stepney, and it was to him that I posted another copy of my CV and a rewritten letter of introduction, neatly penned and presented within a glossy, new display folder (I had bought a packet of them shortly after my Onyx trip).

I had included an extra line in my letter too: 'following on from recent conversation where an interest was expressed in my transverse gearbox experience, I have enclosed a copy of my CV for your perusal. I would be delighted to attend your office for an interview at any convenient time'. I hadn't spoken to Nigel before, but what I had written was true enough: there had been a conversation about my gearbox experience (with Greg, at Onyx); I had enclosed a copy of my CV and I would, most certainly, be delighted to attend for an interview. There was a possibility, I thought, that adding this extra line might prompt Nigel to contact me sooner rather than later. 'Has someone asked this chap to send his details through to me personally? Perhaps this is just who we've been looking for? Maybe I should see him before he gets snapped up by another team? I should contact him today; this very morning!' It was worth a go. Possibly my letter was a mite forward and the wording may have contained a modicum of ambiguity, but if it helped to get me through the Benetton doors for an interview I could then explain who it was I had chatted with about transverse boxes. Getting the interview in the first place, that's the difficult thing; the clarifying of details can always be done over coffee and biscuits when the desired meeting is actually in progress.

...

For those lucky enough to already be working in Formula One, the 1989 season was swiftly drawing to a close. On the Sunday afternoon that I wrote to Benetton, the Grand Prix circus had assembled in Estoril for round thirteen of the World Championship. I remember watching the race on TV, and while I was checking the spelling and grammar of my new application letter, the mechanics were leaving the grid as the drivers set off on their formation lap. It was to be a memorable Grand Prix, well, at least it was for me.

The race was well over half run with Mansell's Ferrari leading from Berger in the other 640 and the two MP4/5 McLarens of Senna and Prost, the two Championship protagonists. On lap 39, Mansell stopped for tyres but for some reason he overshot the Ferrari garage on his way down the pit-lane. He pulled up and waited to be moved back, but total confusion broke out amongst the mechanics as they debated what they were and were not allowed to do in such a situation. Were they forbidden to touch the car in its present position, leaving the driver to reverse with the risk of hitting any mechanics hidden from view behind the rear wing, or was it against the regulations to select reverse gear in the pit-lane? Should the mechanics pull the car back, or was it an infringement of the rules to undertake any work beyond their designated pit area? Was it the case that only the circuit marshals were allowed to move a stranded car? Was the car stranded? Certainly no one would expect the marshals to have a comprehensive understanding of Grand Prix regulations – they are all local volunteers, not FIA employees – so the team couldn't count on them for a correct ruling on the matter. Arms flapped, some mechanics rushed forward, some backed away. In the end, by selecting reverse and pottering backwards, Mansell made the decision himself. The mechanics regrouped and renewed the tyres before dispatching Mansell back into the race. With no harm done, an innocent and accidental situation had been rectified by the driver. Mansell was immediately disqualified from the race. 'Whilst in the pit-lane a car cannot be driven in reverse under its own motive power.' The FIA informed Ferrari of their decision to vanquish car number 27 from the event, inviting the team to call their driver into retirement, thus saving both team and driver the ignominy of the black flag and the public humility of being so brazenly evicted from the Grand Prix.

However, Mansell – now dog-fighting with Senna for second place – ignored the radio and the pit-board messages from his team, later claiming that he was concentrating on Senna's driving so much that he wasn't aware of anything else. This left the race officials no choice but to show Mansell the black flag, and this was duly unveiled and shown to him above the start/finish line (along with a board displaying his car number). He ignored that too. The next lap he did exactly the same. I couldn't believe what I was watching! How could a driver of Mansell's calibre blatantly ignore such a stringent order? The issues and arguments that lead the FIA to find it necessary to display the black flag may be open to many long and multi-sided debates, but these debates can only take place after the event. It is utterly pointless to argue the rights, the wrongs and the mitigating circumstances at the same time as the flag is being unfurled. The black flag means Game Over; no ifs, no buts. Finished. A driver or team may try to defend their actions and contest any imposed penalty at the post-race enquiry (though I cannot recall a single successful appeal being lodged against an FIA ruling), but to dishonour the black flag and drive on is simply asking to suffer greater and greater penalties.

Mansell drove down the pit-straight and ignored the flag for a third time. He was very close to Senna's rear wing now, poised to make his move on the McLaren. During this lap Ron Dennis tried to make radio contact with Ayrton, telling his driver to yield to Mansell's Ferrari, as there was no reason to race against a disqualified car. Apparently Senna struggled to hear the message and asked his boss to repeat the message. But by then it was too late; Mansell made his move, dashing down the inside of the McLaren. As the pair of cars approached the corner Ayrton stayed true to his racing line and the gap that Mansell had bolted towards quickly melted away. The cars collided and instantly the McLaren's right-rear suspension was destroyed; both cars were out of the race.

The consequences were far-reaching, and with Senna still chasing Prost for the

Drivers' Championship he should never have been fighting with a car that had been disqualified several laps prior to their shunt. The whole situation struck me as being quite bizarre. Why hadn't Mansell responded to his radio, his pit-board or the flag? Why hadn't Ayrton been informed of Mansell's disqualification as soon as the situation became clear? Indeed, why hadn't Senna seen the black flag and the number of the car that had been disqualified and himself realize that Mansell's race was effectively over? Surely, Ayrton must have noticed the black flag? After all, until he had identified the number of the car to which the penalty applied there was a possibility that the flag was being shown to him for some reason. Yet the details of what was happening and the facts of the dilemma between Mansell and the FIA officials obviously weren't clear to him.

Mansell was later fined $50,000 and banned from participating in the next race. His explanation was that he was concentrating so hard on following Senna that he never heard his radio, and because of strong sunlight he never saw the pit-board and never saw the flag. And Senna was also unsure about what was happening on the start/finish line that day. I watched that Estoril Grand Prix completely fascinated by all the confusion and misunderstanding between the mechanics, the team managers and the drivers. Also, what of the race officials' inability to impose their black flag disqualification? How were they proposing to stop Mansell if he hadn't stopped himself by shunting into the McLaren? It became clear to me that day that the orchestration of Formula One wasn't note-perfect after all.

That night I mailed my letter, and on my way back from the post-box I called into the Boat for a Sunday evening beer. I thought about these questions and came to the conclusion that the whole black flag procedure was totally inadequate. The basic facts of what had happened in Estoril proved it too. At that time, Nigel Mansell and Ayrton Senna were among the very top of the world's elite racing drivers, the creme de la creme; both talented and gifted with natural speed and superb reactions. Yet neither of them – apparently because of the sun – saw the black flag which the officials were showing the Ferrari driver; certainly Mansell would have been in no doubt about the severity of the penalty for ignoring it. We must, therefore, believe them and assume that they simply did not see it. The marshals, stationed at numerous posts around the perimeter of the track, each have a full set of flags, and any visual communication is passed on from post to post. However, the officials' procedure for instant disqualification only allows for a solitary flag to be displayed, shown above the start-line, a place where the drivers would normally never look, and if the sun is streaming towards them then they will never see it. Throughout the duration of the whole lap the drivers are subjected to only one, momentary flash of the flag as the cars scream past; but if the marshals' posts were all issued with a set of numbers and a black flag, then the message could be clearly and continually displayed to the intended driver on each and every lap until he responded. It would seem a simple answer.

Whatever solution the FIA finally decided upon, I reasoned, I felt certain that any potential future problems arising out of a lack of clear communication between the race officials and the drivers would be swiftly addressed. Surely, the governing body of such a prestigious sport wouldn't allow a repeat of such a farcical situation to occur in the years ahead, would they? Time for bed; leaving the chatter and the hoppy smell of the pub behind me I headed off home.

I don't know the reasons for their swift reply but just over a week after posting my CV another white, business envelope lay on the hall carpet. Benetton Formula Ltd had written back. On the envelope, a little green bunny rabbit hopped next to the company name. A small detail – no bigger then an inch long – but I took the inclusion of this little rabbit as a sign that this team was just a bit different from the rest. It seemed to imply a slight tongue-in-cheek knock at the establishment, as if the rabbit was whispering 'Loosen up a bit, boys, you're all taking this sport a fraction too seriously. We're all here to do a good job and try to win races, but we can still enjoy ourselves while we're at it!' And if the Benetton rabbit was indicating that then it was echoing a philosophy similar to my own: to live is a tremendous privilege, simply to experience a little of the world and to devour the skills and ideas of those who have gone before. But life is a gift on loan, and in comparison with our surroundings, even a long, full life of a hundred years is but a passing moment. We should be resolute in enjoying the experience of the fleeting time we have, and we should try never to regret a second or waste even a moment of it in bitterness; yesterday has already gone forever.

...

Oxford, 'that sweet city with her dreaming spires', that great and noble seat of English learning. Imagine everything that is both exciting and vibrant about Oxford: the carved facades and exquisite stonework of her majestic college buildings with their long centuries of values and heritage and tradition. Her celebrated Bodleian library, containing at least one edition of every book to be published in Britain; the athletic challenge of the Isis river, whose waters flow past the college boat-houses, with teams of devout rowers constantly in training for inter-collegiate competitions and the chance for the lucky few to defend Oxford's honour against the might of Cambridge. The emotion and inspiration of Mozart's Requiem heard within the surrounds of the Sheldonian Theatre; the grand elegance of the Randolph Hotel; the intimate snug of the Eagle and Child where C.S. Lewis planned his next excursion to Narnia. Let your mind meander through the glorious sunshine and gentle breeze of a lazy summer's afternoon spent in the tranquility of Christ Church Meadow. Imagine all of these splendid things; rejoice in them, treasure them, hold them, lift them to the skies. Now drop them, see them shatter and lose them forever. What you're left with is a vision of Witney. Witney is a small, dull and utterly uninspiring provincial market town, about twenty minutes drive north-west of her infinitely more distinguished relative. And it was to Witney that I drove for my interview with Nigel Stepney.

The one overriding memory I have of that first trip to Benetton was how fantastically uncomfortable the chairs in reception were; black leather and chrome, with the seat raked backwards at a jaunty forty-five degrees. And low, so that when you sat down your buttocks slid to the rear and downwards, leaving the feet just touching the carpet. In sharp contrast to the height of the seat, the armrests were incredibly high – only slightly shy of being parallel with the shoulders – while the chair's back was but a token strip of leather. Thus, if a potential employee, trying to maintain an air of unruffled calm, despite boyish excitement, was foolish enough to slide into one of these contraptions while waiting for the company's chief mechanic, he would find himself deprived of all leverage from either legs or arms when he tried to stand again. This made for a most undignified initial introduction to his next likely boss. The chairs' complete inability to offer the user even the most scant comfort left the sitter in no doubt that these design objects were the pinnacle of all that was totally groovy in the art of interior fashion design. Totally groovy and totally useless.

In complete contrast to the pleasing vista of the Onyx manor house, the Benetton factory was located in a small, drab, enclosed industrial estate, just out of the town centre, in an area known as Station Lane. The factory – like the team – had started small and had slowly grown over the years; as soon as an adjoining unit, or one on the other side of the yard became available Benetton would grab it and take over the lease. Thus over a period of time the factory had expanded in haphazard fashion, giving the impression of a rabbit warren.

The chief mechanic's office was housed above the race-bay, overlooking the main workshops where the cars were stripped, rebuilt and prepared for the next Grand Prix. Nigel shook my hand with a polite but definite firmness, which immediately conveyed that he was a man who meant business and who didn't suffer fools lightly. It has always been my experience that a handshake tells worlds about a person's personality; a weak, limp shake is a sure sign that one is about to embark on a damp and vague conversation, while a bone-crunching clamp is but a reinforcement that it is pointless to proffer any views or opinions in the ensuing exchange of dialogue. Fortunately, Nigel's handshake fitted neither of these two extremes, but was an impressive I'm-a-busy-man-but-let's-see-if-we-can-do-business type of a shake.

Nigel had only recently joined Benetton after many years service with Team Lotus where he was Senna's Number-one mechanic before the Brazilian moved to drive for McLaren International. Over the next few months I quickly discovered that Nigel was extremely ambitious and he would only spend an absolute minimum amount of time away from work. He would regularly work from 7 am until 6 pm, go home for an hour and then work from 7 pm until 2 or

3 am the next day; and four hours later he would start again. He simply loved his work: designing pit equipment; using the mills and lathes when the machinists had gone home; reading through endless paperwork; pushing the production staff to come up with the new parts for the cars; badgering the race engineers to finalize their set-up sheets so his mechanics could finish the car builds. It was non-stop, he was always doing something.

Nigel began the interview with a brief history lesson of the company, the rough gist of which, albeit somewhat embellished with a few of my own observations, follows. In 1986 Luciano Benetton, the Italian multi-millionaire and founder of the enormously successful Benetton fashion house, bought the struggling Toleman Formula One team, which he had previously sponsored, finally deciding that it made infinitely more sense to own a team rather than merely rent part of the paint-work. If he owned the cars Luciano could dictate exactly how the livery and the sponsors' logos should look without having to negotiate a deal with some tediously pretentious marketing assistant with a bulging filofax and a dormant pager. Luciano's great expertise lies in image and marketing and as an owner, he could carefully cultivate the team's image to maximise Benetton's exposure on these 200 mph carbon billboards which he had just bought. Plus, owning your own Grand Prix team is an enormous earner (and don't let anyone try to convince you otherwise).

Luciano Benetton is far too rich to run a motor-racing team himself, so he appointed Flavio Briatore to look after it for him. He had been running the New York arm of the Benetton fashion business for Luciano and, by his own admission, he knew absolutely nothing about Formula One. In which case, thought his boss, you will be perfect for the job. The engineers will run the cars, you go in there with a fresh approach and a clear sheet, sell the advertising space and find the money. Fancy the job? Good, you start on Monday. Flavio did a good job too; the cars were bright and colourful, and the money kept coming in, perhaps not massive amounts but enough to keep the team in business.

He then persuaded one of his colleagues from New York, Patrizia Spinelli, to leave America and join him in Oxfordshire. Patrizia is a PR genius; in the States she specialized in organizing sleek photo-shoots of the latest Benetton collections and getting the perfect exposure for the fashion company's fresh offerings by placing them in just the right publications. Her appointment to Benetton Formula proved an inspired choise and she enormously enhanced the public image of the race team; through her contacts with the world of chic lifestyle magazines, she managed to promote the team in areas of the media whose editors would normally choke on their low-cal spritzers at the very idea of including photographs and articles about stinking, oily race cars.

Being owned by such a big concern as the Benetton Group meant that the team had a strong financial basis from which to grow, but results on the track had been poor. True, they had won a race in their initial year as Benetton Formula Ltd but one lone victory wasn't really what Luciano had in mind for his new team. People (read: big, well-heeled sponsors) like to be associated with a winner and for the Benetton marketing formula to work, the team had to win a lot more than just once; it was, therefore, time to restructure the technical side of the company.

Halfway through 1989 Ferrari announced that John Barnard would not be staying with the team for the following year. At the time Barnard was considered to be among the leading Formula One designers in the business (some said the best), and if Ferrari, for whatever reason, wished to part with him then so be it, but Barnard certainly wouldn't be out of work for long. Cue, Flavio and the Benetton Formula cheque book. And in October, after all the details had been finalized and the contracts had been read, rewritten, reread, signed and finally exchanged, a Witney press release stated that Mr John Barnard would be joining Benetton Formula as the team's technical director for the 1990 season onwards.

Even when working with Lotus, Stepney had always held Barnard's design work in high esteem; when the prospect of becoming Benetton's chief mechanic arose, Nigel jumped at both the chance of promotion and the possibility to work alongside the great man himself. Next came the announcement that, for the next two years, three-times World Champion Nelson Piquet had been contracted to the team as their Number-one driver. With the finance in place, Barnard as designer, and Piquet in the car, it was now quite obvious that Benetton was looking to Formula One big-time.

...

Back to Stepney's office and my interview. The team was growing and it wanted to increase the sub-assembly department to cope with the expansion. It was almost certain that Barnard would be designing and testing a transverse gearbox for his car and Nigel was impressed with my working knowledge of the Ferrari systems. I looked enthusiastic and thanked him. (I then moved the conversation quickly on, choosing not to expand on the subject of just how deep my knowledge of these boxes actually was.). 'Of course,' he explained, 'we wouldn't let you loose on the gearboxes straight away. You'd start by building the uprights and steering-racks; little by little'.

'Well, there we are,' said Nigel, smiling, 'that's us and what we're up to. Now, financially, what will it take to drag you away from BMW?' Drag me away? I'd have started work for them there and then! I told him what I was earning and said I'd be quite happy to be paid the same. 'We can do that,' he assured me, 'we could even go a little more, how does £15,000 sound?' An instant £4000 pay rise? I would have taken a drop in wages if he had asked but I didn't tell him that.

Okay, well, thank you for coming to see us Mr Matchett, we'll be in touch in a week or so.' Another firm handshake. 'Oh,' added Nigel as I walked towards the

Escort, 'I liked the presentation of your letter, it looked quite striking in that folder and I liked the way it read too; nice touch that. I like it when people push a bit!' I felt my face beginning to warm; now it was Nigel's turn to use slightly ambiguous wording. 'Sorry,' I said, 'perhaps it was a bit...'

'No, it was good,' he interrupted, 'very carefully written! I'll be in touch.'

This was perfect. Here was a chance to work with real professionals, in a company that looked financially secure, and judging by the casual atmosphere of the factory (the mechanics were all wearing team-issue Benetton jeans embroidered with the team's logo) my initial impressions about their relaxed philosophy to the job seemed correct. This was the team for me. If I was excited by the possibility of working with Onyx, I was doubly so at the idea of joining Benetton.

...

9th October 1989

Dear Mr Matchett,
Further to your recent interview on 4th October.
We are unable to offer you a position as detailed in our discussions on your recent visit to us. Up until the 6th October you and another candidate were in the running for a position within our team, but due to certain policy changes within the structure of our company, we have withheld any further employment of personnel in certain departments, of which Sub-assembly is one.
We shall be reviewing our staff recruitment situation at the beginning of 1990 and your name is high on the list of contenders.
Yours sincerely,

FOR AND ON BEHALF OF BENETTON FORMULA LIMITED

Nigel Stepney,
Chief Mechanic

...

What a devastating blow to morale. That morning, when I saw another of Benetton's rabbits hopping around the hall, I really thought that this was it: game on! But no. It took some minutes of gentle persuasion to carefully separate the letter and the envelope too, as Heidi – Mum's black and somewhat loopy collie cross – had tried to eat most of it before declaring it tasteless. Heidi, an unwanted pup who had decided to adopted us some years before, had grown into a wonderful friend: ferociously brave at the sound of the door bell, docile as a lamb with children and calming, easy company at night. In other words, the perfect house dog. But not once, throughout her long and distinguished life, did she ever allow the post through the door or the milk to arrive on the step without making a massive scene. I still have that letter from Nigel – perforated by the bites of a hundred eager teeth – which is how I've managed to reproduce the exact wording of it here. On first reading it I swiftly concluded that it meant 'thanks, but no thanks'. However, at work later in the day, where I read it again, feeling a little more optimistic, I decided that, perhaps that final, slightly enigmatic line might contain just a glimmer of hope. Before bed, when I read it a third time, I settled on the idea that I had been right in the first place and that it really did mean no.

The next morning I rang Onyx and asked to speak to Greg Field. The voice on the other end of the line told me that Mr Field was no longer with the company. I asked to be put through to the new team manager, who told me that things were a bit chaotic at the moment and that he could find no record of my interview taking place. I asked if I could see him and go through the interview process again? 'Why not send me your details in the post,' he said, 'but when we do need someone we normally advertise our vacancies in the national motoring press. Why not keep an eye on the appointments page in *Autosport*?' he advised before giving a curt goodbye. Less than two weeks after receiving the letter from Nigel Stepney, Benetton went on to score their second Grand Prix victory, with Alessandro Nannini being elevated from second place and declared the race winner. Ayrton Senna, after that infamous coming together with Prost, was disqualified from the results despite winning the Japanese Grand Prix, a decision which also deprived him of the Drivers' Championship.

It was a result filled with bitterness for Senna, although not directed towards Nannini or Benetton, but the FIA were later to feel the full force of the Brazilian's anger; and it certainly wasn't the most desirable way for Benetton to claim another win, but in Formula One you grab the trophies when and where ever they are offered. Whether declared the winner or not, even to be able to follow Senna's McLaren across the finish-line was sufficient to indicate that Benetton was finally getting its act together and was clearly destined for much greater things.

However, if my interpretation of Benetton's chief mechanic's letter proved correct, it was also pretty clear that I wouldn't be joining the team in the quest to become Formula One World Champions.

Chapter three

1990

*A sleepless night…A call from Nigel…Taking a
correct address…Pulling up roots…First day at
school…Joining the race team…A whole new language…
Metallurgy for beginners…The first race…A one-two finish in
Japan…A pledge of allegiance in Adelaide*

It was freezing outside, and at first the inside of the flat felt even colder. However, it was a little warmer once I'd heaved the mattress off the bed and dragged it downstairs to be near the fire, whose one glowing mantle, smelling strongly of the burning dust of disuse, was the sole supply of heat. In the layout of the flat it was true that the fire was fairly centrally located, although it scarcely fulfilled the role of supplying central heating; five hours after spluttering into life there were still traces of ice on the inside of the windows.

At some point during the evening the musty smell of burning dust finally subsided, only to be replaced by the even stronger whiff of grilling mackerel: my headless and gutted dinner wrapped in foil, which Mum had given me as I set off for Woodstock. It would need only a few minutes under a hot grill. I love grilled fish (hate their bones), and for years after I'd left home Mum would give me fresh fish to take back with me whenever I visited. I wasn't familiar with the oven settings and so I managed to burn the fish with no effort at all. I hadn't eaten since breakfast, I was hungry and despite a certain burnt, dry quality the fish still tasted pretty good. Besides there was nothing else in the kitchen to cook/burn even if I'd felt sufficiently inspired to try. I'd buy a few things tomorrow.

I flung the thick duvet over the mattress and my old clock quietly marking time by the makeshift bed, a little familiarity in an otherwise foreign setting. After two or three days of being lived in, perhaps the flat would start to come back to life and, hopefully, after a couple of weeks it would even start to feel like home. I'd finally rolled onto the mattress at around half-past midnight and had spent the next three hours listening to the traffic growing less frequent and the slight hiss of the gas fire, which I had left burning to try and encourage some semblance of warmth back in the place.

Now it was either very late or very early, close to four o'clock in the morning. I was very tired, completely washed out, my eyes sore from night driving, my arms complaining from lugging boxes up long, steep stairs. By rights I should have been asleep ages ago but a potent mixture of excitement and apprehension was making any worthwhile rest impossible. I lay there, still and quiet in the dead of night, trying to identify the slightest sound: an occasional drip of the kitchen tap; the slow creak of an upstairs floorboard (how do they do that when there's no one else there); the scratching of tiny claws on a roof slate: presumably an owl or a mouse (or ten huge rats getting ready to pounce). Within a few days I would feel more at ease and the calm of sleep would come much easier, but on that first long night, half awake in the dark, as I tried to remember where the light switches were, and how I could stop the windows rattling whenever a truck drove past, my surroundings all felt very alien.

> *'Twas brillig, and the slithy toves*
> *Did gyre and gimble in the wabe:*
> *All mimsy were the borogoves,*
> *And the mome raths outgrabe.*

...

Wednesday, 31 January had been a long and busy day, and as I huddled for warmth beneath my quilt I went back over the events which had brought me to this icy flat. The move. The big move. The pulling up of twenty-seven years of family-tied roots and finally moving away from home. Complete independence; a big moment. I kept telling myself that this is one of life's great events, a time that everyone remembers but I'd been so busy all day that the real significance of what I was doing hadn't registered.

On that Wednesday morning I had gone to work at the BMW dealership for the last time. On 2 January, I handed the service manager my letter of resignation; I would be leaving at the end of the month. He seemed saddened by the news at first, but when I explained why I was leaving and where I was going he broke into a broad grin 'No! Really! But that's fantastic news; well done! Bloody well done! I knew you were planning something, but I never imagined for a second it was a move into Formula One; bloody well done!' He seemed quite excited but he was nowhere near as excited as I had been when Nigel Stepney phoned me just after Christmas. 'Still interested in the sub-assembly job?' he asked casually. 'Good. Now, can you come down and see me tomorrow morning, just to go over a few details: start date, confirmation of salary, etc.?'

Ten o'clock the next morning I was back in Oxfordshire, and thirty minutes later I left Nigel with another firm handshake and a contract of employment to read, sign and return by post. 'We'd need you to start as soon as possible, so if you have to give a month's notice can we say you'll start here on the first of February at nine o'clock. Is that okay?'

'Of course, yes; February the first, nine o'clock. I'll see you then Mr Stepney.'

'Nigel,' he smiled.

'Nigel; okay. Thank you very much. Thanks very much indeed!' I'd done it. Just like that; right out of the blue. Still want the job? Yes, good, well you're in then! All those months of letter writing; all that messing about and confusion with Onyx, and that strange chap with his Mars wrappers and his short temper and it finally happened quicker than the blink of an eye. Light, dark; noise, silence; waterfall, millpond; I don't work in Formula One, I do work in Formula One. The throw of a switch. I didn't realize it at the time but looking back on that late December day, with that wonderful clarity of vision which hindsight allows, I now understand that if I could spread out and study the network of roads, loops and cross-roads on life's map, I had just arrived at a bright and clearly marked fork in the road. My growing interest in Formula One, the letters of application, the resulting telephone calls and interviews were all a series of road-signs, directing the flow of traffic on my own particular motorway.

'Road divides ahead. Left to steady-living, via Ferrari, BMW, nine-to-five and wife, dogs and kids all crammed into a small semi on Foxcote Drive. Or right to not-entirely-sure-where-yet, via Woodstock, Chipping Norton, constant fatigue at Benetton Formula, *Life in the Fast Lane*, F1 Constructors Championship and a derelict old farm in France. One day to major decision, get in lane now.

As I left the Benetton factory with my new offer, everything seemed a little hazy, almost dream-like, my mind a turmoil of emotions: excitement, apprehension, exhilaration, self-doubt, achievement. I parked the car in the centre of Witney and strolled. I needed fresh air, a little time to relax, time to come to terms with what I had just been offered before setting off on the trip back home. And despite my earlier descriptions, as I walked through the town's old area known as the Butter Cross with its big village-type green and its ancient market building, I discovered that this part of Witney is, in fact, very picturesque. God only knows what happened to the rest of it.

As I ambled around the shops I was unsure what my next move should be. I had been offered the job, but the factory was too far from home to commute to

Oxfordshire everyday. If Nigel wanted me to start work at Benetton in just over four weeks it didn't leave me much time to sift through endless property papers looking for flats; and I could spend months driving up and down looking at houses with rooms to let. I decided to try and find somewhere to live there and then.

I'd never searched for rented accommodation before and I had no real idea how many rooms I would need or how much anywhere in Oxfordshire would cost. An estate agent's window was advertising property to let, so I asked the woman inside for advice. She seemed to scrutinize me for a moment, as if weighing up the pros and cons of having to assist me. I told her why I was looking for something and where I would be working, and slowly a faint smile crept onto her otherwise disinterested face. She had one place coming up for rent from the beginning of February, just one. Very busy time of year for rented property (apparently). A two-bedroom, two-storey apartment above an old shop in Woodstock. Just being decorated now. Did I know Woodstock, she had asked. No, I confessed, but I remember the name from school (though probably more because of the legendary music festival and Snoopy's yellow bird friend than for any recalled history lessons). 'Beautiful,' she enthused, 'really charming, and very famous too. Oh yes, very, very famous! About fifteen minutes drive from here, twenty at tops. The flat is right next door to Blenheim Palace, in fact. Blenheim Palace! All in all, Woodstock is a very correct address; very, very correct. Interested?' she asked, raising her eyebrows a little. Interested? A palace built next door to an old shop? Not so much interested as intrigued (what on earth did she mean by 'a very, very correct address')?

Number 18, Oxford Street, Woodstock. A single black door to the right of Banbury's, the Gentleman's Outfitters. Located right in the middle of this historic town (which, in reality, is little bigger than a large village), the flat was directly above the shop, a single, steep flight of stairs leading up from the street below. Standing directly opposite the Crown Inn, and with a small Co-op just to the left, the flat's position seemed ideal, and two weeks later, after a rapid exchange of paperwork, the keys arrived in the post.

The agent's claim that the flat was built right next door to the palace was a little exaggerated, but a well-aimed stone thrown from my top window might just make it onto the two and a half thousand acres of beautifully manicured lawns which serve as the eleventh Duke of Marlborough's back garden. (When the Americans debate how to increase engine performance they have a wonderful phrase: 'You can dick around with the frills all you want, son, but there ain't no substitute for cubic inches!'). The title of duke, the parklands and the money to build Blenheim Palace were gifts from a grateful Queen Anne – with the gentle persuasion of a delicate twist to her parliament's arm – to John Churchill (great, great, great, great, great, great-grandfather to dear old Winston), back in 1704. He had planned and directed an inspired military victory over the allied forces of Louis XIV near the little town of Blenheim in Bavaria. Apparently, the Queen was thrilled at the outcome of the campaign and thought the result would deliver a marvellous crushing blow to the fighting morale of France. Certainly, the battle of Blenheim did alter the entire course of this tediously long and awfully costly war. She quickly rewarded the first Duke of Marlborough with a small token of her appreciation. By today's prices that small token would be worth somewhere in the region of £50 million. Not a bad tip for a day's work; it takes Schumacher and Villeneuve nearly all year to earn that sort of money.

After loading my tools into the Escort and saying my goodbyes, I finally managed to leave work at six o'clock. I was sad to go since my time with BMW had been great fun. Everyone wished me well; they gave me some music tokens and reminded me that if ever I needed a job I could always come back. I was genuinely very touched. I had worked with BMW for exactly a year on the very day that I left. Back home I loaded every spare inch of the Escort with clothes and books and things for the flat, and when it was full to bursting I rearranged everything and managed to get in a few more books. After a big hug from Mum, the handing over of my foil-wrapped dinner and a lot of fuss and tail-wagging from Heidi, it was time to go. Fully laden, the car felt decidedly reluctant to either accelerate, brake or change direction, which was a bit disconcerting. However, on the plus side, with the back of the car being so low and the front so high, the driver's seat offered me a much better view of the stars. I was in no great rush (just as well) and together, under a frosty, though brilliantly clear night sky, my old Escort and I slowly plodded along the roads to Oxfordshire. Off towards a new life.

...

The last time I remember looking at the clock it was 4:45 am, and I must have dropped off about five-ish. The next moment the alarm was ringing in my ear, loudly celebrating the arrival of seven o'clock. I awoke totally disorientated and without the slightest idea of where I was. When I tried to climb out of bed I couldn't understand why the floor was only six inches away. I went to find the kitchen and make coffee. It was freezing cold. The kitchen smelled of fish.

I was at Benetton by 8:30, half an hour early, keen to set the right impression. Already the race shop was a hive of activity with people bustling in and out, most drinking coffee from smart white mugs, decorated with the brand-new Benetton Formula emblem. The rabbit had gone, replaced by four brightly coloured flashes; quick streaks of yellow, red, blue and green, as though roughly applied from freshly loaded paint brushes. The result was a simple but striking design, another success by Benetton's image-makers. I wondered if they'd miss one of these mugs if I was to take it back to the flat. I later discovered that these coffee mugs were brand-new, delivered to the factory only a few days before. Apparently, everyone else liked the idea of taking one home as well, and within three weeks nearly all of them had disappeared. More were ordered but they swiftly went the same way. As an experiment, plain white undecorated mugs were ordered instead, which lasted for well over five years.

I was presented to Dave Butterworth, the sub-assembly foreman, and he in turn introduced me to the other mechanics. I was given a blue lab-coat to wear − again adorned with the Benetton flashes on the breast pocket − followed by a tour of the factory. I was both apprehensive and exhilarated. The sub-assembly department was built along one side of the race-shop, glass panels making up one wall, so that when the mechanics stood at the single long work surface, they looked out into the race-shop. In reality it was a room within a room, built this way to keep the working environment as clean as possible and to separate the department from the relative vastness of the race shop.

Directly on the other side of the glass panels, in the race-shop itself, were the three bays for the cars. The two race cars were housed at each end, while the third, known as the spare car, lived in the middle bay. The cars' bays were basically three squared-off U shapes, with work surfaces and waist-high tool cabinets around the sides. Simple melamine walls, built about a foot higher than the cabinets separated the area into three distinct bays; their low height allowing the race-team mechanics to lean over and chat with one another. When they did this their inevitable poses reminded me of old photographs taken in the 1930s of women hanging out their washing and exchanging the day's gossip over the garden fences.

Each bay contained a B189 monocoque, which the mechanics were preparing for a forthcoming test. Each year Benetton numbers its cars in a systematic fashion: the B standing for Benetton; 1 for Formula One; and 89 for the year; so the 1990 cars would be numbered B190-01; B190-02, depending on the exact chassis number. It is usual for the leading teams to produce seven to ten chassis per year, depending on the amount of shunts they suffer. Back in 1989 I was told that the average cost of the materials to produce a Formula One chassis (I'm just talking about the monocoque) was in the region of £30,000. In 1998, just before I left Benetton, I inquired how much a chassis cost in raw materials and was again given a figure of about £30,000. With inflation and the cost of living constantly moving upward it's good to know some things never change. A Grand Prix chassis is as astronomically expensive to produce today as it was ten years ago. And if you have to produce ten of them it soon gets rid of £300,000 worth of carbon a year. I once pointed these ludicrous figures out to someone at Benetton and he said: 'Steve, listen and learn. No one ever said it was going to be cheap, and if it was cheap then everyone would be doing it.' So, if you ever wondered why Grand Prix racing is so expensive, there's your answer.

...

I was set to work alongside another fairly new recruit from Australia, Carl Gibson. We were to rebuild the uprights (the stub-axles, drive-shafts and hubs) for the three cars prior to the race mechanics fitting them to the gearbox and front wishbones. Every time the cars return to the factory they are stripped, cleaned, checked and rebuilt, regardless of whether the driver has reported a potential problem with a particular component. I was used to working in a clean atmosphere, but I was amazed at the precautions some people took to ensure total cleanliness. When the race mechanics removed the parts off the cars they would (should) wipe them clean with blue paper towelling, known as blue-roll (tons of this must get used in Formula One every year) and a chemical solvent such as trichloroethylene, a degreasing solution. To make life that little bit easier everyone but the most pretentious refers to the myriad of different solvents that are available simply as brake-cleaner or chemi-clean. As soon as the race mechanics hand the parts to the sub-assembly mechanics they are given a further spray with chemi-clean and another wipe.

Each mechanic had a big, soft cork mat to work on, which protected the white plastic-coated work surface from damage and allowed everyone a certain space of their own on the one long bench. I can't really explain why but I always thought this cork mat was a good idea, and the one I used on that first day stayed with me throughout my entire time with Benetton. Even when the team moved to its brand new factory in Enstone I made sure that my cork mat made the journey too. Joan Villadelprat, who later joined us as team manager after a spell with Tyrrell, used to grumble at the sight of it in his new factory, moaning that it made his bright white race-shop look untidy. I have no idea why I was so attached to it; since it was just an old cork mat, but I never felt comfortable working without it.

Anyway, it was on these cork mats – which some mechanics carefully wrapped in lengths of blue-roll for double-extra-cleanliness (I always thought this was going a bit too far) – that the axles would be stripped from the uprights and pressed from their bearings with a selection of special tools, all of which were made in-house. Then the bearings would be pressed from the uprights. At this stage the internal grease would be thoroughly washed from everything in one of several cleaning tanks, and the parts again dried off with chemi-clean. I found all of this attention to detail fascinating to watch, and it felt similar to working conditions in an operating theatre.

Carl would explain how he had been taught to proceed and then I'd have a go at the different stages of the rebuild myself. In many ways it was like being back at school. Much of what was being demonstrated was just standard mechanical procedure, all of which I had learnt ten years ago throughout my training as an apprentice. The work may have required no more than basic common sense and a few helpful guidelines, however the important thing for me was that I was working on components of a Grand Prix car. The tasks were quite straightforward and I was happy to do them, to be patient and to do whatever I was asked. I understood that I was a newcomer working in a totally new environment and the company had to gain confidence in my abilities before they would ever allow me to progress on to more demanding work. A simple 'drop-off', a careless assembly error by a nervous mechanic can cause a Formula One car to stop on the circuit, perhaps on the last corner of the final lap, and Sod's law would insist that the car was leading the race too! Best to take it steady and learn the trade stage by stage.

...

A few weeks later another big break came my way, directly after the first two races of the season. The engineers, Nigel Stepney and his race mechanics had left for America and round one of the World Championship. It was to be held in Phoenix in early March and the team didn't return until after the second race, held in Sao Paulo, Brazil. On their return the race mechanics reported that they had found these first two races terribly hard work and the long hours had nearly drained them. Along with most of the other teams Benetton had suffered with brake problems in Phoenix. It was a street circuit and therefore consisted of a series of several short straights and very tight corners; all very demanding on brakes, which never received sufficient airflow or time to cool down before the driver was standing hard on the pedal again. This had given rise to overheating and very rapid wear of the material. Combined with this problem the mechanics had discovered hairline fractures running in between the ventilation holes around the circumference of the discs; as a result the discs and pads were being constantly changed throughout the course of the race weekend to try and stay on top of the problem.

Most people use one of two different makes of discs and pads, which are produced either by the French firm Carbon Industrie, which is one of the world's leading manufacturers of composite racing brakes or by an American company called Hitco. Carbon Industrie supplies the teams with several different brake specifications to choose from, three different disc widths are available as is the choice between either small or large carbon pads, depending on which size and make of caliper is being used. The brake calipers and master-cylinders are manufactured by two more companies, either AP Racing or Brembo, and these parts also come in a huge array of different sizes depending on track design and the team preferences.

Throughout these first two race weekends Nigel had been trying to keep ahead of all the extra work that these brake problems had provided, in addition to the multitude of other duties that his position as chief mechanic required. It had proved too much; the increasing brake work alone was enough to keep someone in a full-time job, and with Imola being the next race – another circuit notoriously demanding on brakes – the anticipated workload would only increase. Nigel wanted someone to travel with the race team and take control of this whole, somewhat chaotic, brake situation for him.

The moment I got wind of this potential job offer I put my hand up to volunteer. Working in sub-assembly was fine, but in the few short weeks I had been with Benetton I could already see that working directly with the race team would be the way forward. Purely on the basis of job security this seemed a sound move too, as actually running the cars on the world's circuits is the main preoccupation of any Grand Prix team, and should the ugly head of redundancy rear upwards, it seemed obvious that the people directly involved with making the cars work would be the last to go. Also, I supposed that looking after the brakes would be something I could handle easily enough, regardless of my lack of race experience, and a position working with the race team would give me a good vantage point from which to observe the race mechanics and learn how their work is done. Besides, I wanted to travel and see something of the world, and if Benetton would take me and pay for me to go, then so much the better.

Despite my eagerness, Carl Gibson, my Australian work-mate, was offered the job first because of his slightly longer service with the company than me. However, miraculously (for me, certainly) he turned the position down, saying he was adamant that he wanted to progress through the ranks of the sub-assembly department and to train as an Formula One gearbox builder. He didn't want to merely look after brakes for a living and he considered such a move as being a retrograde step. That decision and his reasoning were absolutely fine by me, I could see several major advantages in joining the race team, but if he wanted to organize his career via another avenue then good luck to him. I shook his hand in genuine thanks and gratitude. Actually, Carl resigned at the end of the season, leaving Benetton to join Eddie Jordan's race team for their debut year in 1991. Some years later he met a Swedish girl in Estoril during a Portuguese post-race test. A budding relationship blossomed and shortly after she moved to England to stay with him. Carl ended his Formula One career with TWR Arrows, working with Damon Hill in 1997 – then the current World Champion – before finally waving goodbye to the pit-lane and heading back to live with his girlfriend in Australia directly after the 1998 Monaco Grand Prix.

When Carl turning the chance down, the job of running the Benetton race team's brake department was offered to me. I eagerly accepted.

...

I was allocated some space out in the race-shop, on the mezzanine floor above sub-assembly, a space which also served as the travelling composite and fabricators area too. When I looked over the railing the floor's height gave a good view of the three car bays and the mechanics working below. I was given a couple of Lista cabinets – robust storage units with sliding steel drawers – to keep the brake stocks in. Nigel Stepney seemed pleased that I had volunteered for this new job ('I like people who push a bit') and introduced me to Steve Cook, the chief truckie, who would assign me some drawers and a work area on the race truck. When Nigel had gone back to his office the chief truckie told me not to bother calling him Steve, everyone knew him as Tats (he has several colourful tattoos, including one of Donald Duck on his leg). 'Okay Tats,' I said, 'thanks very much for sorting out the drawers and workspace.' Tats walked off, then paused for a second and looked back at me, 'Just don't even think about making a mess in the back of my truck with those stinking brakes; one smudge of black carbon on my clean paintwork and I'll tip'. He rounded the back of the truck and was gone, leaving me to ponder what he had said. Certainly, I got the general gist of what Tats expected of me, but I'd never heard anyone say 'I'll tip' before and had no idea at all what he could possibly mean. Later I made a few discreet enquiries, discovering that 'tip' is an abbreviation for 'tip me right over the edge'. This was the first time I'd heard it, but over the coming years up and down the pit-lane 'tip' became a common enough expression to hear; there are a few unusual variations too, my favourite of all being 'That's it! Now I'm really tipping; big-time bad and I mean it as well!' (as well as what?).

If you spend long enough with the same relatively small group of people it's inevitable that a certain idiosyncratic vocabulary builds up, and I imagine that working with the Benetton race team would be a little like being in the forces in this respect. For instance, people would constantly refer to one another as Gambit, 'Quick, Gambit, have a look at this!' And if someone had just arrived on the scene and wanted to know what was happening they'd ask what the 'sketch' was, or if the same action was being repeated – such as another practice pit-stop – it would be introduced with 'Okay everyone, same sketch'.

Tats had joined the team after years working with McLaren, where he was also chief truckie and tyre-man for Prost and Senna (at the circuits the truckies look after the preparation of the tyres and fuel). At the end of the 1993 season, after four years with Benetton, he was made an offer to return there and promptly left to be reunited with Ron Dennis in Woking. There is no rushing Tats with regards to forming a friendship – it is something that builds over time with a long trial period, and a relationship of mutual trust and understanding has to develop first. But once friendship is established it makes for a good strong bond. It took me more than two years to get to know Tats well, and on that first encounter in the back of the Benetton truck I was politely but firmly put on the first step of the ladder of respect.

After familiarizing myself with the layout of the race truck and measuring the internal size of the drawers, I wandered off to the fabrication department. I wanted to cut some material and make some drawer dividers in order to better organize and separate my precious cargo during their future trans-European treks. It would be awful to have to tell the chief mechanic that all his brand-new brake discs had chaffed on each other for the last 2000 miles and were now completely useless!

I asked one of the fabricators which of the multitude of materials in the metal storeroom I could use without leaving them short for their work. 'Anything,' I was told, 'use whatever you need, none of it is reserved or allocated yet'. I had never seen such an array of different metals: mild-steel, stainless-steel, several grades of aluminium, and countless pieces of brass, hydural and copper. Some of it was in large sheets ready to be marked, cut, folded and welded; others were in great ingots and blocks, waiting to be machined. Most of the material had been marked with a colour code or a series of letters and numbers, which to a fabricator or machinist familiar with what the pinks and blues and whites or the Ns and Hs mean will identify the material's type and grade. It was all Greek to me. I decided on a big sheet of matt grey material, the colour of which suggested that it was a nice new piece of high-quality mild-steel; when I picked it out of the rack I was surprised at how light it appeared for such a big sheet. After setting the backstop on the automatic guillotine to produce the right sized cut, I quickly chopped the sheet into twenty small divider-sized pieces.

Pleased with how easy and quick the job had seemed I returned to the race truck to fit out the drawers. Ten minutes later Tats came in carrying a set of tyre blankets and asked how I was getting on. I explained that I was organizing the drawers, proudly showing him my new dividers.

He picked one up, 'You've made these,' he asked me.

'Yes,' I said, 'a few minutes ago; how did you know I made them, aren't they very good? They seemed both strong and light enough to me.'

'They're certainly good enough, too good I'd say. Who gave you the material?'

'I just got it out the rack; why, what's up with it?'

'Nothing's up with it, but I wouldn't show them to anyone else if I were you,' he said, tossing the divider back on the others. Tats started to walk off but I called him back, keen to know what the problem with my first fabrication job was.

'There's no problem with them,' he reassured me, 'it's just that, personally, I wouldn't have bothered using an entire sheet of titanium costing several hundred pounds a go, to have made them from. About three quid's worth of NS4 ali' would have done the job just as well. You've managed to produce the most expensive drawer dividers in the known world; well done!' Tats went back to his growing stack of tyre blankets.

Back upstairs, after confessing my sins to Nigel, I began organizing my new department, collecting the new carbon discs and pads from the stores en route. Thankfully, Nigel understood that it had been an honest mistake with the titanium; he didn't seem at all overly concerned to be honest, but he did tell me to make certain I checked with a fabricator before I cut anything else into little pieces. I asked him if I should go and tell the fabricators what I'd done, but was advised that it would probably be more prudent to leave them well alone, at least for a couple of weeks. I had simply never seen titanium before; no excuse, I know. However, the upshot was that I did end up with a set of rather jaunty drawer dividers, which would have been the envy of the pit-lane if ever I'd dared show them to anyone.

...

Each disc and pad that I received from the supplier was first weighed and labelled with indelible ink. Regardless of the fact that a particular batch of, say, a hundred pads should, in theory, be identical, I would weigh each of them and record their weight to within a single gram. This would show me which pads were slightly more dense than the others, and due to the front brakes working harder than the rears it was these denser, heavier pads that would be allocated to the front of the car. Not only that, but on a clockwise directional circuit (which the vast majority are) the most heavy pads would be given to the left-front brake, which will see marginally more work. So, the order of density would go, left-front, right-front, left-rear, right-rear. The same would be done to the discs too, and once the individual pieces had been graded into sets I would etch each part with its own serial/life number. This would allow me to wear-check the brakes at the end of each running session and keep track of exactly how every disc and pad was lasting in comparison to each other. The thickness of each component would be recorded before the cars ran and be recorded again at the end of the session. Subtracting one figure from the other would give the amount of brake wear for a known number of laps, and armed with this information it should be possible to calculate, on the Saturday night of a race weekend, which thickness of brake disc was needed and how much ducting the brakes would need to get the car to the end of the race. In theory, at least!

While I was engrossed in all of this weighing and marking and etching of the brakes, and cleaning and inspecting the numerous calipers, Gordon Message, the team manager, climbed the stairs from the race-shop and introduced himself. He apologised for not meeting me sooner (I had been at Benetton for several weeks now) but, apparently, he'd just not had a spare minute. Had I settled in? Was everything okay? He'd heard that I'd joined the race team and the news had pleased him (I thought it best not to mention the titanium incident).

'Yes, everything's fine, I'm loving it. It's like being in a different world,' I said, nodding at the stack of fifty brake discs, each one costing close to a £1000. Gordon laughed, looking at the £50,000 worth of soon-to-be scrap discs, and then glanced over the railing at the three race cars, collectively worth over £1.5 million, with their teams of mechanics carefully installing the Ford V8 engines 'I suppose you're right,' he agreed, 'it is another world. Problem is I've been in it so long I can't remember another one anymore; this is all that's normal to me now!' He gave another slight chuckle. A quietly spoken man and instantly likeable; we were to became good friends in later years.

'Come and see me tomorrow morning,' Gordon said, 'now you're going racing we need to get you kitted out with all your team gear: shirts, trousers, shoes and whatever.' The next night I went home with a big travel bag full of team kit, all made by Benetton (they even supply their mechanics with team-issue socks). That evening I tried on a pair of light blue work trousers and baggy white race shirt, a big Benetton emblem emblazoned on the back. I didn't recognize the person who gazed back at me from the mirror.

In a couple of days I would be flying off to Italy, a member of the Benetton Formula race team, to contest our cars in the 1990 Grand Premio di San Marino. Ferrari and Mansell would be there. McLaren and Senna and Ron Dennis would be there; Williams and Patrese too. How odd! Patrese, Senna, Mansell, Prost, Piquet. Nelson Piquet – three times World Champion – would be driving one of our cars; he and I work for the same boss. Nelson Piquet and I are team mates! None of it seemed real. However, I wasn't dreaming and over the next few days I definitely woke up. At Imola the reality of my new job hit me with a massive jolt too. Welcome to the wonderful world of Formula One!

When I wrote *Life in the Fast Lane*, it wasn't necessary to describe the lap-by-lap events of each round of the 1994 Championship, and it isn't my intention now to describe the individual events of each race I attended throughout my time with Benetton. After all, there were exactly a hundred of them and much of what we do at one race is merely a repetition of what we did two weeks prior. However, Imola 1990, my first Grand Prix working with Benetton, was quite an exceptional race and those four days in early May remain etched in my memory.

...

We left the factory at five o'clock Thursday morning. I set the alarm to wake me at four, which left me an hour to shower, dress and drive to Witney. Ample time. However, I had never had need to rise that early before in my life, and I soon found out that getting up at such a stupid hour wouldn't come easy to me (and over the next few years I never really improved). Certainly, I was excited by the thought of going to Imola, but fatigue was making sleep come very easily. I'd been working quite late over the last few days, eight and nine o'clock, making sure that everything the chief mechanic and the engineers had asked me to take to Italy was carefully stowed in the truck and that all the paperwork was up-to-date. This event was going to be a baptism of fire for me, a very steep learning curve, and I didn't want Nigel to change his mind after just one race and find myself back in sub-assembly.

I must assume that the alarm did go off at four, but it was much closer to half-past by the time my subconscious had given up trying to conveniently fit the bleeping into the vague story-line of a dream. The bleeping persisted, and eventually I was left with no choice but to slowly open an eye and blink at the clock. I didn't really approve of what I thought I saw. I opened both eyes and had another go. This was swiftly followed by hopping around the room trying to pull two socks on the same foot while throwing everything else to the floor in an attempt to find the car keys (I'd left them in the ignition so I wouldn't lose them). It really was quite pathetic. Finally, though, most of the relevant brain cells flickered back online and I made the factory with five minutes to spare. I climbed on board the coach sporting a look which I hoped would convey to the team manager that everything was calm and under control. However, Gordon wasn't there, and we had to wait half an hour for him as he'd overslept. When he did arrive, looking tired but completely unflustered, he apologized to everyone, gave a relaxed chuckle, lit a cigarette, and told the driver to get on with it. As the coach lurched and groaned towards Oxford and the M40, Gordon handed me an envelope, 'Steve, this is for you, you'll need it to get in the circuit, it's your FOCA pass; It'll get you in the paddock, the garages and the pit-lane. And they're a real pig to get hold of, so please don't lose it'.

To put it mildly, Imola was absolutely physically and mentally exhausting. I had never felt so utterly washed out and drained in my entire life, and I had serious doubts that my feet would ever recover. To this day I have no idea how I managed to keep going from Thursday morning until Sunday night; I was completely knackered. On returning to England I slept in a deep trance-like state for twenty-four hours; Monday ceased to exist. When I finally did wake I was in exactly the same position, the pillows and quilt unruffled, I hadn't turned once, even murmured, in all that time.

On several occasions since that first race I have had to work for two or three days without any sleep at all (as, of course, do all Grand Prix mechanics), and the prospect of doing another terrifying 'all-nighter', or two, or three, becomes no more than an occupational hazard. They are detested, without doubt, but one just gets used to it, the mind adjusts. I never worked an actual all-nighter on that inaugural race in Italy, I came close, but I did manage to get a couple of hours back at the hotel. Some of the other mechanics weren't so fortunate; a few, working directly on the cars, went right through from Friday morning to Sunday night (and they still looked fresher than me).

I had no idea that the mechanics were expected to work so many hours. I just assumed that if the team encountered the sort of problems requiring extensive repairs or modifications they would simply withdraw the cars from the following day's sessions. I supposed the mechanics would work until six or seven o'clock before going back to the hotel for dinner and a beer, then come back in the following morning to finish off. Then, if there was still time to get the cars out and get some lap-times in, so be it. How blissfully naive I was.

After the first eight hours at the circuit my new, team-issue Timberland shoes started to pinch a little and rub the back of my ankles. After twelve hours my feet were actually quite sore. At fourteen hours they really started to hurt, and after sixteen hours I kicked them off and started beating them with a heavy plastic mallet. I hoped this might soften the leather a bit, but just the sight of the damn things being repeatedly squashed seemed to bring some comfort. I tried walking in just socks, and for a while the cool of the concrete floor in the garage was like heaven but, sadly, this brought only temporary relief and I was soon forced back into my flattened shoes. Now, after years of wearing them, I find Timberlands the most comfortable shoes on earth (this is not an endorsement), but the stiffness of that first pair combined with the long hours nearly had me in tears.

The first practice session of my career started at 10:00 am precisely, on Friday, 11 May. I could sense the tension mounting as the hour drew closer. At nine o'clock everyone seemed fairly relaxed, sitting on the Lista cabinets, chatting, drinking coffee or standing at the front of the garage sharing a joke with other teams' mechanics. I wasn't sure if we were encouraged to talk with personnel from rival teams or whether it was a case of wishing them a polite good morning and moving swiftly on. I was relieved to discover that this wasn't so; I'd already had a chat with one of the McLaren mechanics and hoped that no one had seen. (Caught by the Formula One Thought Police on my first day at the track.) At 9:30 the engines were run up to operating temperature in order to check that all was well and to put some heat into the water system. Nelson Piquet and Sandro Nannini walked into the garage at 9:45 am, the tyres were fitted with ten minutes to go and at 9:55 the whole team was ready. As the siren signalled the opening of the pit-lane the engines fired into life and my first frantic Grand Prix weekend really began.

I managed to cope with the work without problem. During the practice and qualifying sessions I would dash between the three cars (in that era the team could use the spare car throughout the whole weekend), monitoring the brake temperatures and checking for any slight cracks that might appear in the carbon discs. The spare car would be built with one particular set-up and, depending who had use of it, either Piquet or Nannini would swap between his race car and the spare, comparing the differences. To minimize lost time, while one car was on the circuit the mechanics would be changing the wings, or springs, or roll-bars, of the other; then that car would be driven while the mechanics worked on the other. Everything was done double quick, flat-out, not a second was wasted. Push, push, push, get the car back out! This was totally different from the relaxed atmosphere of the factory. Time is a very precious commodity in Grand Prix racing, and when the cars are allowed to run they must do so. Ten minutes of lost track-time could make all the difference to finding that slight edge over the opposition.

After the running was over I would measure the discs and pads, fill out a wear-check form and report my findings to Nigel or the engineers. At night I would prepare the fresh brakes for the next day's running by bolting new discs onto the mounting-bells, which is a Benetton piece, a machined centre-hub allowing the one-size-for-all-teams disc to be adapted to the Benetton stub-axles (to suit their own cars, McLaren, Ferrari, Williams and all the other teams have their own mounting-bell designs).

The Saturday night race preparation seemed endless, with new brakes, fresh engine, fresh gearbox, different rear suspension and modifications to increase the brake-duct intakes; basically the cars were totally rebuilt. By three in the morning, when Nigel finally allowed the mechanics not working directly on the cars to go back to the hotel, I was really struggling to stay awake. I couldn't understand why we didn't finish the work tomorrow. We had been at the circuit since seven the previous morning and in four hours' time we would be back again. It seemed sheer madness to be working these hours, and all just to put two cars on the starting grid for Sunday's race. I don't think I'd ever been awake that late before. My feet throbbed, my fingers were numb; it was terrible. The glamour and the glitz of working for a Formula One team! I sat in the back of the minibus seriously questioning what on earth I was doing there. I had made a huge mistake, that much was certain. As soon as I got back to England I would try and get my old job back again with BMW; it was good there, a normal life, but this was plain insanity. How could the people around me still feel like chatting and joking? I felt like shouting: 'For God's sake! It's three o'clock in the bloody morning, please just shut up!' But I didn't say anything, I just watched the blackness as the minibus bounced over the deserted mountain road towards the hotel and quietly planned my escape.

Back in the bedroom my last conscious thought was how cool the marble floor felt and what a wonderful tonic it was for my two aching feet. Then, at the same instant as I sat on the edge of the bed, I was asleep. Two milliseconds later my room-mate, Paul, was shaking me awake, 'Steve, come on, it's six-thirty. We've got to go.'

I owe Paul Howard a great deal of thanks. Throughout my first year with Benetton he was always looking out for me, constantly waking and forcing me up in time for work the next day. Without his help I would have been sunk. In 1990 Paul was a gearbox mechanic, then he worked on the back-end of one of the cars, and he is now one of Benetton's number-one mechanics – and currently (in 1998) he is running Alex Wurz. He is fabulously calm and meticulously well organized. If ever anyone had forgotten something or needed a special tool, Paul Howard would be able to help. Of course, he couldn't help with everything, I mean, it would be most unlikely that he would have a street map of Springfield in his briefcase, but he might just have a rather dog-eared photocopy of the exact area you wanted to look at. Such organizational skills are a black art to me, but to him they are second nature. As an example: in 1996 during the quiet winter period known as the 'off-season', I was keeping myself occupied by assembling a B193 show car from the contents of several cardboard boxes which, apparently, contained everything I'd need. Eventually I found everything but one special bolt, a mounting for the rear suspension. I asked in the stores, but as the car was three years old they no longer had the part lists and couldn't help. I thought I'd ask Paul, just on the off chance. Within thirty seconds of asking he had found his copy of the B193 assembly drawings, had written the part number down for me and told me exactly where, in the myriad of old parts kept at the back of the stores, I would find one. It's a sort of magic with him.

Anyway, I digress. Sunday, back at Imola, and I was in for another shock (it can't be right when your feet still ache as you stand up the next morning). Gordon Message, the team manager, said he had a little job for me during the race. He needed someone to operate one of the two pit-boards. Stewart Spires, who ran the motorhome, would operate Nannini's and Gordon wanted me to work Piquet's. I quickly told him that I'd never used one before and that I thought he was asking the wrong man. But he seemed quite undeterred by this news, telling me not to worry and that I'd soon get into the swing of it. Get into the swing of it? I'd never used a pit-board before in my life, never even picked one up, never really studied what was displayed on them either. And now, the first time I was going to handle such a thing it would be used to communicate with a treble world champion in a Grand Prix which was only an hour away from starting. Piquet's pit-board? Had everyone gone completely loopy? How could I ever hope to work it correctly without any sort of training? And then I would have to confidently show the board to Nelson Piquet (Nelson Piquet!), telling him such things as his position in the race, how many laps to go, how much time he was behind the car in front; and, oh, by the way, Mr Piquet, can you just stop racing now and pop into the pits for some fresh tyres? Who was I to inform him of anything? It was like being asked to mix paint for Michelangelo. 'Thanks very much, Steve,' smiled Gordon, 'I knew we could count on you; ask Stu if you're not sure of anything.'

Mike Coughlan was Nelson's race engineer. After leaving Lotus he was recruited to Benetton thanks to his former working relationship with John Barnard. Mike is enormously self-confident and nothing appears to phase him. He is a big, tall chap and radiates great presence. He can walk into a pub a complete stranger and within minutes the landlord and the four locals at the bar will be chatting with him like they've known him for years. Throughout the race Mike and I were in contact (or not in contact, as the case may be) via an antiquated intercom system; any attempt at verbal communication was strictly a one-way affair: Mike was able to speak to me (or shout over the constant screaming of twenty-six racing engines) through the ageing CB-style microphone, I could hear (nothing) through the old headphones. The communications system was fantastically inefficient, and after a couple of laps we both gave up and reverted to good old sign language. I managed to pick up the use of the pit-board pretty quickly, and within a few laps of watching the ever-changing lap times flicker away on Mike's TV monitor I was setting the pit-board with any relevant info myself. The top line was used for Nelson's position in the race, displayed as: P5 or P3, or whatever the case may be. The second and third lines displayed the time difference and the name of the driver who was directly ahead of Nelson in the race, shown as a negative figure, for example: -1.6 Warwick. The fourth and fifth lines represented the difference between Nelson and the car behind him, this time represented as a positive figure: +2.3 Nannini. Finally, the bottom line would show the number of laps to the end of the race, and this would simply be reduced by one number every time Nelson drove past. So, an example of a set pit-board might look like this:

P3
-1.6
Warwick
+2.3
Nannini
L32

The only real difficulty I encountered using the pit-board came with being able to reset all the information before Nelson came back past the pits. At that time a racing lap of Imola took about 1 minute 27 seconds, an amount of time which sounds easily sufficient to reset the board, but when you have to change everything – and one of the drivers' names seems to have vanished from the box – believe me, it was quite possible to finish setting the board and swiftly swing it over the pit-wall only to find I was just in time to see the rear wing of Piquet's Benetton at the end of the straight, as it shot left towards Tamburello.

Fatigued and overtired as I was, the constant attention that operating the pit-board demanded, combined with the adrenaline and excitement of the occasion kept me going. I'm sure if I had just sat down and watched the race on the garage monitors I would have been fast asleep from lap two onwards. However, this way, working with Mike Coughlan on the pit-wall the sixty-odd laps of the race seemed to flash past in a matter of minutes. Nevertheless, as soon as the chequered flag came out I started to wilt. We finished the race third and fifth, but notwithstanding this impressive result I was simply too worn out to walk to the podium and watch Sandro receive his trophy. I slept in the minibus on the way to the airport and I slept in the departure lounge too. I wasn't aware of any of the flight to Heathrow and I slept during the coach trip to Witney.

. . .

Obviously, I didn't leave Benetton after that first race, though, I freely admit to contemplating the idea. What a blow to the senses that first Grand Prix was! However, the thing that really prevented me taking the idea any further was the constant pressure of time. Before I knew what was happening the race trucks had returned from Imola and everyone was back at work preparing the cars for Monaco. (Now, that race really did see my feet and Timberlands having the most enormous falling out.) Then we flew to Montreal for the Canadian Grand Prix, stopped over in America for a couple of days, and then flew down to Mexico. Back to England and straight off to France, followed by Silverstone, Hockenheim in Budapest and Spa and on and on. Build, race, build, race, build, race. There was no opportunity to try and organize an escape route; sometimes we would work at the factory until midnight or one in the morning (sometimes later), I can't imagine any service manager from the road car industry in his right mind consenting to an interview at 2:00 am.

The other thing that was preventing me trying to leave was the fact that by the third or fourth race, certainly by the time we went to France, I was actually beginning to enjoying myself. I was adjusting to the stupid hours, getting to know the other mechanics better and, at last, my feet had finally made friends with my heavily battered shoes. And on 31 May, shortly after the Monaco race, I received a letter from Gordon in which he praised the commitment and effort I had shown (he also increased my salary by £3000, upping it to £18,000 per year).

As the season progressed we constantly picked up Championship points, and when Nannini secured another podium position by taking third place in Jerez, it made a running total of five rostrum finishes for the team (although, as yet, none were on the top step). This meant that we would finish no lower than fourth place in the Constructors' Championship. In fifth place, Ken Tyrrell's team was trailing Benetton by thirty-two points, so even if some bizarre twist of fate resulted in Tyrrell finishing the final two races of the year with consecutive one-two results, and we failed to score anything at all, they would still be two points behind us (remembering that in 1990 a race win was only worth nine points). However, the battle for first place in the Championship was well beyond us and it was left to the might of Ferrari and McLaren to fight for the final honours. But we were only two points behind Williams, and if our drivers continued to show their current form – and the B190 remained reliable – it was possible that we could snatch third place by the end of the season.

At that point in Benetton's short history, to beat Williams with all its widely acknowledged technical expertise would be a tremendous result. Back in Witney, as we made the final preparations to transport the cars and equipment to Suzuka, the whole team seemed in buoyant mood. On a purely personal note, I was thrilled at the idea of visiting Japan. I never imagined I'd be able to see such exotic cultures; I had romantic images of huge mountains enveloped in a gentle dawn breeze of light mist and save for the delicate ring of a lone wind-chime everywhere would be silent. As it turned out I didn't see any mist-covered mountains and jingling wind-chimes on that particular trip, though I could give you lucid accounts of vast bustling crowds and talking vending machines and multi-tiered golf ranges and trucks draped with a billion flashing lightbulbs.

A couple of days before we were due to fly out the team had some devastating news. Sandro Nannini had been involved in a terrible helicopter accident. He was alive but he was, nevertheless, in a serious condition, his right hand severed by a shattered rotor blade. Tragic, awful news. The magic of micro-surgery had managed to reattach his hand and there was optimism that he would retain some use of it too. However, his Formula One career was over. I didn't know him very well (and I don't know him any better now), but we had chatted from time to time as we stood around the coffee machine and I liked what little I knew of him. Throughout the years I worked in Formula One he is the only driver I have ever known to smoke – and not try to hide the fact too. When he worked with Benetton he was addicted to espresso coffee (presumably he still is) and I blame a certain amount of my own craving for espresso on him; whenever he poured himself a coffee, which was often, and he saw me preparing the brakes in the back of the truck he would always pour one for me too. An all round decent chap. How many other drivers would do that? Two? three perhaps? The vast majority of today's 'up and coming great talents' would willingly fling themselves from the top of Beachy Head rather than waste any precious PR time chatting to their mechanics. 'Pour one of the mechanics a coffee! Have you lost all sense of profitable time management? I've just spent an hour with them getting their damn car to fifteenth place on the grid! I'm feeling weak just at the thought of the idea, where are my personal Post Qualifying Stress Assistants? Fetch them to me now. Interview over!' There are exceptions, of course. A few.

The Brazilian driver Roberto Moreno, was brought in to replace Nannini for these last two rounds of 1990, and as history shows, the team went on to win both the Japanese and the Australian races. Moreno finished second in Japan, about ten seconds behind his old friend and mentor Nelson Piquet, making the result Benetton's first one-two finish. Moreno couldn't believe what had happened to him, he had been plucked from total obscurity to become an instant hero. With his old team, the struggling Eurobrun outfit, he had failed to even pre-qualify for the Spanish race, and then the team collapsed and folded for good. Talk about clouds and silver linings!

It was a fabulous result for everyone: for the team, for Moreno, for Piquet and certainly for me personally. My first Grand Prix win. What a wonderful feeling of achievement. I couldn't imagine myself working in any other industry, this was the ultimate in job satisfaction. We had come to Japan under a dark cloud and ended the weekend in total jubilation. After the podium celebrations Roberto was so overcome with emotion that he was unable to speak; he walked into the garage and burst into tears. Standing amongst us, warmly hugging every one of us, it was all he could do to stammer out just two words, and he kept repeating them over and over: 'Thank you. Thank you. Thank you'. The drivers brought their half-sprayed bottles of champagne back to the garage and we passed them between us, each savouring the sweet taste of a Grand Prix victory, a one-two victory at that. It was strange to think that we, Benetton Formula Ltd, a relatively small concern of about a hundred people operating from a handful of old units in a Witney industrial estate, had beaten the full might of the established Grand Prix elite of Ferrari, McLaren and Williams.

The dominating result of the Japanese race had pulled us ahead of Williams too. We proudly stood in third place in the Championship and two weeks later, in Adelaide, when Nelson yet again took the first place chequered flag, our position in the 1990 Championship was sealed. Once more the victory champagne was handed round, and as I slowly lifted the weight of the bottle and felt the sparkle of the wine touch my lips I knew that I wouldn't leave Benetton – indeed, couldn't leave – until we had finally secured our team colours to the bright silver of the Constructors' trophy. I didn't know how many years it would take but I knew I would stay until we became World Champions.

Chapter four

1991

Three men in a balloon...Another promotion...Pit stops...John and Luciano part company...Victory in Canada...Senseless hours in Imola and Monaco...Stepney leaves...Walkinshaw arrives...Moreno leaves...Schumacher arrives...Piquet leaves

It is impossible to take any holidays during the Formula One season, there is just no spare time to fit them in. This means that by the end of the year everyone is as keen as mustard to take time off and enjoy themselves. Because the last race of the 1990 season was in Adelaide I thought it made sense to see a little more of the country I was already in. One of the great perks of the job is the chance to travel. My return flight had been paid by Benetton, so all I had to do was delay my flight home by a couple of weeks. The life of a Formula One mechanic isn't all work – at least one percent of it is non-stop play. I teamed up with two other Benetton mechanics, Bill Harris and Jorg Russ, and together we set off to explore.

Queensland, Australia, eight o'clock in the morning, the sun was just peeking through the branches of a thick forest clearing while the three of us lazed on the ground munching our breakfast. Close by were two old ladies, whose combined ages we estimated to be about 150 years, giggling like teenage schoolgirls and having the time of their lives. Next to them sat Dave and Phil, our two tanned and muscular hosts. They were all tucking in too. It had been an extremely busy morning for us all.

'And if none of you need to be rushing home,' invited Phil as he cut up more cheese with an enormous bowie knife, 'we'll call into a beaut of a hotel I know on the way down the hill and have a tube or two before lunch'. It was an invitation we couldn't refuse. After all, there was little chance of getting out the rain-forest without his guidance and certainly not without the use of his mate's van. Besides, I wouldn't have missed any of their antics for the world; so far that morning we had been driven at high speed through a burning forest; crash-landed a balloon and been pursued across fields by an irate farmer before making a dramatic escape into the depths of a rain-forest. And all this before breakfast.

In normal circumstances, our two mild-mannered though eccentric Australian hosts dressed in shorts, heavy boots and singlets would be beyond belief but here, in the far north of Australia, they fitted perfectly. Queensland still has a strong flavour of the frontier. When it rains it does so by supplying thick, torrential sheets that last for weeks on end, and when it decides to warm up it does so with such ferocity that it becomes an act of sheer madness to attempt to do anything out of doors. Our two guides were born and bred in this strange, harsh environment, a pair of genuine Crocodile Dundees.

We had seen a leaflet advertising dawn balloon flights a few days before, and immediately Jorg and I were keen. Jorg is game for any sort of adventure, brimming with enthusiasm for any sporting activity that smacks, even slightly, of potential life-threatening danger: parachuting, abseiling, potholing, white-water rafting. You name it and Jorg's name will be at the top of the list. Bill, on the other hand, is not keen on dangerous sports, and is one of life's great connoisseurs, a man for whom the words luxury and extravagance were invented. Don't misunderstand me, Bill is a true gentleman and would always support his friends faithfully and to the hilt. He would, for example, willingly accompany Jorg if he attempted to sail a small dinghy across the Atlantic, providing, of course, that Bill could watch events unfold from the sun-deck of the QE2. Bill didn't think that floating in a basket, hundreds of feet in the air, was quite what he had in mind for a holiday treat, but we finally convinced him.

The day had begun at four in the morning when Dave Dundee collected us in his van. We jumped inside and drove into the pitch black hills to rendezvous with Phil and the hot air ballon. As Dave drove us further into the depths of the rain-forest we could see dim orange flickers in the distance and were surprised to come across small areas of woodland merrily burning away; the van speeded up as Dave attempted to outrun the thick smoke hanging in the trees. When we asked who would come to extinguish the flames, Dave told us that it would probably be left alone and allowed to burn itself out naturally. 'You put one fire out and another starts, you put that one out and a third starts. They're natural; best just to let em slowly go.'

Finally we arrived at the launch site and through the half gloom of the near sunrise, we saw a figure who turned out to be Phil Dundee. He was busy unrolling

The two cars cross the finish line at Monza, 1988,
to record an historic one-two finish for Ferrari.

Unable to believe the end result, the Tifosi stream towards
the podium in celebration at the end of the race at Monza.

Gerhard Berger at Imola in 1989 prior to the massive
shunt at Tamburello on the following Sunday.

Despite Berger's dramatic accident at Imola that
year, Ferrari made the brave decision to restart.

Imola 1990 was my first Grand Prix as a
Benetton mechanic – one of the hardest
and most memorable races of my career.

Away from the madding crowd, Benetton team manager, Gordon Message and Sandro Nannini in the sanctuary of the F1 paddock at Imola in 1990.

Engineer Andy Le Flemming (Alf), and Roberto Moreno discuss progress at Suzuka in 1990. Prior to firing the engine on the B190 the battery drill behind Moreno's helmet was used to obtain initial fuel pressure.

The author, sporting the useless headphones of the equally useless pit-wall intercom system at Suzuka.

Briatore and Moreno. The Brazilian is so overcome with
emotion at Suzuka he is barely able to walk and talk.

My first Grand Prix victory, and what a feeling of pure elation the result brought at Suzuka in 1990.

Flavio, drenched with champagne after accepting Benetton's trophy at Suzuka.

The Foster's girls rehearse their routines prior
to the race day parades in Adelaide, 1990.

Piquet driving the Benetton B190 at Adelaide.

Nelson with his victor's trophy in Adelaide. It was Benetton's second race win in my first season with them.

A Grand Prix novice, a young German called Michael Schumacher, is given his race debut in a Jordan at Spa, 1991. Benetton is so impressed...

... that they immediately set about signing him to drive a B191 in the next race at Monza.

The deal is done, the ink on the contract has dried. Flavio has secured the future services of Michael Schumacher, for and on behalf of Benetton Formula Ltd.

One of the first, hastily arranged publicity shots at Monza – so hasty, in fact, that Michael is sitting in Nelson's car.

With Moreno gone, Alf meets his new driver and talks him through the initial settings of the B191 at Monza.

Then down to business. Although this was his first race with Benetton, Schumacher already has the determined look of a future World Champion.

Regardless that the event was Nelson's 200th Grand Prix, the
entire focus of the picture centres on the chap standing behind
Flavio: Mr Bill Harris, a man for whom champagne was invented.

While delving through the LAT archives, I came across this beautiful forgotten
picture of Ayrton Senna in the McLaren in Canada, 1991, which I had to cut
out of a long strip of other miscellaneous transparencies.

Flavio congratulated Nelson immediately after the race in Canada in 1991. Notice how simple and uncluttered the steering wheels were before the explosion of instrumentation in the mid-nineties.

The author helping Schumacher into the car prior to
the shortest Grand Prix in history at Adelaide in 1991.

Standing on the grid in the pouring rain in Adelaide.

The shortest race gets under way...

... and is shortly stopped. The McLaren mechanics try to shield one of their cars from the driving rain while they inspect the engines prior to the restart, which never came.

the balloon and the gas burners. As the sun lifted itself over the trees and bathed the scene with fresh morning light the balloon lifted upright, the basket held firm with ropes and metal stakes. The light of the new day introduced us to our fellow travellers: two aged women who were enjoying a last burst of excitement and discovery while their health stayed with them. Dressed in thick khaki shirts and skirts and each sporting a broad jungle hat, they looked like early pioneers. While most of their peers were content to sit and watch countless hours of TV soaps, these two brave women were living life to the full. I admired their spirit.

Phil Dundee would be our pilot today, and he was already in the basket taking charge of the burner controls. Dave Dundee would tail us in the pursuit vehicle (their old van) and collect us when we achieved touch-down. The basket was divided into six separate compartments – like a large wicker milk bottle carrier – so that if the basket fell over we wouldn't crush each other in the resulting melee. Bill was already in, picking what he considered to be the safest spot. Then the first pioneer was heaved aboard, 'Quick, everyone in the basket,' called Dave, 'we're off!' I jumped aboard and helped haul the second pioneer inside while Jorg pushed her from behind. The balloon had started to rise before Jorg had scrambled in next to me. The basket lurched from side to side as Phil fought to unleash the final restraining rope. And then it was free, the balloon rising swiftly, lifting the basket into the bright morning sky of North Australia. Up and up we soared, and within minutes we were sailing high above the bright green canopy of the rain-forest. Magnificent views. My first balloon trip, something I had always wanted to do, and what a place to experience it. Phil switched the burner off, the balloon levelled out and we began to drift along the roof of the mighty forest below. How wonderfully silent it was without the roar of the burning gas, just the creak of the wicker basket and Jorg's laughter as he surveyed Bill's gaunt expression. Our two pioneering women were full of life, 'Higher!' called one. 'Oh yes, let's go higher, much, much higher!' called the other.

Dave, however, insisted that we were riding in the perfect thermal current now and that to go any higher would alter our intended course. 'Bugger the intended course!' laughed the first old lady, but Dave was the ship's captain and the ship's captain wouldn't be moved. We left the green of the forest behind us and glided over immense flat fields. Dave radioed Phil on the balloon's radio that all was well; we looked down to see the old van chasing us along the dirt roads below, a great cloud of billowing dust behind.

A lone farm house appeared in the distance, and Jorg asked if that was our landing sight. It wasn't. Dave explained that he and Phil didn't really get on with the owner. They had landed on his fields from time to time and the farmer had accused them of damaging his crops. Big arguments had broken out; Dave had tried to explain to the farmer that it wasn't always easy to land his balloon exactly where he choose. The farmer wouldn't have any of it and had threatened to shoot the balloon down if it flew over his house or landed in his fields again. The balloonists now kept as high as possible above the farmer's house and fields and tried to land a few miles on the other side of his boundary. The CB crackled into life. 'Yeah Dave, it's Phil here, mate; it looks like you're pretty low over Taylor's farm there.'

'You're right mate, I'll lift her up a little,' answered the balloon's captain. The farm was growing much bigger now. Dave fired the gas burner to put a diplomatic height between the balloon and the farmer's house. The farm grew bigger still, the burners were full on, yet we really didn't seem to be getting any higher. The radio sparked into life again. 'Dave, I would lift it up a bit there, mate,' suggested the pilot's friend, and I thought I noticed the merest hint of concern in the tones which were normally so laid back.

'I'm trying, mate, but she isn't really lifting up quick enough,' countered Dave. 'I think we might be in for a slightly premature landing again,' Dave added down the CB.

'Oh, bloody hell, mate, not again! Well good luck, I'll try and get to you before Taylor does!'

The balloon had dropped a little lower now, though still clear of the approaching farm roof by a good 150 feet. The door of the farmhouse burst open to reveal a big man pointing something at the balloon. Our two ladies whooped with delight, 'Gun!' exclaimed one, 'He's got a gun!' Taylor then jumped into his pickup, sped out of his gate and set off down the road towards our direction. 'Don't worry,' said Dave, 'he won't do you no harm, he's just a little pissed at us that's all, but all the same I'd appreciate a little help getting the balloon packed away and loaded into the van before he reaches us.' We had dropped to 100 feet now, and Dave pointed at two approaching dust clouds. 'The one on the left is the farmer's pickup, the one on the right is Phil.' The race was on.

The balloon was losing height very quickly now, making it easier to see just how fast we were actually travelling. 'Assume crash positions!' shouted Dave. Bill and I looked at each other, while Jorg laughed so hard that he was clearly having trouble breathing. The two old ladies applauded loudly, telling Dave what a fantastic morning they were having. The balloon finally came back to earth in a tilled field, the basket hit the ground and tipped on its side as the deflating balloon pulled us along. The lip of the basket acted as a plough, digging into the soft ground and filling the inside with soil, pebbles, straw and grass. Our ageing pioneers were in the two compartments nearest the ground and took the full brunt of the inbound debris. We bumped and scraped our way across the field until we came to a grinding halt. One by one we rolled ourselves from the basket; how no one was injured I'll never know; even the two pioneers survived the landing without receiving so much as a scratch. They jumped up and down with the thrill of it all and gave Dave another spontaneous round of applause. 'Thank you ladies,' he said, returning their great praise by removing his hat and giving a low gracious courtly bow.

The two plumes of dust were getting nearer and we rushed to help wrap the balloon inside the basket. Phil's van shot into the field and we heaved and shoved the basket roughly inside and quickly loaded ourselves too. 'Go, go, go,' enthused Dave, slamming the door of the van as we roared back down the road heading for the sanctuary of the rain-forest. 'Right,' asked Phil, with a big, broad grin on his face, 'everybody worked up enough appetite for breakfast?'

. . .

Back in England after our winter holidays were over, I was asked to join one of the three car crews. Nigel had been pleased with how I had taken control and run the brake department, and he'd been impressed with my confidence and commitment to the job. And when, on occasion, I had been forced to stand my ground with Georgio Ascanelli, the team's chief engineer, about whether a brake disc was cracked or not, or how many miles a certain set of calipers had been used in between servicing, Nigel was pleased that I had refused to be dictatorially managed. I always enjoyed working with Georgio (another ex-Ferrari man who came with Barnard), and any disagreements we had were always conducted with great civility, but I wasn't going to be pressured into agreeing with him merely because of his superior status within the team. The chief mechanic agreed: 'If you know you're right, then you must stick to your guns, otherwise there's no point in having you doing the work; we may as well just let the engineers get on with everything – and what a total catastrophe that would be.'

A vacancy for a mechanic on the spare car had arisen and would I like to join Bill Harris and Jorg Russ, the other two mechanics running the car. Throughout 1990 I had got to know Bill and Jorg quite well, and after surviving the Dundees' ballooning trip we had formed a good friendship. I would be more than happy to work with them. The job would be another promotion with a little more money, and with a little more job security too. I accepted Nigel's offer and on 8 January a letter from the accounts department informed me that my new salary would be £19,500. I would work primarily on the front of the car – the chassis, front suspension, pedals and steering rack and wiring loom. Jorg would be at the rear, taking care of the gearbox and rear suspension. Bill, the car's Number One mechanic, would look after the fuel tank, engine installation, make any executive decisions, drink the champagne, all that sort of thing.

In my new role I would have to give up my race-day pit-board job too; as a race mechanic I would become a member of the pit-stop crew. Nigel assigned me to the left-rear corner of the car, with responsibility for taking off the old wheel during the stop. To be honest it wasn't an aspect of the job I relished either. For the past fourteen races I had stood on the pit-wall and watched the action of the pit stops as the inbound cars screamed down the pit-lane towards the waiting mechanics. It looked bloody terrifying.

Unfortunately, the medium of TV belies the truth of the cars' real speed and video footage of the races portray the cars looking deceptively slow (as you watch the cars flash past the screen this seems hard to believe, I know, but from first hand experience I know it to be so). Pit-lane speed limits weren't introduced until after the tragedies of that hideous Imola race of 1994. Before that horrible accident, cars would hurtle past one pit-crew and towards their own at something approaching 150 feet per second. One tiny error of judgement and lives could be lost. Now, some may think that what I have just said is a gross over-exaggeration, but those who disagree with me have never stood in front of a ferociously hot, 800 horsepower, ear-splittingly loud race car which is spitting fire and careering straight for them at 100 miles an hour.

> *The Jabberwock, with eyes of flame,*
> *Came whiffling through the tulgey wood,*
> *And burbled as it came!*
>
> …

In any event, Nigel had offered me the job of working directly on a car, and part of that job was to carry out the work of the pit-stops. I had accepted the job and so I had accepted the inevitable role of being a pit-stop mechanic too. My choice.

As for our driver line up, Nelson would remain, but because of Alessandro Nannini's awful accident with his new helicopter (he had only just taken delivery of it, a treat to himself because of his recent race successes) his seat was taken by Roberto Moreno. We had a totally new car too: the John Barnard-designed B191. It looked nothing like anything else that Benetton had ever produced but this wasn't surprising. Barnard had started the design work of the B191 with a completely clean sheet; it was intended that nothing should be carried over from previous Benetton creations. The only way to move forward is to innovate, I suppose. It must be said that what he came up with was a beautiful-looking car, endowed with some very sleek body lines. In essence it looked much more like a Ferrari than a Benetton; the shape could have been a perfect successor to Ferrari's 1990 car, the 641. The reason for this was that John Barnard and his design team had drawn the 639, the 640 and the 641, and their new design seemed a natural evolution of that series of cars. If the B191 had been painted red and fitted with a V12 instead of a Cosworth V8 it could easily have carried a 642 chassis plate too.

John Barnard is a perfectionist, his attention to detail is legendary, and there were some fine details to the design of the B191. It is usual that the radiator side-pods of a Grand Prix car are secured to the chassis with a number of individual bolt fixings around the edges of the pod. However, as the side-pods are removed two or three times each day of a race weekend this becomes a tedious and time-consuming matter – plus one always runs the risk of 'rounding' an over-tight bolt in the process of trying to remove it. In an ingenious way of improving this situation, Barnard's team had developed a flush-fitting quick-release catch. Operated by a special two-pronged key, this simple, though brilliant design feature enabled both side-pods to be removed from the chassis in a matter of seconds. I have never understood the real reasons why but those catches were never carried over to any other Benetton designs since the '91. I don't know if it was just a matter of pride ('I can't use that idea because I didn't think of it first') or what it was, but it was a superb idea that has since been wasted.

However, one feature of John's car which has remained on every Benetton car since, and has now, in fact, been copied onto every Formula One car in the pit-lane is his quick-release catch for the nose and front wing assembly. This was another brilliant piece of ingenuity, and one which should have won his team a trophy for Formula One design excellence. The idea wasn't new, since it was based on the plastic snail-cam fasteners found in quick-build kitchen units in the big DIY warehouses. Push a doweled peg into the body of the snail-cam and an Allen key turns the cam through 180 degrees, locking the two parts together. Job finished. Brilliant!

On the other hand, the nose of the B190 was secured by four small pins, retained in the chassis by internal spring clips. The idea was to grip the head of the pin with a pair of pliers, pulling them out of the nose in order to detach it. They were terrible. The pins would either stick in the nose, resulting in the pliers constantly slipping on the tiny removal flange or, occasionally, the pins would work loose and disappear out on the circuit somewhere. Other teams were using bolts to hold their car's nose to the chassis, though most soon relented once they noticed a possible alternative, but Williams continued to use this method until relatively recently. Although bolting the nose in place was a very secure method of retention, in an emergency pit-stop following a front wing shunt, the mechanics would take far too long trying to replace the damaged nose. I remember that at one time, in an attempt to speed things up, Williams had a couple of small air-guns in the pit-lane, set and reserved just in case of a possible nose change; to me this was a case of treating the symptoms instead of curing the illness. Nevertheless, in the end, even the great strength of Williams Grand Prix Engineering couldn't hold back the tide any longer and they too fitted a version of the Barnard nose catch.

. . .

The year 1991 turned into a strange season for us, a time of mixed fortunes and sadly, despite his great technical skills, the first major upheaval was with our illustrious technical director, John Barnard. The B191 was supposed to take the world by storm, the car to catapult Benetton amongst the dogfights of McLaren,

Ferrari and Williams for race victories. Maybe it was not the car to clinch the Constructors' Championship in its first year, but the next evolution of it, the B192, should have been in a position to have the bounties of glory heaped upon it. A contract had been signed with Pirelli, and they had agreed to help Benetton develop a tyre for the B191 which should challenge the dominance of Goodyear, and in 1991 a shot at second place in the Championship should have been a distinct possibility.

However, it wasn't long into the season before one could sense that things weren't going as smoothly as we had all hoped, and the relationship with Barnard and Benetton was becoming increasingly strained. Benetton had shovelled huge amounts of money into structuring its revamped race team and it was – quite rightly – expecting to see some pretty impressive results from this vast financial investment.

Right from the beginning John had no desire to move to Witney and had wanted to relocate the entire team further south, to Godalming, next door to where he lived. That Benetton was even considering relocating its entire operation, notwithstanding the huge inconvenience it would cause to over a hundred other people, has always struck me as being quite incredible. However, the mere fact that Benetton were prepared to do this shows the extent to which the Benetton management valued the merits of their new technical director. Temporary buildings had already been leased in Godalming; a test team and a research and development department had been established; and the hunt was on to find a suitable building site for the team's brand-new headquarters.

Meanwhile the entire staff of the old Witney factory was invited to Godalming so they could observe the temporary facility, witness for themselves the picturesque beauty of the Surrey landscape, and see what an irresistible, golden opportunity they were about to be offered by having their place of employment shifted two hours' drive away. If the staff didn't relish such a long trip, ten or fourteen times a week – and we knew one chap who didn't – then they could always look to relocate. That generations of their families have lived in Oxfordshire; that their children were happily settled at school; that their grandchildren lived just two minutes round the corner; that their husbands and wives were in full-time jobs; that their lifelong friends and cricket clubs and gardening societies were all within a short stroll away; surely all of these things were just minor irritations? 'Earth calling Planet Formula One, we're losing contact with you, can you still read me?'

It was a similar story when Barnard worked with Ferrari. He is a happily settled family man and had no wish to relocate to Italy. And, surely, it was unthinkable speculation that Ferrari would uproot from Maranello and relocate to sunny Surrey? (I wonder if they were asked?) Despite this stand-off, both parties could see obvious advantages in working together, and an agreement was reached whereby John would open a drawing office and research facility in England, called the Guildford Technical Office, known as the Ferrari GTO. Unfortunately, trying to run a successful Grand Prix team from two different headquarters was never going to be easy and their remoteness provided both parties with all sorts of logistical problems. With Barnard's appointment to Benetton it was agreed that the only way forward was to house everything under one roof. Again, I think this is good sound policy, but trying to move everyone and everything down to Surrey, that bit never really gelled with me. However, the Benetton group is a very professional organization, with brilliant financial tacticians, and they must have gone through the figures and the pros and cons of such a move in great detail and found that it was both possible and feasible.

A few months later, as the solid stone of history proves, debating the pros and cons of a proposed move to Godalming became purely hypothetical. It never happened. The temporary buildings were closed and the quest for a suitable building site in Surrey was cancelled. Of course, as a mere mechanic I was never privy to the reasons why the business relationship between Flavio Briatore and John Barnard collapsed; I guessed it was because we weren't achieving the race results quickly enough, but there may have been many other considerations too. Whatever the reasons, I feel the details are private and between the parties concerned. I've never claimed to be a journalist (in fact, I've always claimed not to be) and I had no need or desire to delve further; it was the net result of the situation that was of concern to me. Just after the Monaco Grand Prix it became apparent that John would be leaving and, sure enough, he didn't attend the Canadian race. And in Mexico, the second race of the North American double-header, we were all introduced to a Mr Gordon Kimball, the team's new technical director. He seemed a pleasant enough chap. I had never heard of him before, although that didn't count for much, but it was as if the team's management had decided that they just needed someone (anyone?) to carry the mantle of technical director until they had more time to reorganize. Poor Gordon Kimball was replaced by the end of the year.

The most poignant aspect of losing John at that moment was that in Canada, the very race he didn't attend, Nelson Piquet won the Grand Prix for Benetton! It was rather an odd victory; in the closing stages of the race Nelson was in second position trailing behind Mansell, who had rejoined Williams for his push to become world champion, and they stayed in this order until the final corner of the last lap. Suddenly, as Mansell prematurely waved to the crowd, his Williams ground to an undignified stop, with Piquet nipping past to take the chequered flag. Very bizarre! Afterwards, Mansell absolutely, categorically and unconditionally denied that he had flicked the ignition switch by accident as he lifted his hand from the cockpit. Well, we're all only human and we all make mistakes from time to time. After carefully inspecting the car, I understand the Williams mechanics never found fault with it. Conclude from that what you will.

So, for whatever reason, Williams lost one and we won one, the team's fifth ever victory and my third. Sadly, that lone fortuitous win in Canada would be our first and last of the year, and it was a great pity to have parted with John Barnard when we did. Given sufficient development time I'm convinced that the B191 would have proved its full potential and perhaps we could have squeezed more than just a single victory out of it. However, the problem that Barnard was forced to accept was that there is no spare time in Formula One. The life of a successful Grand Prix car is glittering but brief: it is drawn, born, lives a glorious life of eight or nine months, and as soon as the last flag falls it instantly becomes a pile of ageing scrap.

The B191 was scheduled to be introduced for the third race, the team sticking with the B190 for Phoenix and Sao Paulo. Nevertheless, despite the added comfort that this two-race buffer provided, the 1991 car arrived late and its first build turned into a series of all-nighters. When it left the factory for its initial shakedown we didn't even have a starter for it, we couldn't get fuel pressure and we had to resort to towing it along the road to try and fire the engine into life. We were slipping behind schedule and needed more time, but try telling that to the FIA. The races will happen when they're planned, and no one is going to put the San Marino Grand Prix back a couple of weeks because Benetton isn't quite ready. We had problems with the gearbox, problems with the engine's cooling system and constant problems with fuel pressure. The knock-on effect of all this was that the Imola race was much worse than 1990. There was not so much as an hour's sleep for anybody throughout the duration of Thursday, Friday, and Saturday. We flew back to England on Monday morning, which meant that we finally got to bed at nine o'clock Sunday night.

Monaco, the following race, was another massive epic. On Friday, at five in the afternoon, on a day curiously known as 'the day off' (as the cars run on Thursday instead), we started building a jig to try and set the gearbox selectors. Not building the gearbox itself, you understand, but building a jig to try and help us build the gearboxes. At midnight the gearbox mechanics were still down at Riva Boat Services on the harbour front, borrowing mills and lathes, trying to machine the jig into submission. We barely managed to finish the cars in time for Saturday's practice and qualifying sessions. Saturday drifted on, melting at some point into Sunday, and we were struggling to get the cars back on the track for the morning warm-up. And come the race, after all that extraordinary effort, Nelson's car was clipped from behind, forcing him to retire from the race, halfway through lap one!

Normally this sort of news would have been soul-destroying, leaving us utterly deflated but we were so tired I don't think anyone even bothered to comment on what had happened. It just meant there were fewer pit-stops to do. However, Moreno was still pounding round so we were still on duty, although one of the gearbox mechanics was so exhausted he fell asleep while standing in the pit-lane, coming very close to hitting the floor like a dropped sack of potatoes, a procession of cars constantly screaming just inches away from where we stood. After the race was finished, while we were loading everything into the race trucks, I remember a chap with a thick American accent telling us how lucky we were to be working in Formula One and how he'd give his right arm to able to join us, 'Gee,' he said, smiling at the cars, 'you guys have got it all!'

...

Nigel Stepney was the next to go. Again, there were perhaps several contributing factors in his decision to leave, but I think the main cause was the departure of John Barnard. One of the chief reasons he had moved from Lotus was to work with John, and he would have been more than happy to follow him to Guildford too. However, it wouldn't be the last that Formula One would see of a Barnard/Stepney partnership, for in 1993 when John was reunited with Ferrari, Nigel soon joined him in the role of chief mechanic. Nigel has pushed and fought his way forward from the very first day of his career, and with the arrival of the press release from Maranello announcing that he was to be the first English chief mechanic appointed to the legendary Italian marque, Nigel Stepney made Grand Prix history.

The departures of Barnard and Stepney were followed by two arrivals. First on the scene was Tom Walkinshaw, a big, stocky-looking Scot. Walkinshaw had been in racing for years, although never in Formula One. A one-time driver, he had gradually built an enormous motor-racing empire, Tom Walkinshaw Racing (TWR) and secured a huge personal fortune too. I have memories of him driving Mazda RX7s when I was an apprentice at Terry Howlett's back in the 1970s; I never imaged then, as I fitted the extra-zoomy TWR spoilers to the RX7 sales cars, that we'd end up working together! He's progressed a little since then. Touring cars; Group C cars; Le Mans GT1 cars; a string of prestigious dealerships; Walkinshaw is a real motor engineering entrepreneur. He and Benetton had made an agreement to consolidate the loss of Barnard and to increase the technical skills of Benetton by bringing in key members of TWR's engineering staff. I seem to remember that he was given the title of engineering director.

Walkinshaw's first priority was to locate suitable sites for a new Benetton factory. If the team wanted to grow it needed to ditch its decrepit old rabbit warren and move into a purpose-designed building, although any proposed site would certainly be in Oxfordshire and not two or more hours drive away from Witney.

The next person to arrive on the scene was another driver, a young German chap new into Formula One, from a career with Mercedes driving for their Group C sportscar team. The fresh-faced young upstart was called Michael Schumacher. At first, the news of his appointment caused little interest with the mechanics (just another damn seat to have to make) but at least Jorg seemed relatively pleased, as Schumacher's arrival would give him someone to converse with in his own language.

Schumacher had only driven in one Grand Prix before, a couple of weeks earlier at Spa, for the brand-new Jordan team. However, his debut outing lasted less than a tenth of a lap before the Jordan's clutch gave up. Regardless, Walkinshaw knew of the German's potential from the years that the TWR Group C Jaguars had raced against Mercedes in the World Sportscar Championships. Walkinshaw's advice to Flavio was simple: that he should sign him and sign him really, really quickly. If this driver was allowed to get away, Benetton Formula would regret it for the rest of its existence.

I first met Michael in the Benetton pit garage at Monza after he had just signed a contract with Flavio. Somehow, Eddie Jordan had taken his eye off the Formula One ball just for a split second, but that was sufficient time for Flavio to introduce himself to Schumacher and his manager. Eddie, in that first year was perhaps still a little green to the way some things work in Grand Prix racing, but after all the political dust had settled, the upshot was that he had let Schumacher slip through his fingers. And he must have been seething too, for without doubt, if he had kept Michael in one of his cars, Jordan Grand Prix Ltd would be Formula One World Champions two or even three times over by now. In that one slip Eddie saw untold millions in lost revenue escape through his fingers. Good job it's only a sport and we can all shake hands and have a drink together on the flight home.

The brief Benetton/Schumacher courtship was shrouded in secrecy, and the press release was withheld until the very last minute. However, prior to the team flying out to Italy, Michael had already been to our Witney factory for a seat fitting, and we had taken this seat with us as hand baggage on the plane from Heathrow. It was èven marked with a large MS in white paint-pen on the back – all seats are marked with the relevant driver's initials – but as the teams are constantly sending all sorts of last-minute components out with their mechanics everyone seemed oblivious to this rather blatant clue as to what we were about to announce to the world.

As it transpired, Walkinshaw was perfectly correct in his predictions and the Schumacher signature on a Benetton contract was a tremendous scoop. The ground-work was all carried out somewhat furtively and involved the rotten deed of firing dear old Roberto Moreno halfway through the season. At a hastily arranged meeting at Nice airport he was informed of Benetton's desire that he should pursue a possible career change (Roberto later told us that this wasn't the first time he had been summoned to Nice airport for such a meeting and that he suspected bad news). He was more than a little miffed about it too but his performances during the first half of the season were nowhere near as impressive as that stand-in job he did for us in Japan. He's a slight chap and he just didn't seem to have the stamina to run at a competitive pace for the duration of a race. Great shame, but Formula One is a tough game. Presumably Benetton paid him handsomely for his trouble, and he probably made more from that one golden handshake than we'll earn throughout our entire working lives.

As I said, the first time I met Michael was in the Monza garage, and when he introduced himself he went amongst us making a special point of shaking everybody's hand. He stood back, leaning forward to proffer his right hand, his left remained securely in his back pocket; a sign I took to mean that he was feeling a little shy, a touch unsure of himself in these new and strange surroundings. I knew nothing of him and, of course, he didn't know me from Adam. On that, our first meeting, I had no idea that he would soon develop and mature to become the greatest Formula One driver of his generation, and a few years later I would be writing my first book, describing the unprecedented sequence of events which would eventually lead to his first Drivers' World Championship (and he had no idea that he would volunteer to write the foreword for it either!).

As Benetton team-mates we worked side by side for four and a half years. Our relationship culminated in securing both the Drivers' and the Constructors' Championships in 1995, and as far as my career as a mechanic is concerned, those times were the best years of my life. Indeed, I feel as though all the years of training and mechanical work I did prior to that zenith lead inexplicably towards that goal. It is the ultimate achievement for any mechanic, the final rung of a very high and sometimes unstable ladder: secure the Formula One Constructors' trophy and there is no more to secure. Cross 'mechanic' off the list and decide what to try next. And now, the paths of Michael and I have once again separated; he, still pursuing his Formula One career, searching for further glories by driving for Scuderia Ferrari; me, a retired mechanic, scribbling my books in France. I wish I had a photograph of that handshake in Monza, two strangers meeting for the first time, a fleeting moment frozen in time. That morning as we drank coffee and chatted, none of us had any idea exactly what was about to be unleashed into the world of Grand Prix racing.

…

In the same year that we welcomed our future World Champion driver, we were preparing to bid farewell to a previous one; 1991 would be Nelson Piquet's last year in Formula One. In Adelaide, the last race of his long and highly distinguished career, I had the unforgettable privilege of being with him on the very last occasion he climbed from a Formula One car.

For me, the 1991 Australian Grand Prix was special for three reasons. It was Nelson's last race; my mother had flown out to Adelaide to visit friends and watch the race from the grandstands; and the temperamental coastal weather turned it into another historic event, as the deluge of rain which fell, literally a few minutes prior to the start, would mark the race as the shortest Grand Prix ever run in Formula One's history.

After the warm-up Schumacher wasn't happy with his own race car and the decision had been taken to put him into the spare car. In fact, when I was scouring through the LAT archives digging out relevant photographs for this book, I came across one of Schumacher just climbing aboard our car as I held the belts clear of the seat (you can easily tell it's the spare car because it has both Michael's and Nelson's names on the side). In the next photo, where Michael is holding the umbrella, you can see our gearbox mechanic Paul James standing near the rear wing; his expression sums up the mood of the occasion! Actually, it was an exhausted Paul who fell asleep in the Monaco pit-lane a few months earlier. Formula One, it's a glamorous life!

It was a bit daft to have started the race in such aquatic conditions, and if the officials had delayed it for just an hour, the storm would have passed and we would once again have been bathed in bright South Australian sunshine. But I suppose global TV times are all prearranged and to delay the start would have proved catastrophic for screening the race; this, I'm sure, is the only reason why the Grand Prix was sent under way at the scheduled time. However, appeasing global scheduling or not, it soon proved quite farcical to continue racing Formula One cars in these adverse conditions, and the whole show lasted a mere fourteen laps before the chaos of cars aqua-planing into each other every few seconds forced the officials to bring the red flag out and stop the race.

For a while, with a grey blanket of clouds hanging overhead and torrents of thick rain still gushing upon us, it was assumed that the race would be restarted. The cars were pushed back onto the grid and the teams of mechanics reformed around them, most holding nylon covers over the exposed engines and gearboxes in an attempt to stave off the water. The spare car had been damaged and so, out of a job, I helped the mechanics preparing Nelson's car, mopping out the chassis with masses of blue-roll. Nelson's race boots were sodden and I'd ran back to the garage to fetch new ones. With these the first job was to cut the toe off the right hand boot, something he insisted on to avoid his boot touching the steering column as he flicked his foot between the throttle and brake pedals. Next they needed the soles scuffing, to increase the grip on the pedal pads. He handed me his old wet boots, complaining that his socks were wet too.

'What do you want me to do about it?' I asked, 'you're all wet, your overalls are soaking, everything's wet. You've just been driving in a major bloody rain storm!'

'I don't think we can do anything about it,' he laughed, 'I'm just telling you that my socks are wet, that's all! My last race and I've got cold feet!'

We finally got Nelson back in the car and waited for news of the restart. Of course, it didn't come. There was a lot of bustling from the officials, several pieces of damp paper exchanged hands, teeth were thoughtfully sucked, but eventually the Grand Prix was declared abandoned, the results from the first race would stand.

Georgio Ascanelli was engineering Nelson that day, and he stood at the front of the car as he explained to Nelson that the race was over. Nelson looked back at him, his deep, expressive eyes betraying the realization that his Formula One career was also over. He beckoned for his engineer to come nearer, and when he did he quietly asked Georgio to allow the mechanics to fire the car up and let him drive off round the circuit for one last lap, a final slow tour to wave goodbye to the world of Formula One. Of course, with the race now abandoned, the circuit was officially closed to traffic and to have let Nelson go would have broken all sorts of sporting regulations. Georgio considered the situation and slowly shook his head as he explained to Nelson that he couldn't let him drive off; to allow such a thing would be a grave failing.

'Come on Georgio,' he said, 'let's go, one last time!' but already I could sense that Nelson had resigned himself to the impossibility of the request. Georgio's position was one of great responsibility, he simply couldn't allow it.

'No Nelson, the track is closed; we can't let you go, you know we can't. There's nothing we can do. The flags are out, Nelson, let's go home'

Nothing happened for a moment or two, then I heard the click of the belt buckle and he gently pulled the steering wheel from the column. 204 Grand Prix starts (the third highest in history), 24 pole positions, 23 race victories, 485.5 points (the third highest in history) and three Drivers' World Championships. It was finished. It was all finished. The shortest race in Formula One history; Ayrton Senna's final World Championship winning season; Nelson Piquet's Grand Prix career. All over.

And for us, despite Nelson's lucky win in Montreal, we only scored a total of 38.5 points throughout the year, the odd-looking score a result of half points being awarded in Adelaide (Nelson was running in fourth place when the race was stopped). The final standings in the 1991 Constructors' Championship saw us drop back a place from the previous year, finishing the season in fourth position. With a magnificent score of 139, McLaren International claimed their forth consecutive Constructors' trophy. Their dominance over Formula One had been incredible, and as I walked over to their garage to congratulate the mechanics on securing another McLaren plaque to the winners' cup, the team looked as strong and professional as ever. I have to admit I felt a little deflated as I shook hands and chatted with them; it seemed certain that their winning form would continue for many more years to come too. With the power of the fabulous Honda engine, Senna's brilliance behind the wheel and Dennis calmly controlling the engineering, I could see no reason why they shouldn't continue holding the trophy for another ten years or more. In fact, I couldn't have been more wrong and 1991 would be the last year they would clinch the title during my career as a Formula One mechanic! How quickly the balance of power can shift in this sport.

Ferrari had finished the year in third place – seventeen points ahead of us – but notwithstanding the fact that Alain Prost was driving for them, they had failed to win a single race, the first time such a thing had happened to them since 1986. Throughout the course of the season the great Italian team seemed completely disorganized and as the season drew to a close it seemed to be in out-and-out panic mode. The team manager was fired and then Prost was fired too. Alain Prost fired by Ferrari! A three-times World Champion driver sacked by an eight-times Constructors' World Champion. What a sad, shambolic end to the season and unfortunately it would only get worse for Ferrari in 1992.

Of course, we too had suffered a retrograde step, a problem undoubtedly caused by internal wranglings and too much coming and going. No consistency to the mix, that was the problem, though no where near as catastrophic a situation as Ferrari's. On the bright side, however, a new and very special ingredient had recently been added to Benetton's simmering pot, a rare and precious spice that would gradually impart its improving qualities over the next couple of years. All of a sudden its perfection would suddenly explode, transforming the Benetton recipe out of all recognition. I didn't know it then, of course, but the Constructors' Championship was coming, it would just take a few more years! But for Ferrari there would be little or no improvement in their fortunes until the start of 1996.

All that was years away in the future, and back in Australia in 1991, standing in the rain-soaked pits of Adelaide, it was time to dry off, pack everything away and head off on holiday for a couple of weeks. Back at the factory, it was time to calm everything down too. Time to take careful stock of things and begin detailed planning for next year's campaign. Holiday time. That seemed to have come back round jolly quick.

Another year done!

Chapter five

1992

Another promotion thanks to Nelson...Joan Villadelprat...Appreciating F1 racing for what it is...Tom Walkinshaw...New factory site...Brawn arrives...Brundle arrives...The B192...Michael's maiden win

The first year I joined the race team I looked after the brake department. The second year I was promoted to the spare car. In 1992 I was promoted to work on one of the two race cars; little difference, but a promotion nevertheless. Actually, the whole of the spare car crew was promoted with me, and we swapped roles with what was Nelson's race car crew. Not surprisingly, this produced some rather unhappy looks and comments from a couple of the chaps who had effectively been demoted, but the decision was out of my hands.

Of course, I can't deny that I was pleased by the news – everyone likes to be thought of favourably – and I was looking forward to working with the team's new driver brought in to replace Nelson Piquet. Actually, the reason for the change of crews was really down to Nelson. Throughout much of 1991 he had always favoured using the spare car. I don't want to go into the details of why and it would be most immodest of me to make any suppositions. Nevertheless, the line was that during the Sunday pre-race meetings, Nelson would normally insist on racing the spare car. In fact, come the end of 1991, I think there were only two or three races during the season where Nelson had consented to use his designated race car, one of which was for the Canadian Grand Prix, so at least his race car crew had the satisfaction of claiming his final victory. Perhaps a personality clash with some of the other mechanics sparked the situation off, I don't know and I didn't care. If Nelson felt happier with me strapping him into the car, as opposed to mechanic X, then so be it. It is difficult to imagine for a moment that one car felt in any way consistently different from another car, and to eliminate the possibility of a flexing chassis we had even interchanged the two chassis between the crews without informing the driver of the switch (twice, I seem to remember) but still Nelson maintained his preference for using the spare car. Anyway, whatever his reasons, it was undoubtedly Nelson who forced the internal reshuffle at the start of 1992, and I have him to thank for my promotion onto a race car.

Another year, another promotion and another pay rise too; things were going well! 'I am pleased to advise you,' wrote Joan Villadelprat (pronounced *Joe-ann*), our new operations manager, 'that with effect from 1 January 1992, your salary will be increased to £22,790 per annum. Where relevant this review takes into account a number of factors including your performance during 1991.' A touch enigmatic that last line? I was longing to ask him what he meant by 'where relevant' but I was too scared and settled with being happy just to accept the rise.

Catch his expression in the right mood and Joan's features – his dark hair, dark watchful eyes and his thick dark moustache – remind me of the posters of Big Brother from the old black and white adaptation of Orwell's *1984*. I always fancied the idea of hanging a huge poster in the race-bay, showing an enlarged photo of Joan's head and shoulders, his deep, thoughtful eyes seeming to follow every move, carefully observing what everyone was doing; the words 'big brother is watching you' written underneath. But, again, I was always too scared to go through with it; some people said his bark was much worse than his bite. Others didn't. As the years went on, Joan and I formed a strong mutual appreciation of each other. I hesitate to use the word 'friendship', as this may be overstating things. I mean, we never phone each other to chat about how well Tiger Woods is playing at the moment; we never exchange birthday cards; nor do we meet up on our free weekends for a beer at the Chequers (though, at several Benetton parties, we've both ordered far more drinks for each other than was particularly very wise). However, we are certainly friendly towards each other; he was genuinely thrilled when I had my first book published, telling me that it was a great achievement for me to persevere with writing the text and negotiating the contract with the publishers, while still forging ahead with the 1994 season. He told me that it was something that he too would love to do, but that he knew it would never happen. He has always been supportive of my writing, and in return I am genuinely impressed with what he has achieved with his career too. Maybe writing books is something that Joan doesn't see himself doing, but, by the same token, running a Formula One team is certainly something that I don't ever envisage doing.

Joan is Catalonian, married, with a family and, in common with all people from northern Spain, he is also a very proud man, proud of his heritage, his land, his origins. He has worked incredibly hard for his success, and like Nigel Stepney, he has dedicated much of his life to Formula One. He spent years with McLaren working as a mechanic, then to Italy and Ferrari, working as their chief mechanic (the last chief mechanic to work directly for Enzo Ferrari before his death in 1988. In fact, Joan was the Ferrari chief mechanic in Monza at the time of that historic one-two finish). After his stint with Ferrari it was back to England, employed by Ken Tyrrell as his team manager, and to Benetton to work alongside Gordon Message.

In 1991, when Stepney resigned from Benetton, Joan also deputized as replacement chief mechanic for a while. There are few roles he hasn't played at one time or another. A tight bond soon formed between him and Flavio, helped enormously by the fact that Joan speaks fluent Italian (as well as Spanish, English and French), and before long he was given the title of operations manager, with responsibility for overseeing the day-to day running of the factory, the production department and the organization of the test and race teams too. A year or so later Joan had risen to the rank of operations director.

Flavio would be the first to admit that he knows little of mechanical engineering, and having Joan in the team was a great help to him. Unlike McLaren, or Williams, where Ron and Frank are capable of overseeing the running of their own teams, Flavio could pass all of those day-to-day chores over to Joan, allowing him, in his position as commercial director, to concentrate with the team's marketing department. This is where Flavio's skills lay, and to improve the marketing and sponsorship of the team is precisely what Luciano Benetton had brought him in to do.

In this respect, Flavio was one of the best bosses one could hope to have. For example, during the lunch hour I could be working away, repairing the carburettor from my road car, or making a bookshelf bracket in the fabrication department, and if Flavio walked past he would have no interest whatsoever in what I, or anyone else, was up to. As far as he was concerned, perhaps the selection of air-correction jets, diaphragms and throttle-pump springs were from somewhere underneath the bodywork of the B192. He didn't know what the bits were, he didn't need to know and he didn't want to know either. Flavio is a marketing man, not a mechanic. As long as the cars were polished and the correct sponsors stickers were on the right bit of the bodywork Flavio was a happy man. Organizing the mechanics and the preparation of the cars he could leave to Joan. However, if Joan was on one of his lunch-time prowls round the factory and found parts of a carburettor being cleaned and rebuilt on his beautifully clean, white work surfaces it was impossible to explain the situation away.

He was my boss and I was his charge, and if he told me that we had no choice but to work all night, then that was that. I might not like the idea (most certainly didn't like the idea) but it was part of the job and he knew that I would always do as I was asked. And, by the same token, if there were only five minutes to go before the pit-lane closed and I shouted over to him that I needed a helping hand in order to get the car to the grid before the deadline, I knew that he would do whatever he could to help. 'Hold this! Pass me that! Get me one of those from Paul Howard!' When we were really struggling to finish the cars, with tears of sweat stinging the eyes, and the engineers all conspiring to do everything they could to thwart us by constantly producing ever-growing and ever-changing job lists, when the clock was truly against us and it was proving near impossible to even see the car due to the masses of corporate guests milling about the garage, when it was genuinely Now-Or-Never time, I knew that I could depend on him, and he knew he could rely on me.

Joan is also quite aware of my perception of exactly what Grand Prix racing is. Being inside Formula One is a very demanding and dedicated life, full of highs and lows, a life full of tears and heated emotions. At times it can seem like it's one of the most important things in the world. However, for some of the more impressionable souls it does become the only important thing in the world, the true reality of their situation is lost to them. The reality is this: Formula One for all its associated passions, is a job of work, another way of earning a living. The fact that a newly designed suspension 'upright' has no intention whatsoever of fitting the wishbone may cause all sorts of arm-waving and general gnashing of teeth and result in a vast stream of faxes, phone calls and e-mails back and forth between the circuit and the factory as people try to pin the blame on one another, and some of those people may well refuse to speak to each other for weeks, or even months afterwards as tempers continue to brew and simmer, but take just one step outside of Formula One's micro-universe and nobody living in the real world gives a damn about the upright. In the real world the only concerns are that the cat needs feeding, the puncture on Gran's bike still wants looking at and that the video must be unplugged to stop it desperately trying to record the *Dad's Army* repeat over what remains of the Monza highlights, half of which have already been lost due to the kids taping the *Mr Blobby* weekend special on top of it. Real life in the real world, where Grand Prix racing is something to be enjoyed as a distraction, a weekend hobby.

Formula One is just another job, but treated properly it can also be terrific fun, and as the teams stump up about 99.9 percent of the costs, it's a wonderfully cheap way to see the world too! It's also a colossal stepping stone if you wish to move on to other things and are prepared to take full advantage of it. My first book is an example: it would have been infinitely more difficult to have persuaded a publisher to have taken me seriously if it weren't for the huge lever that working for Formula One gave me. If you work for a Grand Prix team and have written something of merit about them, then people in the book world are immediately interested in taking a closer look at your efforts. If, on the other hand, you work for a Vauxhall dealership and have written a truly revealing and scintillating account of your experiences, then there is every likelihood that your manuscript will stay firmly at the bottom of the slush pile, gathering dust, remaining unopened and unread.

You have to be professional, of course, to work in Formula One and you have to work to the world's highest standards, but the key is to get Formula One to work for you, not letting Formula One use you until you're no more than a burnt-out wreck. There are many examples of people who have worked in Formula One for year after year, just because it is F1, once young men who have given too many of their best years to Grand Prix racing. But come the first race for which they feel unable to continue, they will, inevitably, be immediately replaced by somebody younger, stronger, more enthusiastic and fitter. Replaced and forgotten in the blinking of an eye. Twenty-five years here, gone tomorrow. The way of the sport. No one (with the possible exception of Bernie Ecclestone himself) is indispensable to Grand Prix racing. No one.

Along with other high-profile activities, such as art, opera, music, film and fashion, the realization that Formula One is just another commercial industry is rarely discussed in such base, businesslike terms amongst the people who actually produce the finished work. For such people to talk openly of their work in simplistic financial terms would be thought of as giving the game away. To an extent it is the same in Grand Prix racing; it is a passionate business, but a business all the same. Some people know this, some people will never understand it, even if you sat them down and patiently explained it twice a day for the rest of their lives. In 1992, when I told a long-serving Benetton mechanic how much I enjoyed the chance, provided courtesy of Formula One, to see and explore a little bit of the world, he snapped at me, saying that the job wasn't about travelling and looking at things and writing diaries and talking to people and taking notes. He said the job was about making sure that the cars were polished and ready to go, each and every time the drivers wanted to jump into them. At first I felt a little sorry for him, thinking how sad it was that he should miss such golden opportunities, but after the first couple of years I just gave up on him; he was incurable, too set in his ways. He must have swallowed a Formula One conditioning pill with his morning coffee every day for the past fifteen years. The perfect employee, I guess! However, I wonder how keen on Formula One he would have been if a Grand Prix season consisted of sixteen races, all run only in the freezing Thruxton sleet, being paid half as much and receiving no media coverage whatsoever. 'It's not about travelling, it's about being totally pissed off and wanting to top yourself.'

Joan knew my thoughts on all of this, even though we never openly discussed such things. The odd passed comment and the occasional wry smile made it clear that we both understood the rules of the game. Perhaps in me he saw a little bit of himself although we are very different people. Joan has always been terribly ambitious, very career-orientated, always searching for more responsibility and more authority within the sport – mechanic, team manager, operations manager, operations director and on and on, no doubt. Me, all I wanted out of Formula One was to win the Constructors' Championship and have my photograph taken holding the trophy just to prove it had actually happened. I didn't know how long that would take, but I knew that whenever it did happen I could then wrap up my mechanical career and start planning for the next challenge.

...

Just like Joan, Tom Walkinshaw is also very much a hands-on sort of a chap and I'm quite sure that he could have spotted a 'homer' going down from a range of a thousand paces. However, despite his title of engineering director, I never saw much of him at the Witney factory, and I didn't see an awful lot more of him at the new Enstone factory either. I suppose he carried out most of his duties from his TWR base at Broadstone Manor which was just outside Chipping Norton. Looking back, it is now much easier to gauge Tom's impact on Benetton's success, but at the time it was not clear at all. His arrival was viewed with mixed feelings by many of the Benetton staff. Of course, everyone knew of TWR and they knew that Walkinshaw was very successful in all the categories in which he entered his racing teams. Therefore, it was safe to assume that his involvement with us could be extremely beneficial from an engineering point of view. But TWR is a huge conglomerate and we were apprehensive about what might become of us and of our individuality. We didn't relish the prospect of a TWR buyout and to wake up one morning to discover that Benetton had been incorporated as the gemstone in Walkinshaw's motor-racing crown. If we were taken over we would cease to be Benetton Formula, our identity would pale and our four bright primary colours would have to fade in order to blend and comply with the rest of the TWR empire. I didn't want that and the same feelings were echoed by many of my colleagues as well.

The TWR buyout never happened, and on reflection an awful lot of good resulted from Walkinshaw's involvement with Benetton. Furthermore, I don't think that Tom ever really received the thanks or appreciation which he rightly deserved for his input. I may be wrong here, and I can only speak from my own feelings on the matter, but the entire duration of the working relationship between Walkinshaw and Flavio Briatore seemed permanently unsettled. As a mechanic it was difficult for me to pinpoint exactly why that should be, but I always got the impression that things were never as comfortable as they should have been.

As far as we were concerned, one of the main problems of the linkup between TWR and Benetton was one of communication and clear understanding of exactly what was supposed to be happening to us, the mechanics and indeed, to the rest of the Benetton staff. Was TWR buying Benetton Formula from the Benetton family? Was the Benetton family buying TWR? There was some suggestion that each had bought half of the other's business. No one was certain which stories were exciting, exaggerated rumour and which were no more than boring fact.

At the conclusion of the 1991 season, just a few months after this partnership began, the entire Benetton staff was invited to attend the TWR Christmas party, held at Tom's Broadstone Manor headquarters. But few people seemed interested in going; it was nothing personal, nor was any offence intended against Tom or any of his employees; it was just the fact that it wasn't a Benetton party, it was a TWR affair. What had happened to our end-of-year celebration? People felt slighted (silly, perhaps, but some can be easily offended). When word reached the Benetton management that the majority of its staff seemed disinterested in attending what was primarily somebody else's celebration, it all became a rather political affair. Apparently, Benetton's staff was supposed to be engaging in a session of affable *entente cordial* with our new friends; at this point, I suspect, some people felt they were being toyed with. Finally we were more or less ordered to go, and if we couldn't make the party then we had to have a damn good excuse why we wouldn't be there. All a bit daft really, but I can understand the reservations about producing such forced gaiety. If people wanted to go, then fine, but if they didn't, then that was, surely, their own prerogative? In the end, come the night of the party, quite a few Benetton people did attend, and as soon as the petty politics of the event had been brushed aside it turned into a bloody good night out too. I'm all for a good bottle of wine, a Christmas kiss and a chicken vol-au-vent.

The first task that Tom turned his hand to was finding a new home for us, or at least a suitable site on which we could build a new home. And this he did with great success. The chosen land was a disused quarry in the middle of nowhere. The site was owned by the Reynard organization, which had bought it as an intended base for its own Formula One project. However, before any building work had commenced at the quarry, Reynard decided to shelve its proposed Grand Prix plans for a few more years. Walkinshaw knew of the site and of Reynard's intended use for it, and before long the deeds of the old quarry had changed hands. Building work began as soon as the appropriate consents had been granted. The postal address of the building site was actually given as Enstone, Chipping Norton, but in reality the site is neither in Enstone nor Chipping Norton. Instead, it nestles between Gagingwell and Middle Barton, two quiet villages which had managed to avoid any sort of media attention for the last 900 years. Benetton Formula Ltd was about to change all of that.

At the same time as negotiations for the new factory were under way, Tom was also sorting out the position of the team's technical director. Exit Mr Gordon Kimball, enter Mr Ross Brawn, a man who Tom knew well and who had worked with TWR as technical director of their Le Mans, Group C, Jaguar project. Certainly, it seemed that Kimball had been given a raw deal in the few months he had been with the team, but as far as I could make out it never looked good for him. With Barnard's swift exit it had appeared to me that the management had needed a quick stopgap and it seemed that Kimball had been just that. He was upset by his treatment but still went to the trouble of sending everyone in the team a Christmas card, pointing out that he bore no ill feelings towards the staff and wished us all the best for the future. A nice gesture from a pleasant man in a sad situation. What more can one say other than Formula One is a harsh environment?

Next on Tom's list was a replacement for Nelson Piquet. The logical choice was Martin Brundle, another man who Tom had worked with and again a man who would become a valuable asset. Joining Benetton from the struggling Brabham outfit was a big break for Martin, and I liked him from the first moment we met. He always struck me as being just a normal bloke, a genuine chap with no tedious pretensions in his makeup. Of course, he was also the first driver I worked with in my new role as the 'front-end' mechanic of a race car, and I enjoyed my time with him very much indeed. He would chat like an old friend, listen to his engineer's advice and work hard in the car. What more can you ask from a team-mate?

Tom was instrumental in bringing Michael Schumacher to the team, building the new factory, signing Ross Brawn as technical director and bringing Martin Brundle to us. The South African aerodynamisist Rory Byrne rejoined the team too. Rory had worked at Benetton before as chief designer, chief aerodynamisist, chief engineer, call him what you will, he got involved with everything. As soon as Barnard had been appointed to the company as technical director, I suspect Rory began to feel the carpet being pulled from underneath his feet. He left Benetton in October 1990, working instead for Reynard, drawing its proposed Formula One car which never happened; when the project was cancelled Byrne had the perfect opportunity to return to the Benetton flock. He was given the title of head of research and development, although whether this meant working alongside or underneath Ross Brawn's leadership, was difficult to say.

I'm not entirely sure what the word maverick means, but I'd probably use it to describe Rory Byrne. He is a true character, some may even say slightly eccentric, a man who relishes his race car work with the same vigour and excitement as a young boy playing with a new train set. In qualifying sessions, I have often seen him staring at the bright, sun-filled sky, his outstretched hand trying to filter the strong light as he patiently waits for a cloud to float between the sun and the track. He wouldn't allow the drivers to take to the circuit before this happened because he had a theory that the passing cloud would drop the ambient temperature by a degree or two, perhaps just enough to give the engine that minuscule fraction more power. And only when Rory was quite sure that the fabled qualifying cloud was in the correct position would he signal for us to quickly remove the tyre blankets and fire the engine into life.

So, the team's instability problems had been settled and we were now all set to start again and have another bash at the championship. And Tom Walkinshaw had done far more for us than anybody will ever give him credit for.

...

Unfortunately for us, 1992 was not to be the year Benetton would claim any championships, since Williams and their two drivers, Nigel Mansell and Riccardo Patrese would clinch just about everything there was on offer. Over the winter Williams had continued to test and finely hone its previous year's car, the FW14, to such an extent that they considered it unnecessary to introduce the FW15. A new car always carries an element of risk in its reliability, so Frank Williams and Patrick Head, the team's technical director, took the decision to reissue the race team with a revised version of the 1991 car, calling it the FW14B. This would allow Williams the luxury of being able to test the FW15 thoroughly throughout the opening months of the season, and only when it had reached a stage of development and reliability to out-perform its predecessor would the FW15 be introduced into the chase for the Championship. However, the FW14B proved quite devastating and soon confirmed itself equipment enough; it remained in use from the opening round in South Africa to the closing round in Australia.

Throughout the racing season, during our evening breaks for dinner, I used to drink my coffee strolling up and down the pit-lane, occasionally chatting with other mechanics, mostly just observing other teams at work. Watching how other teams operate and how their set-up procedures differed from Benetton's was a practice taught to me by Nigel Stepney. He used to say that it was important to keep an eye on what everyone else was doing; you never know, their system may be simpler or quicker or lighter than our own. All the teams constantly watch each other, all on the lookout for any slight advantage that they can employ themselves. The clearest example of this is the teams' pit equipment, much of which is copied and recopied from team to team: air-jacks, quick-lift jacks, overhead gantries, banners, even the design of the litter bins. Benetton stipulated the use of clear plastic bin liners in its garage because they look smarter than black or grey ones when the top of the bag hangs over the rim of the bin. Now Benetton has gone a stage further and completely redesigned the bin, so the liner is no longer visible at all. Can you imagine Benetton Formula even contemplating trying to qualify its cars for Sunday's Grand Prix, knowing that the whole world can see the top two inches of its bin liner? That's Formula One, though, always pushing forward!

In sharp contrast, the Williams garage always looks like a garage: clean and tidy, of course, but, nevertheless, a garage, not an operating theatre. A few simple banners, airlines, tools. I somehow doubt that Frank would have any strong views on what colour his plastic bags were; I rather imagine his thoughts on the matter would be something along the lines of 'who cares what colour the bin liners are, let's just win everything and go home.'

The FW14B was a fully 'active' car, meaning that its suspension movements were controlled by a sophisticated, computer-controlled system using high-pressure hydraulic fluid to control the mechanical handling of the car. The system that everyone else was using, known as 'passive' suspension, relied on teams having to carry a huge range of fifty or so progressively stiffer springs, twelve or more different ratings of roll-bar, three different types of bump-rubbers and a myriad of different specification dampers to each race. Then we, the mechanics, would be constantly changing them and resetting the 'roll' and ride-height throughout the two days of practice and qualifying, until a reasonable balance was achieved (then, as likely as not, we would alter it again on the grid and go back to the original settings we had on the car when it left the factory).

Apart from the massive amount of work it creates for the mechanics, the disadvantage of a passive suspension system is that the performance from the suspension is relatively limited. Along the straight sections of the circuit a car needs to feel very stiff, at other times it needs to feel softer, more roll is desirable for some corners, less for others. But with a passive set-up – despite all the options stored in the garage – there can only be one choice of set-up on the car at any given time. This single set-up, obviously becomes a compromise of the best options for all the different sections of the circuit.

However, an active system is altogether different, and regardless of its initial added complications, once the system is up and running it is a dream to work with. First, there is no need to carry any of the vast array of parts. The onboard computer processor and hydraulics can reproduce the entire range of changeable suspension options, the desired settings merely programmed into the controller by the engineer before the car leaves the pits. Stiffer, softer, more roll at the rear, less at the front, whatever the driver and the car are happiest with, it is just a matter of changing the software settings. Wheel speed sensors feed information to the controller to allow the suspension to automatically adjust to the velocity of the car, and ride-height sensors detect any suspension movement such as bumps and dips in the track, or any undesirable acceleration squat or nose pitching on braking. The controller is constantly fed with information and is constantly adjusting the actuators and rate of fluid flow to the four corners to guarantee the car maintains its optimum trim. On the fast straights the rear ride-height is slightly lowered, just enough to stall the efficiency of the floor's diffuser, which reduces the car's downforce at a time when it is not wanted and is merely limiting top-end speed. As the car approaches the corner and begins to decelerate, the rear ride-height is picked up again, bringing the diffuser into play and restoring the available downforce to its maximum.

In-car adjustable wings are banned in Formula One (which would be the technically correct way to alter downforce settings on the circuit) but the versatility of active suspension can go some way towards replicating the same effects. When reliable and functioning correctly, active suspension is brilliant, lending the car all the poise and grace of a prima ballerina. Engineering excellence. However, when it's not reliable and the systems are functioning incorrectly, it is, quite simply, bloody terrible. Either it's spraying the mechanics with boiling oil at pressures of 2500psi and more, or else the car just sits in the garage violently shuddering and shaking, refusing to listen to any sort of electronic reason. Worse still, if it decides to fail while the car is actually pounding around the circuit, it could just give up altogether and flop to the ground, dumping the car and driver to the tarmac (which at speeds approaching 200mph can be a mite disconcerting).

Sipping my coffee, I often used to pause outside the Williams garage, and during 1992 I found it fascinating to watch the three cars going through their exercise programmes. Whenever an active component is disconnected or replaced on the car, the hydraulics have to be purged of air; known as bleeding, this process requires a flushing-rig to be connected into the car's system. The rig uses its own high-pressure pump instead of the car's own engine-driven pump, which will obviously not work without the engine running. The flushing-rig also contains a reservoir of hydraulic oil to allow the car's system to be replenished. With the rig connected, the suspension is then worked up and down throughout the full range of its possible travel, as this will gradually persuade any trapped air to find its way round the system and out to the rig. This process can sometimes take as long as half an hour, so to avoid wasting the mechanics' time while they waited for the car to be bled, Williams had written a 'bleed' programme for the onboard controller. While the mechanics sat down to dinner, the three cars would be left alone to run through their stretching exercises. Up, down, up, down. Squat to the right, up, down. Squat to the left, up, down. And again, up, down. In the gloom of the pit-lane, with no one else around, the whole thing had a strange, almost surreal air to it, like the toys coming to life in *The Nutcracker*. As I watched from the obscurity of the darkness, it felt as though the cars would instantly fall still and silent as soon as a Williams mechanic walked back in the garage. Whoops! They nearly caught us that time! To me, the FW14B seemed like the ideal race car. I have never worked on one, but from what I could see and discover, it must have been close to mechanical perfection.

The year 1992 was to be Mansell's great one too, the year he would finally win the Drivers' Championship. He was a different man that year, one who had obviously decided that it was going to be now or never. He knew that the Williams car was leagues ahead of the opposition, and that it would give him a major advantage over any attempt by Senna to thwart him. He had shed many of his surplus pounds in the gym and emerged from hours of rigorous training looking trim, alert, determined and committed. There was to be no stopping him, not this time. He secured his Championship in quite unbelievable style too: fourteen poles, nine victories, and three second places. That was it! No other placings at all, if he wasn't on the first or second step of the podium he didn't finish the race at all.

Patrese finished second in the Drivers' Championship, but regardless of picking up a useful ten points for winning the Japanese Grand Prix he still finished the season fifty-two points behind his team-mate. Williams claimed their fifth Constructors' Championship too, sixty-five points clear of McLaren's second place, a staggering demonstration of what a committed team and two equally committed drivers are capable of.

. . .

Our car, the B192, pleasantly surprised me. It was, of course, no match for the Williams (no other car on the planet was a match for the Williams) but I had genuinely expected to find that the new Benetton was no more than an evolution of the old B190, with scant regard shown to anything connected with Barnard or his car. Perhaps if Rory had been left to his own devices that would have been the case, but now with Ross Brawn on board, things would never be as they once were. The order of things was different, we were once again on the move. The old Benetton regime had come and gone; the Barnard era had come and gone too; now we were entering our third generation and this was to be the team that would win the World Championship. Looking at the B192, it is easy to see a similarity in aerodynamics with the B190, and as Rory had been deeply involved with the drawing of both chassis that's no great surprise, but there were some aspects of the 1992 car which were taken and reworked from Barnard's B191 – the lifting of the nose profile, for example. Ross, in contrast to his colleague, is far more of an engineer than an aerodynamisist. He had studied the merits and the faults of Barnard's mechanical designs and had incorporated several of these ideas into our new car.

The earlier Benettons (pre-Barnard) tended to be big, bulky affairs, which sported huge slabs of coolant radiator. Everywhere one looked there seemed to be scores of small brackets and clips and brackets on other brackets; the front wings and their end-plates were made up of countless interchangeable spacers to allow the wings to be set to different specifications. On the rear wing, support wires would stretch from the wing, pass through the bodywork and be fastened to turrets on the gearbox. Whenever the bodywork needed to be removed (which was each and every time the car returned to the pits) the support wires needed to be disconnected first. On the B190, the rear brake ducts were cumbersome one-piece things, without split-lines (as opposed to being separate halves which could then be bolted together). They were probably quite efficient in the wind tunnel – as there were no bolt heads to interfere with air-flow – but to install or remove them from the car meant that the mechanics had to unbolt and remove the entire 'upright' and drive-shaft assembly from the car. If the duct had been a two-piece design it could simply be assembled around the drive-shaft leaving everything else in place. As it was, this almost Dali-esque one-piece duct turned what could have been a five-minute job into a potential half-hour epic! It seemed to me that the design of the early Benetton cars showed little to no interest in their serviceability; the priority was all aerodynamic.

Now, some may argue that it doesn't matter that the mechanics had to remove the drive-shafts to change the ducts. Who cares? After all, the mechanics are there to work on the cars, if it takes them six times as long to finish the job because of a particular design, so what? They choose to work on the cars, so let 'em work! Well, my riposte is this: what happens if the brake duct needs changing with ten minutes to go in qualifying? It's been tipping down all afternoon, the driver has posted a slow lap-time because of the rain and on returning to the pits the mechanics notice the duct has been smashed by a stone, leaving most of it lying out on the circuit somewhere. However, the rain has now stopped, the track is rapidly drying and the qualifying times are tumbling. The driver needs to get out again or his pathetic-looking lap-time will see him starting the Grand Prix from the very back of the grid. Yes, he could use the spare car or his team-mate's race car, providing they haven't been shunted, of course, but the fact remains, that for want of a bit more practicality, the car has been put out of commission. And if the duct needed changing on the grid, then forget it! It would have to be bodged up with tape and ty-raps. Formula One cars must be designed so that they can be worked on as quickly and as easily as possible. Wherever it is practically possible, all jobs must be able to be completed in twenty-five minutes – the time the teams have with their cars on the grid – for Sod's law decrees that it is always going to be then that the damn things will let go.

As engineers, both Barnard and Brawn could appreciate these mechanical concerns perhaps far more that the aerodynamisists; certainly the 1991 and later Benettons seem to suggest this. In Formula One, everything is a compromise.

The biggest advancement on the B192 (apart from the introduction of two-piece brake ducts) was the installation of the front dampers. They were mounted on top of the chassis and covered by an easily removable carbon panel. As far as Benetton was concerned, this was a major breakthrough. The B190 had dampers mounted inside the chassis, in an X-pattern: the bottom-mounting of the right damper attached to the left of the chassis, the left damper to the right of the chassis, allowing the driver's legs to pass underneath. Access to the springs was gained by the two holes in the chassis where the top mountings of the dampers attached to the push-rods. All very awkward.

The B191 was even worse, but there was good reason for it. The 1991 car had the dampers running parallel and above the drivers' legs. Gaining access to them in order to change the springs, the bump-rubbers or the ride-height involved the rather intimate business of sticking one's arms in between the driver's legs and groping around, unable to see, with one's head resting in the driver's lap. All rather undignified. The reason for this was that John Barnard had originally intended the B191 to be an active car. Hence, after the actuators had been initially fitted at the factory, there would have been no need to adjust them during the practice and qualifying sessions; all that would have been done via an engineer's computer. However, as we now know, the B191 was late coming into production and the active programme was shelved in order to try and meet the immovable deadlines of the season. The solution was to fit dampers and springs instead of hydraulic actuators, temporarily turning the suspension into a passive system, but because of all the political upheaval it was a temporary solution which lasted for the entire life of the car.

On the B192, having the dampers mounted atop the chassis was bliss. No further need to stick one's head inside the cockpit, only to hear Nelson fart and have to listen to him crack up with laughter while one was delving in between his legs, unable to move for fresh air for fear of dropping the spring or a bolt inside the chassis. What a relief! Thankfully, Nelson's replacement, Martin Brundle, never struck me as the sort of chap who would expel gas onto his mechanics but, nevertheless, being able to readily see and adjust the dampers and not having to blindly grope between the driver's legs, made for altogether more dignified working conditions.

Oddly – despite its rather unsavoury side effects – the fact that someone can possess the ability to pass wind, almost on cue, has always struck me as being quite a talent. I remember reading somewhere that many years ago, around the turn of the century, a Frenchman became so good at it that he managed to produce his own stage show entirely based on that very skill. Apparently, he became famous throughout the music halls of Paris and as his fame spread, people would pack the theatres to listen to his nightly performances, where – using just the lower half of his body – he would recreate amusing incidents of daily French life. What a curious evening's entertainment.

...

With all the comings and goings throughout the latter months of 1991, the development of the B192 was considerably behind schedule, something which was only to be expected as the design of the following year's car normally begins in June or July of the previous season. So, knowing that we had lost over six months' design time, the decision was taken to start the season with the 1991 car and introduce the B192 as soon as it was feasible to do so. The B191 was used for the first three races, the long-haul, intercontinental 'fly-aways' of South Africa, Mexico and Brazil. The car was renamed the B191B (although, as far as I can remember, there were no significant changes made to it to really warrant the B suffix). Certainly it was sound logic to use the old car for these three long-distance races; when the team is out of practical reach of the factory, they want a car that they are familiar with, that they thoroughly understand and that, above all else, is going to be reliable. When you're stranded in the middle of South America, having new-car teething problems can be a terrifying prospect. When racing in Europe the teams can easily have new parts machined and flown out to them within the space of a few hours of encountering a problem at the circuit, but when encamped on the opposite side of the planet, things aren't that easy.

This gradual phasing-in of new cars was something that was quite common at one time: for example, Benetton issued the B190 in Imola, the third race of the season; the B191 was introduced at Imola too; the B192 in Barcelona; and as we mentioned earlier, Williams didn't bother issuing a new car in 1992 at all. But the constant rule changes that the sport has been undergoing since 1994 have meant that it has proved impossible to continue with such a useful policy. A car that was built to the 1994 rules was outside the 1995 regulations, therefore the B195 cars were unable to be raced the following year (the same thing happened in 1996, 1997, etc). The 1992 season might not have brought Benetton or our drivers any championships, but it wasn't a disaster by any means. We were making progress, and we finished the year with a third place in the Constructors' Championship, just nine points behind McLaren.

...

Martin Brundle didn't win a race during his year with us in 1992. In fact, he failed to win a race throughout the whole of his Formula One career. However, he should have done, there's no doubt about that at all. He was good, he had the talent, but it just never quite happened for him and that was a great shame. He did everything right but sometimes that just isn't enough. In Canada he most certainly should have won. He was comfortably reeling in Berger's McLaren and the race looked to be in the bag; but then we experienced an incredibly rare mechanical failure: a bolt broke in the transmission and destroyed the diff'. It was a most bizarre fault caused by a slight machining error, one missed by the machinist, the inspection department and the gearbox mechanic. A rare fluke, but we lost a Grand Prix victory because of it. I suppose that for Benetton it was a case of good fortune and bad fortune in Montreal, remembering Nelson's lucky win there the year before. You win some, you lose some, but that philosophy was scant consolation for Martin Brundle's valiant and wasted efforts. For reasons which I won't ever understand, he was replaced at the end of the season by Riccardo Patrese from Williams.

My defence of Martin is in no way a condemnation of the arrival of Riccardo, who was another terrific character, but I just do not understand why we had to lose Brundle. He wasn't as quick as Schumacher (but then none of Michael's team-mates ever have been) and this hurt his qualifying performances, but in the race he was very useful. Martin has great 'race craft', the ability to preserve the car, to take care of the tyres, to conserve fuel and not to take stupid chances in the early laps. We scored points in every race of 1992, which was due to having bright, intelligent drivers who thought about what they were doing. Schumacher's team-mate was replaced every year until he finally left to join Ferrari, a situation I didn't agree with. What the team needed was a competent, stable partner for Michael, one who could constantly bring the car and the points home. Let Schumacher battle for the Drivers' Championship while his team-mate keeps racking up the extra points for the Constructors' Championship. However, it wasn't my decision and Martin left us after Adelaide.

Martin had great rapport with Pat Fry, his engineer. He would describe the handling of the car in the most extraordinary ways to Pat, using terms like 'wishy-washy' and 'speed-boaty'.

'I just can't get on it!' he would say, 'It's all wishy-washy, I just can't get on it, it's like a speedboat!' Another memorable line was, 'I feel like the car's riding on the track, not in it, I need to get into the track more!' Pat would listen and scribble copious notes, translating his driver's colourful descriptions into mathematical percentages of understeer and oversteer, and calculating possible solutions to reduce the car's speed boaty-ness. Martin is quite aware of the technicalities of car set-up, it's just that he loved to play the game with Pat. In Adelaide, the last race of the season, he finally had Pat completely stumped. The mechanics had primed Martin before the practice session and he carried it off flawlessly. After completing a five-lap run in the car, Martin returned to the garage to discuss the need for any changes. As we pulled the car back inside the garage, Pat keyed his radio and asked Martin how the car felt.

'I just can't drive it, Pat, it's way too stage-coachy!'

'Sorry, I think I missed that, Martin, say again.'

'It's way too stage-coachy, we'll have to do something.'

'Sorry Martin, did you say "stage-coachy"?'

'Yes, you know, much too like a stage-coach!'

'Yes, I understand that stage-coachy must mean taking on the characteristics of a stage coach, Martin. It's just that I haven't got the faintest idea what on earth you're talking about!'

...

Michael Schumacher had been improving his form constantly throughout the year and had stood on the podium no less than eight times. Four thirds, three seconds and on 30 August, at the circuit Spa-Francorchamps in Belgium, exactly one year after his Formula One debut, he took his maiden Grand Prix victory. He was elated, we all were, but I have never seen a driver so absolutely ecstatic at his achievement. He didn't weep in the way that Moreno did in Japan, he was simply utterly elated. For Roberto, Japan was an unbelievable result, something that he never expected, but for Michael winning a Grand Prix was always coming; we didn't know exactly when and if it wasn't Spa, then it may have been Barcelona or Hockenheim or Monza or Adelaide, but it was coming.

His rapture at winning that race is something that he has continued to show with every successive win. Here is a man who delights in winning and takes no win for granted. He understands that to cross the finish line ahead of all the others involves a massive amount of effort – effort by the whole team, as well as the driver – a simple fact that some other drivers have clearly forgotten. On the occasion of that first win, as with each of his subsequent wins, Michael's sheer happiness is recognition of all that team effort, from the work of the fabricators, the machinists, the composite specialists, the electricians, the mechanics and the drawing office. The toil of hundreds is reflected in the utter joy of his podium celebrations.

On returning to the garage he shook everyone by the hand, thanking us all individually for our help, another genuine show of appreciation that would continue with each subsequent win. I have never felt such an integral part of a team than when working with Michael and sharing in the pleasure of one of our victories.

As the crowds bulged from the circuit gates and we began packing equipment in to the back of the race trucks, Michael changed out of his overalls. He waved us farewell and set off on a bicycle, his victor's trophy strapped to the back to meet his parents who were staying in one of the local hotels. As he peddled off, weaving up the steep hill leading out from the La Source hairpin, the road was still bustling with people making their way home. Michael gradually disappeared out of sight, ringing his bell, gently turning left and right, avoiding the small groups that were slowly plodding up the road. What a marvellous sight. Here was Michael Schumacher, the winner of the Spa Grand Prix, cycling among the dispersing crowds, off to show his mother and father his new trophy. The people, most with their backs towards him, had no idea who this bloke on the bicycle was, or why he was making off with what they must have assumed to be a cheap replica of the winner's trophy.

How times have changed! These days, Michael can't move without being recognized and if he ever decided to try to cycle off in Monza with the winner's cup, I imagine he'd need to be surrounded by at least half the Italian police force.

Chapter six

1993

A note for future historians...Moving into the new factory...Formula One's geographical relocation...Patrese arrives...Mansell bows out...Active suspension...Semi-automatic transmissions...A world record is set in Spa...Nunes wins in Estoril

The long hours, the all-nighters and the hectic workloads that we are sometimes forced to endure are terrible facets of work in Formula One, and at times it felt as if we were little more than slave labour. However, I've always thought that the pay I received in return for all my hard work was fair, but if my gross annual salary was divided by all the hours worked and expressed as an hourly rate, it begins to look like pretty poor remuneration. I've been jotting down a record of my earnings, from that first pay packet as an indentured apprentice onward, and I've continued to do this, year by year. I have always kept letters which refer to my wages and have included them to add a little further colour. However, one thing is certain, times are changing. It won't be long before the need for mechanics will evaporate. I strongly suspect that within the space of another fifty or sixty years our skills will have become redundant, and just like the longbow maker, the knight's page, the roof thatcher and the barrel cooper, the mechanic will become near extinct, part of history.

I don't think I'm overstating the situation either. Take this book for example: I'm writing it on a notebook computer (I still want to call it a laptop), powered by a 200MHz Pentium processor with MMX (apparently the MMX bit makes it much more fun), it's just over twelve months old and it cost me nearly £2000 – an awful lot of money, but a necessary investment which, hopefully, I can recoup with my advance from Weidenfeld & Nicolson. (I just hope Marilyn, my editor, likes what she reads or I'm sunk.) In 2001, the start of the next century which is only a couple of years away, this machine will seem like a fossilized artefact, nothing short of a whimsical curiosity. Compared with what will then be the latest machine, this one will be akin to scrawling on slate with a wedge of chalk. Within three weeks of buying my machine, 'voice recognition' software was on the market, and shortly after that I noticed that a 266MHz model was available. The other day a 333MHz machine was advertised in *The Times* for less than half what I paid nearly a year before! If that trend continues, sometime in the next century you'll be able to buy a 1,000,000MHz (should that be 1000GHz?) machine for less than the price of a cup of tea; that can't be right, can it?

Here we are in the very closing stages of the second millennium, with major, almost daily, advancements in microchip electronics screaming past us. I don't think I'm being technophobic but I'm sure that some current traditional trades such as working as a Navy jet-fighter pilot or a NASA shuttle-craft astronaut, or a Formula One Grand Prix mechanic will soon be memories of a bygone era. Hopefully the need to blast each other with air-to-air missiles will soon become rather passé anyway, and all cargo aircraft will be flown by remote, as will the vast majority of spacecraft, with much of the colonization of other planets achieved by embryo transportation and genetic engineering.

And as for race cars, they will quite probably be subject to a total world-wide ban; either that or they will be constructed from a single piece of composite material, with an in-built magnetic repulsion system which allows them to hover precisely 10mm above an electronic track (though, I suppose, the engineers would still want to lower the front float-height by half a millimetre to improve that niggling bit of mid-corner understeer). Many hundreds of technically skilled professions will simply no longer be required. In fact, I reckon the only safe job to be specializing in at the moment is head chef of a good tandoori restaurant. Both now and in another two hundred years' time, people are always going to want a well prepared chicken tikka.

I once tried to converting my salary into an hourly rate while enduring a long session of Terminal Boredom. We were in Heathrow waiting for the flight which would eventually take us to Japan for the penultimate round of the 1992 Championship. I fished out my ancient calculator, held together with several strips of ageing Sellotape, and added up the total number of hours we had worked, both preparing the cars at the factory and servicing them at the circuits throughout the course of the year (one chap always kept a meticulous log of all hours worked). Armed with this information I then divided the sum into my annual salary in order to break it down to an hourly rate. I was expecting to see a figure smaller than the legal minimum wage, and was all ready to start complaining that we would be financially better off working the same number of hours for McGrizzler's or Cheeseburger Yourself Solid.

In fact, I was getting quite excited at the prospect of unveiling the injustice of it all, already imagining a series of organized protest marches breaking out as hoards of mechanics from every team in the pit-lane banded together, walking arm-in-arm, placards held aloft, singing loud and rousing choruses (one or two chaps just slightly out of tune with the rest), the air thick with the scent of rebel spirit. A little fanciful, but there must have been a possibility that a scenario similar to that – even if somewhat tamer – might have occurred as a result of my calculations, but when I pressed the 'equals' button I was more than a little mystified to see the figure 71077345 faintly flickering from the little screen. What was I supposed to make of that? Was that a low hourly rate, or a good one? The thing about calculators is that they never bother to give an explanation for their findings, they merely publish, wait a few minutes, and then quickly switch themselves off. I looked at the calculator wondering what I should conclude from its results and noticed that if you held the thing upside down the numbers spelt out the words SHELL OIL. However, that in itself didn't throw any real light on the hourly rate issue. I tried to work the sum again but, sadly, the calculator's days were over, the yellowing Sellotape finally gave way and several bits of it fell to the airport floor. A shame really, I'd had it for years and my tentative plans for any Great March had to be quickly suppressed. Nevertheless, the day wasn't a complete disaster by any means, and I think the exercise was worth doing just to see the Shell Oil thing.

...

3 February 1993

Dear Steve,
I am able to advise you that with effect from 1 January 1993 your salary will be increased to £23,474 per annum.
Thank you.

...

The year 1993 was a busy one. At the end of 1992 we left for Japan from the old factory in Witney and came back from Australia straight to our brand-new factory near Enstone. As far as the race team was concerned, the whole move was seamless; a very neat, well-organized idea. While we were out of the country for the final two races, the factory staff had been working flat out, moving all the machinery from one place to the other: mills, lathes, drills, folders, guillotines, metal, carbon, everything. On my first day at the new factory two things struck me about the place – it seemed enormous and it seemed very, very white. Some may even say a little too white. Great expanses of white painted walls, white work surfaces, white cabinets, white window surrounds, white litter bins (each sporting a Benetton emblem); we were all issued with brand-new, bright white lab-coats too (each sporting a Benetton emblem). In fact, the only thing that had managed to escape this minimalist colour scheme was the cushioned flooring, which was grey. Presumably you can't get it in white.

At Witney, the stores area had been a small, cramped affair, with John and Alec, our two storemen, gradually becoming buried under ever-increasing piles of supplies and car components. As the team continued to grow, every spare inch of shelf space was eventually filled. The only option then was to store things in boxes on the floor, but the demand for more and more storage space continued unabated. Boxes were stored on boxes, then more boxes would arrive, which inevitably found themselves being stacked on top of boxes which had previously been stacked on top of other boxes. Slowly the stores became completely engulfed, turning the task of finding anything into a sort of black art, requiring John and Alec to make mental contact with the desired component buried deep within the dark reaches of the storage pit.

'John, have you got a Schumacher brake pedal pad, please?'

'Brake pedal pad for Schumacher, now, let's see; they came in from Inspection about two days ago, then they went to be plated, they were picked from there last night so they should be in that bag there, on top of that box to your left, just to the right of the stuff that's just come in for the cleaners. Unless Alec's already put them upstairs, in which case they'll be. . . '

The stores at the new factory appeared gigantic by comparison, with more floor space than the total combined area used by the machinists, the fabricators and the stores when we were at Witney. The machine shop is four times bigger than it was; the same is true for the fabrication and composite shops. The security house and its automatic gate (white) extend an initial warm welcome to any guests; there is even a heli-pad for those harassed, indispensable executives who simply have not got time to travel by road with the rest of us. However, regardless of that little bit of self-indulgent pretentiousness, it must be said that the new factory is a great improvement on what went before. In 1993 it was said to be the most advanced facility in the world for producing race cars; now with the proposed new McLaren building and the recent completion of British American Racing's new facility, I think that claim could be challenged but, nevertheless, the Benetton building is still very impressive.

The nearest town to the factory is Chipping Norton, which lies approximately halfway between Oxford and Stratford-upon-Avon. An old market town on the edge of the Cotswolds, it is a relatively small community of about five thousand people. Actually, the Chambers's *Encyclopaedia* of 1895 quotes the populace as being 4222; reassuring to think that in over a hundred years it has remained exactly the same. Back then at the turn of the century, however, Chipping Norton was a thriving centre for commerce, with its huge Bliss Mill turning out some of the Empire's finest tweed. The thick woven cloth was loaded aboard steam trains and dispatched straight from the station to the world's most discerning clientele. How things have changed. The mill burnt down, the station was closed and the international tweed industry is all but dead. Despite the loss of Bliss Mill, Chipping Norton soldiered on until the arrival of the next great employer, Parker Knoll, the furniture manufacturer. Parker Knoll is well known because of its lounge chair, the Parker Knoll Recliner, which was an absolute exec' must-have in the mid-sixties and early seventies. The company has since been through a very lean period (as have the rest of the planet, of course) but it survived and is still producing a range of quality furniture in Chipping Norton, although I suspect that demand for its magnificent recliner has dwindled since its earlier heyday.

To survive the late nineties, the town has had to diversify yet again, and the main industries now appear to be antiques and tourism. Shops selling such rarities as 'interesting, turn-of-the-century cake tin' or 'an amusing eighteenth-century wooden spoon' seem to spring up all the time (how amusing is it possible for a wooden spoon to be?). At the edge of the market place, right in the centre of town, stands a huge five-storey building, converted and now dedicated solely to the furtherance of the antique trade; they even have a tea room where, after browsing through the myriad of interesting and amusing kitchen implements, you can refresh yourself with a welcoming cuppa, a nice slice of Dundee cake and a good sit-down.

I visited one such establishment – although an altogether much smaller concern – run by a rustic-looking chap who appeared to specialize in what could only be described as the more affordable end of the market. In one corner of his dimly lit premises he had a selection of second-hand books arranged in comfortable, informal style. After an hour of rummaging I selected the three titles which best suited me, including two written in French, which I rather naively hoped would help improve my language skills. I asked the chap how much I owed him and he told me that I had to buy £10 worth. The books weren't priced and there was no sign indicating that his clientele had to purchase a pre-set amount (presumably, pricing books and sign writing were to be the day's priority jobs directly after the reading of the morning papers). I said that I didn't want any more of his books and that a price of £10 was a steep sum to pay for the three somewhat dog-eared editions which I'd just spent the last hour choosing. He said I had to take £10 worth to make it worth his while. I said that I'd gladly pay him a £1, even £1.50 for each of the three I'd picked, but that was it; a sale of £4.50, surely better than no sale at all and quite reasonable remuneration for reading the papers, I thought. No, it had to be £10 worth or it just wasn't worth his trouble. I silently congratulated him for sticking both to his principles and his stringent trading policy, replaced his stock neatly on the floor, hoping not to disturb the look of his dumped-on-the-floor sales display and swore an eternally binding oath never to enter his shop again for the duration of my life.

Over the years people have arrived, people have left, people have been born and people have died, but Chippy still keeps plodding on. I like the place, I like it very much. So much so, in fact, that I bought a house there. As a town it has everything I needed — a superb tandoori restaurant, two wine shops, an excellent bookshop and a cashpoint machine. And, in the Chequers, Chipping Norton undoubtedly has one of the best pubs in the world. The Chequers is a real-life Cheers, a pub where Josh, the landlord, seems to know absolutely everyone. Go in once and the next time he'll remember your name. Standing well over six feet tall with a great mass of greying beard, Josh was born to be a pub landlord. He has that rare, special gift which allows him to chat to everyone, possessing sufficient knowledge on any given trade, pastime, or subject of study, to start and sustain an absorbing conversation. Whatever your own profession or passionate hobby may be, Josh is able to converse in your language. Go to the Chequers alone and you will chat as old friends; go with friends and he will unobtrusively serve drinks and discreetly leave you alone. The pub has won the Best Pub Award so often that in the end the brewery had to omit the Chequers' name from the entry list to give someone else a chance. Difficult to pinpoint exactly what makes it such a compelling place, it's just a pub after all, but it's the perfect pub: good food, good beer, neither too busy nor too quiet, too posh nor too scruffy. I know that such a thing shouldn't influence one of life's major purchases, but if I'm being honest I have to confess that the Chequers was the main reason I bought into Chippy.

There had been one other change to Benetton's company policy since Tom Walkinshaw's involvement: we now had to start work at 8:30 as opposed to 9:00 in the morning. Apparently all the TWR companies started work at this earlier time and the alteration would bring us in line with them. The concept struck me as being rather unfair, for as our finish time was to remain at 5:30 (for whatever that's worth in Formula One), it appeared - technically at least — that the net result was having to work an extra two and a half hours of unpaid overtime every week. I pondered this proposed scheme but decided not to get involved; it wasn't really something to which I thought I could lend my full support. I continued to arrive at the new factory at my usual time; the only difference being that I now arrived fifteen minutes late instead of fifteen minutes early.

The unveiling of Benetton's new facility marked a wider-reaching change too, a geographical one this time. The hub of the Formula One industry used to revolve around Woking in Surrey, to the west of London, with McLaren International, Tyrrell, Ferrari, Benetton and Onyx all, at one time, having their operations based in the south of England. The desire to be based close to one's competitors is certainly not unique to motor racing; look at California's Silicon Valley or London's Fleet Street, for similar examples. Grouping brings many benefits, not least being the increased prospect of successfully poaching staff from one another without the added burden of having to offer the incentive of a relocation deal. Also, around any gathering of big, like-minded companies there inevitably grows a useful plethora of associated small businesses, providing a multitude of outside services which can be easily utilized. In the case of Formula One, this means that a selection of electronic specialists and harness builders, precision machinists and metal finishers, decal manufacturers, composite specialists, even quality dry-cleaners are all close at hand.

However, much has happened over the last ten years: Onyx folded in 1990 (I was so relieved I didn't get offered the job there!); and the Surrey-based Barnard/Ferrari, and the Barnard/Benetton projects folded too. Eddie Jordan went completely against the grain and opened his headquarters next door to the Silverstone circuit, which is in Northampton (north of Oxford). At the end of 1998 Tyrrell ceased to exist and its new incarnation, in the form of British American Racing, has built its new factory in Brackley (very close to Jordan's place). Stewart Grand Prix has opened up at Milton Keynes and TWR-Arrows has built its headquarters in Leafield, just outside Witney. Unconsciously, the sport has gradually moved further north, resulting in a complete shift to the industry's nucleus. Now, McLaren is the most southerly team, with Williams, TWR-Arrows, BAR, Jordan and Stewart all encamped around Benetton.

...

As I mentioned in the last chapter, the Italian Riccardo Patrese joined us from Williams in 1993, replacing Brundle to become Schumacher's third Benetton team mate since 1991. From a point of view of testing and developing our new car, signing Patrese was a perfectly sound move. He had been with Williams throughout the entire evolution of their all-conquering FW14B (in fact, he had been with them for five years), and as the B193 was to be an active car, having such a professional driver on board, one who was thoroughly proficient with the most successful active suspension system in the world, could only be a major advantage. The wealth of experience and knowledge that Riccardo had gained at Williams and which he brought with him to Benetton undoubtedly saved us weeks, if not months, in both our active suspension and our semi-automatic transmission research and testing programmes. In Formula One, where development time is everything, his inclusion in the team was invaluable.

On the downside, however, was the fact that he didn't really want to be with us. It was a sad state of affairs really. Riccardo had been happy at Williams; he had won races at Williams; he had been runner-up in the Drivers' World Championship at Williams (a result he referred to as Vice Champion). He knew the team, the team knew him. But when Frank had announced that Alain Prost would be joining his team in 1993 (following a year's sabbatical after his dismissal from Ferrari in 1991) Riccardo had assumed that this would put him out of a drive. It was a fair assumption too, Nigel Mansell had just stormed the 1992 Drivers' Championship, and the chances of Frank getting rid of Mansell in order to keep Patrese in the team must have seemed close to a billion-to-one against.

It had been announced quite early in 1992 that Brundle would not be driving for Benetton the following year, and knowing that Flavio had not yet made a decision on Martin's replacement, Riccardo moved quickly in order to consolidate his position. With 240 Grand Prix starts, 6 wins and 261 points to his credit, Briatore and Walkinshaw must have been thrilled at the prospect of having Riccardo in the team; here was a seasoned professional, a perfectly able and winning driver (and one that just happened to be carrying all that invaluable Williams active suspension experience) asking to join and drive for Benetton. Yes! Of course you can drive for us, Mr Patrese; please, sign here! I've got a pen if you need one! Then, shortly after Riccardo had signed for Benetton, Mansell's own negotiations with Williams collapsed and the next thing the world knew was that Nigel had left for America taking his Drivers' Championship with him. In light of this development it now became evident that Patrese's job at Williams would still have been open for him, the net result being that he would have partnered Prost instead of Mansell. Damn! Damn! Damn!

Now, I don't know this for certain but I suspect that as far as Frank was concerned, Riccardo could have rescinded his newly signed Benetton contract and stayed with Williams. In fact, he would probably have been more than happy for their working relationship to have continued for another few years (securing Riccardo's knowledge of the Williams active project would have been justification enough for some sort of contract extension). However, I don't imagine that Benetton were remotely keen to let go of such a valuable new employee, though perhaps an agreement could have been reached whereby Patrese was released back to Williams; but the bottom line was that Riccardo decided to stick with his Benetton agreement, and that decision says an awful lot about him. He is a real gentleman, a man of ethics and one who is genuinely true to his word. Despite preferring to have stayed with Williams he had agreed to work with Benetton and as far as Riccardo was concerned that agreement – be it either verbal or written – was as firm as being set in stone.

So with Patrese quite prepared to honour his commitment to us it was left up to Frank Williams to find a replacement for him. Enter: Damon Hill, the Williams test driver, a man who knew the team well and who, like Patrese, had driven thousands of miles in a Williams active car. And who could they find to replace Hill as the team's new test driver? Enter: David Coulthard, promoted into Formula One from F3000.

There was only one aspect that I found unsatisfactory about all of this, and that was the fact that Mansell had turned his back on Formula One and decided to drive in the US Indy-car series the very next year after clinching his Drivers' Championship. To my mind I don't think that decision was ethically correct; I didn't agree with his decision back in 1993, and I still don't agree with it today. I would have no objection to the move if he had decided to go to the States at the end of 1991 or at the end of 1993 (providing he didn't retain the Championship), but to abandon the sport without defending his crown in the following year's competition seems wrong to me. It's probably just a personal thing but I believe that if you win something you should then compete against your rivals to defend the right to retain it or, in the face of superior talent, compete and graciously pass the prize to the new winner. For whatever reason, perhaps Mansell couldn't have stayed with Williams but it's impossible to think that a reigning World Champion couldn't have found a Formula One seat somewhere. Not enough money on offer from a smaller team? Let's face it, when you've just been crowned Formula One World Champion you're not going to be short of a few bob; if you never earned another penny for the rest of your life you'd still be a multi-millionaire. This is not a situation unique to Mansell, of course, there are many such examples (Prost did exactly the same at the end of 1993) but I just cannot agree with it.

My criticism of his departure is in no way a denunciation of the man himself, however. Mansell is a wonderful personality, a true showman, full of character, something that many of the new breed of drivers seem to lack. In his prime years he was the Bulldog Drummond of Formula One, capable of taking an average car and wringing every last drip of performance out of it; either that or driving it so hard that the car would simply blow up under the strenuous demands he would make of it. During one race, I remember watching him drive out of the Ferrari pits with such fury that he tore both drive-shafts out of the gearbox. For a few seconds, accompanied by great plumes of white tyre smoke, the V12 screamed and wailed in complaint, then BANG! Game over.

Another of Mansell's great appeals is that he's capable of producing and sporting the most astonishingly big moustache. A huge, bushy affair, a real classic of a moustache, one which seems to possess a life and a personality all its own. The media loved Mansell too, not merely because of his moustache (although that must have been an added attraction for the photographers and cartoonists), but mainly because he always had a story to tell about how tough his weekend had been, or how much his foot was hurting or that he had a headache like there was no tomorrow. Things like that just don't seem to happen anymore. The sport has changed. The drivers have changed. Anyway. Nigel Mansell did take his Formula One crown and leave for the States, so that's that.

Annoyed at himself, perhaps, but determined to stick by his word, Riccardo Patrese joined Benetton, and he and I started working together as team-mates in the winter of 1992. It was a long, hard winter too; for everyone at the Enstone factory, producing our high-tech B193 resulted in a fiercely steep learning curve. To make life a little simpler, the initial idea was to retain last year's chassis, the B192, but to remove the passive suspension and install our own in-house designed active suspension. The 1992 gearbox was also scrapped; for the new season we were to build and develop a semi-automatic transmission. Because of both of these major modifications, as well as some additional changes to the aerodynamics, the car was sufficiently altered from its original specification to warrant it being rebadged as the B193.

With all of the upcoming test sessions we would have more than enough work to keep everybody fully occupied throughout the winter. However, the FIA then stipulated the compulsory use of narrower tyres for the 1993 season, but in testing, regardless of the assistance offered by our new active suspension, the '92 chassis hated the reduced grip imposed by the new regulations. The only real solution to the car's handling problems would be to design and build a new chassis, one with the weight distribution and suspension geometry perfectly matched to the characteristics of the new tyres. But at this late stage in the year, coupled with all the development work required on the new active system and the semi-auto transmission, to then embark on such a mammoth project would, quite simply, be utterly crazy. Indeed, merely to suggest that such an undertaking was possible would be seen as an act of sheer optimism. The decision was taken – we would build a new chassis.

The glue had barely dried on the B193 chassis plates before they were pulled back off and changed again. This time the revamped 1992 chassis were badged as B193A cars; when it came into production the brand-new '93 chassis would be known as the B193B. It would have been impossible to start the racing season with this true 1993 car, since there just weren't enough hours in the day, so the policy we had used in previous years was deployed once again: we would use the old car for the first two races, the intercontinental races of South Africa and Brazil; then the new car would take over once we had returned to Europe.

. . .

I mentioned earlier that when an active car is performing well it is a dream to work with. In the pits the mechanics are still having to adjust the wing angles, check for leaks, circuit damage, and generally keep an eye on the brake wear etc. but the vast majority of suspension alterations are merely software changes. Connect car to computer, tap, tap, tap, unplug computer from car, send car back to the circuit. How long did that take, about six seconds? Well it possibly took a little longer in reality, but not much. However, the amount of work it took Benetton to get the car to that stage of efficiency was immense.

In Estoril during the winter, where we were testing our new active suspension system shortly after its introduction, we worked on the car for three days and two nights (with no more than four hours sleep throughout the entire test) and it was only on the third day that we finally managed to coax the car into doing one extremely slow lap past the pits. For two frustrating days and two freezing nights the car sat in the garage doing no more than being a completely stubborn bastard. We had the thing sitting on corner-weight scales (four electronic pads, one placed under each wheel, which are used to check for even weight distribution), with the flushing-rig maintaining fluid pressure to the car while Ross Brawn and his R&D engineers tried to get the computerized electronics to communicate and work with at least some slight semblance of harmony with the system's hydraulics. Software was installed and system pressure applied, but rather than react logically to these settings the car would just violently shudder and shake as if in the throes of some hyperactive, convulsive fit. Hydraulic pressure was cut, data was scrutinized, teeth were thoughtfully sucked.

We tried again (several times, in fact), only to achieve slightly more disconcerting results. More sucking of teeth and then the Moog valves were blamed as being the most likely culprits (the electronically controlled flow valves, which regulate fluid movement around the car's hydraulics). The mechanics duly changed the Moog valves, but with absolutely no improvement to the car's attitude whatsoever.

Working on such complex, high-pressure hydraulics was a new experience for me (it was new to us all) and knowing that the system's operating pressure was in the region of 2500psi – certainly more than enough to blind a mechanic or cause an instant fireball in the event of an accident – I was always careful to ask the R&D engineers, the people who had designed and pioneered the concept, for advice on exactly when it was safe to disconnect a particular component. Once, one of them told me it was perfectly fine to disconnect a Moog valve from the car's fluid manifold, 'the system's dead, there's no pressure in the line now,' he continued. I looked at the mechanic standing next to me, he seemed rather unconvinced by this news. I asked the engineer again, just to confirm that we were all happy before I started unscrewing the bolts (working on an active suspension system was a little like defusing a bomb), this time even the engineer seemed a little unsure of the validity of what he had said. 'Yes, it should be okay to remove it; but just be very, very, careful when you do so.' And leaving us with that he disappeared to the back of the garage. Very reassuring.

The problems with the car continued, chins were stroked, heads were scratched and numerous telephone calls were exchanged between Portugal and England. New software was written and installed, more Moog valves were changed, then the original Moog valves were substituted for the ones we had just fitted. More software changes were followed by more coffee-drinking. Moog changes were followed by more bouts of hydraulic flushing. Long and tedious hours were followed by longer, even more tedious hours. For two days the car never turned a wheel, we just continued to exchange one possibly faulty part for another possibly faulty part. We drank coffee, we became more and more tired and we got thoroughly sick to death of each other's company.

It must be remembered that monumentally long hours are par for the course during the start of any Grand Prix year and, regardless of whether a team is designing an active car or not, it makes little difference to the potential workload. Pre-season testing has always been grim and the arrival of any new design is a potential all-nighter in a box. A redesigned chassis, a new transmission, a different engine, new suspension, it makes little difference; until the freshly starched creases of the new design have been thoroughly ironed out, the chances of a good night's sleep between the months of January and April are extremely limited.

This situation is normal and understood, but what really depressed me, right throughout the period of our active suspension troubles, was the fact that as a mechanic there was little I, or any of the other mechanics could do to speed things along. We couldn't see any fault. The parts that we removed from the car because they were apparently faulty looked as good as the parts we refitted. As mechanics, we are used to looking at a component and checking it for serviceability: too much play in a bearing or not enough lubrication on a gear; stretched threads, damaged wiring looms. Locate the fault, see or feel the problem, think of a solution, fix it and move on; but when, for example, the potential fault is caused by one wrong digit in the writing of a software program, what can we do? We feel helpless, our role gone.

I'm all for the advancement of Grand Prix technology, but my formal training as a mechanic never allowed for such speed of advancement in electronics – not even my BMW training included lessons in correcting computer programming errors. Throughout the Estoril test the car crews would ensure that their machines were in pristine mechanical condition, but until the electricians, the lab technicians and the software specialists had worked their magic, no more could be done; the mechanics were sidelined. Terribly frustrating.

That Estoril test was a career low point for me, not the lowest, by any means, but I hold no fond memories of it whatsoever. Well, perhaps just one: another of the mechanics, Kenny Handkammer, came out with a wonderful phrase at some point during those three days when, tired and ashen-faced, he described our active car as being like a moose. 'Steve, you've got to help me,' he said, 'I can't go on anymore! I'm so knackered I can hardly walk, yet it feels like I'm having to carry a huge burden around with me. It seems just like I've got a massive moose flopped on my back! Its front legs draped over my shoulders, its great head lolling to one side, and I'm having to lug it about with me; it's really starting to drag me down. The Benetton Active Moose and I've got it! It's jumped on my back!'

...

I thought I'd explain a little about semi-automatic transmissions at this point. I quite like them and, speaking as a mechanic, I think they are one of the most interesting things to come out of Formula One design. At the end of the 1992 season in Adelaide, I was standing below the rostrum with the other mechanics, watching Michael and Martin receive their awards for finishing in second and third places. Both drivers were delighted of course, and when Martin saw us he lifted a hand aloft, his thumb held up to thank us for the reliability of his car. As he did so I remember noticing the black tessa-tape which I'd used to bandage his right thumb and a couple of his fingers prior to the race. I remember too how odd his bandaged hand looked as he stood there smiling from the rostrum, and thinking that millions of people around the world would be wondering what had happened to his hand. In fact, this bandaging was something I used to do for him as a matter of course throughout his year with us. It was protection for the fingers of his right hand against blisters, caused by the knob of the gear-lever. Regardless of the added protection of his leather racing gloves, the constant gear changes with the Benetton manual gearbox used to blister his fingers. As he stood on the rostrum, smiling and waving to the Australian crowd, I knew he must have been in some considerable discomfort, yet his happy demeanour betrayed nothing of his pain, the adrenaline of competition and of winning keeping the soreness at bay, probably for another hour or so.

The Australian Grand Prix of 1992 was the last time that Benetton used a manual transmission on one of their cars; and now, those old romantic days of stick-shifting the gearbox have long gone; gone forever, I assume.

Back then, and quite unlike the current semi-auto systems, the driver had to be brave enough to take his hand from the wheel and to manually select the desired gear himself. He was also expected to remember which gear he was already using, and be able to study the rev counter to coincide his next change with the engine's peak power output. Not only that but while down-changing he had to blip the engine with the throttle pedal to synchronize the speed of the gear shafts and be careful not to change down prematurely, over-revving the engine as a result and causing pistons and valves to over-react.

All of these gear changes were achieved via a hand-operated control knob connected to a titanium lever, connected to a joint, connected to a carbon rod, connected to another joint, connected to the selector mechanism, mounted on the gearbox casing. Not forgetting reverse, of course, which at one time was selected by pulling a cable mounted behind the driver's shoulder. How terribly quaint. Well, quaint the use of a gear lever may have been but it wasn't very efficient and it wasn't very quick – at least not when compared with the current state-of-the-art, computer-controlled, hydraulically operated systems, which are capable of changing gear within thirty milliseconds (0.03 seconds; doing so with perfect synchronised timing and with zero risk of over-revving the engine.

To make such rapid gear changes the selector mechanism utilizes the same high-pressure hydraulics which are also used to control the active suspension. The greater the fluid pressure is, the faster the fluid reacts and the quicker it can shift the gear selector mechanism. Because of this extreme operating pressure (didn't we say the active pumps worked at 2500psi) the hydraulic fluid has to travel around the car through equally high-pressure resistant hard-pipes and flexible hoses; anything less than jet aircraft specification equipment would result in an instant and most dramatic fire. Every time these hydraulic lines are disconnected, for example, to allow the engine or gearbox to be changed, the system needs to be purged of air in exactly the same way as the active suspension. In order to reduce these delays to a minimum (remembering that track time is a very precious commodity) all the top teams utilize quick-release couplings known as a 'dry-break'. This no-fluid-loss connector is a piece of pure aeronautical engineering magic, a push-and-click-on, click-and-pull-off device. As the dry-break is uncoupled it does so without losing a single drip of fluid, allowing components to be interchanged without the need to purge the system. Dry-breaks are enormously expensive but in valuable time saved, each one is worth double its weight in gold.

With semi-auto transmissions, instead of the driver using a lever to manually change gear, the gears are 'requested' via two micro-switches mounted on the steering wheel, each switch operated by the now familiar-looking paddle levers. Pulling the right lever changes the gears up; pulling the left, changes down. I think it's interesting to note that all the teams have their up-shifts and down-shifts co-ordinated like this. For some reason it would appear illogical – as if against human conditioning – to reverse this, right-for-up, left-for-down design. Given the choice how would you prefer the paddle layout?

When the driver pulls the up-lever all manner of exciting things happen: the micro-switch sends a signal to the computer processor located in the gearbox controller, asking if it would be possible for the selector mechanism to change up a gear. The controller hears the micro-switch and ponders the situation. The controller checks with the potentiometer mounted on the rotary selector (which is similar to a motorcycle system) as to what gear the car is in at the moment. Next the controller checks with the rear wheel-speed sensors to see how fast the car is going, and then checks the same information with the engine revs, courtesy of the crank-speed trigger. Now the controller looks at the ratio of the desired gear, and because the ratios are constantly being altered, from circuit to circuit (or due to a change in wind direction, from session to session), this ratio information is pre-programmed into the controller every time the gearbox undergoes a ratio rebuild. The controller reads the information about the desired ratio, looks at the engine speed, looks at the wheel speed and does some calculations; working out the anticipated rpm that the engine will be running at should it allow the desired gear to be engaged. Armed with all of this information, the controller is finally ready to go to work.

The controller tells the clutch–actuator to engage the clutch slave-cylinder and disconnect the transmission from the engine. The clutch–actuator obliges. Next the controller orders the actuator working the throttle butterflies to blip the engine rpm to a figure slightly higher than it anticipates the engine to be running at once the new gear is engaged. The throttle-actuator does as it is told. Now, to bring the rpm to its correct figure, the controller asks the engine management controller if it could spark-cut the ignition system until the desired figure is reached. The engine management controller checks the operating condition of its engine and, on finding that all is well, it willingly agrees to assist the gearbox controller, and the ignition is momentarily cut. Now the controller orders the actuator working the gear-selector to pull the original gear out of mesh, rotate the selector and engage the new, desired gear. This is done. The controller seems pleased with its work but still has a final check to see that everything is as it should be and that no one has become lost or confused with what he has been asked to do. On finding only good news it then orders the clutch-actuator to re-engage the transmission with the engine. Voila, one gear change satisfactorily completed, all in less than a third of the time it takes to click your fingers. Oh, and just to make life as easy as possible for the driver, the gearbox controller even flashes up on the dashboard which gear has been selected.

All in all, a jolly impressive piece of engineering, don't you think?

...

Finally, after several weeks of such long and arduous tests, the car began to calm down and eventually to respond favourably to treatment. More filtration and purification of the software, more delicate alterations to the hydraulics, and the Benetton active cars gradually matured into a very quick and nimble series of Formula One race car. Throughout its brief life, refinement work never stopped on the B193B, and for the last two races of the year there was a big push to fit a four-wheel-steer system. I don't know why – the car certainly didn't need it – but it was as if the engineers were desperate to produce the most sophisticated Grand Prix car in the pit-lane before the end of the year. We had thoroughly tested the four-wheel-steer system in England before we packed the cars and left for Japan, but when I spoke to the drivers about the effects of this rear steering, both Patrese and Schumacher could find no advantage whatsoever in using it. Riccardo told me that it certainly made the car feel different but it was a feeling he didn't like. I couldn't notice any improvement in lap times either, and as far as I could see, the pre-Japan/Australia test proved that the system was not needed.

True, the system was designed to be able to be switched on and off, so the drivers could elect to use it or leave it switched off (in which case the hydraulically operated rear steering-rack would merely work as a solid link), but it still had fluid lines connected to it, which meant that it remained a reliability risk. The theory is this: any component of a race car carries a potential risk of failure, therefore the philosophy for ultimate reliability is not to have the component on the car in the first place; if it ain't there it can't go wrong. Obviously, it's not possible to do away with every component, otherwise you'd just end up with a block of carbon, but anything that doesn't need to be on the car, shouldn't be on the car; simple common sense really.

In the event of hydraulic fluid loss the rear steering-rack was designed to fail-safe in the straight-ahead position (again, like a solid link) – so there was no danger to the safety aspect of the car – but a loss of fluid would put the car's hydraulics out of operation, effectively finishing its race. I was dead set against the four-wheel-steering being included on the three race cars, but the decision was made to include it on the Japan/Australia race car specification. I think it was a wrong decision, and I think it was a decision driven more by ego than by any principals of mechanical engineering.

I remember that for these last two races, and in recognition of this additional system, the cars were re-designated as B193C, but I don't think anybody took any notice of the new suffix. *Autocourse*, the Formula One end-of-season review, still referred to the Benetton as being the B193B, so either nobody told the book's compilers of the change or they chose to ignore it. In the practice sessions, both at Suzuka and Adelaide, the drivers did a number of practice laps using the four-wheel-steering but both drivers elected not to have the system activated during the races. As it transpired, we did fail to get either car to finish in the last two Grands Prix, but I also have to say that the rear steering system ran trouble-free throughout the Japanese and Australian weekends. However, to me, that gives scant justification for including something on the car that didn't need to be there.

> *Beware the Jubjub bird, and shun*
> *The frumious Bandersnatch!*

...

One of the most memorable events of the year occurred at the Grand Prix at Spa. Unlike 1992 we didn't win the race, though we did finish second and sixth, which was a far better result than we could ever have hoped for, considering the quite atrocious start we made. Half-an-hour prior to the start, as the cars left the pits to form up on the grid, both drivers were asked to try the cars' start-control at some point on the circuit – as a systems check – before arriving at their respective grid positions. Michael confirmed that all was well, but Riccardo said it didn't feel right to him – the engine seemed to bog down – he couldn't define exactly what the fault was, but he advised not to use it. Better, he said, to switch the device off and make a conventional start selecting the gears manually (the start-control software would allow the clutch and the gears to be worked automatically, matching gear changes with peak engine revs for optimum performance, the system interlinked with the car's traction-control software to avoid any wheel spin as the car shot from the grid). While the mechanics fussed over the engine, gearbox and suspension, making their last checks that all was well, the engineers checked the streams of data stored in the onboard controllers. Finding no apparent fault with the start-control electronics the decision was taken to overrule Riccardo's advice and to use the system as planned.

If you ever have the chance to watch the start of that race on video you'll notice that as the rest of the field scream off towards the first corner, both Benettons make the most appalling start, chugging and spluttering off the grid as the other cars dash and weave their way around them. We had qualified third and sixth but by the first lap we had dropped to ninth and seventeenth, so getting Michael onto the second step of the rostrum in those circumstances was a pretty impressive result. However, it was neither the start of the race nor its result which made the Spa Grand Prix so memorable for me; it was one of the pit-stops, Patrese's stop on lap seventeen to be more exact.

I'd now changed my role within the organization of our pit-stop crew. In 1991, Nigel Stepney had set me to work on the left-rear corner of the car, but since the start of the 1992 season I had been in charge of operating the rear jack. I've said before that I didn't enjoy this aspect of the job, but carrying out the pit-stops is all part and parcel of the profession. You either accept it or you leave; there doesn't seem to be a third alternative. There is a small advantage in using the rear jack as opposed to working in any other position on the team. To allow the car to drive into position you have to stand well clear as it speeds down the pit-lane towards the other mechanics (the disadvantage of using the front jack is that the driver is aiming the car straight at you).

The split second after the car had sped passed me, I'd dash in from behind, throwing the jack forward, and engaging the lift-bar onto the two hooks – known as jacking plates – which are located at the base of the rear wing. For increased speed and efficiency, it is best to have the operation completed while the car is still moving forward (the air-guns should also be in position at this stage). As soon as the car stopped I would then lift the rear, allowing the mechanics to finish removing the wheels. The same thing happens at the front of the car, of course. I would then watch and wait until the gun-men had raised their arms, signifying that they had finished fitting the new tyres, and then glance towards Kenny Handkammer on the front jack, just to confirm that we were both happy. If all was okay, the car would then be dropped back to the ground.

Throughout all of this the mechanic with the BRAKES ON board – known as the lollipop – is in total control of the car; it is a position of great accountability and one usually undertaken by the team's chief mechanic. When, and only when he lifts that board away will the driver be allowed to speed off. The man holding the lollipop has sole responsibility for ensuring that all work has finished on the car and to check that the pit-lane is clear of traffic before giving control of the car back to the driver. 1993 was to be the last year before the reintroduction of the stupidity of refuelling, the act of which has slowed even a perfect pit-stop by over seven seconds. So, in Spa that year all we had to worry about was successfully changing the four wheels, and when Riccardo pitted for fresh tyres we managed to service the car in just 3.2 seconds. That remarkable time was a world record, the quickest pit-stop in history. To this day it has never been bettered, and now that the cars have to refuel, the chance of that record being beaten are terribly slim. It is, of course, entirely possible to pit just for tyres – it isn't compulsory to refuel – but in reality all teams do refuel, so Benetton's 1993 record looks safe, at least for the foreseeable future.

...

For me, the world record we set in Spa was the season's high-point, while that winter test in Estoril was, undoubtedly, the season's low point, but I also remember Estoril for a much happier reason: we won the Grand Prix. Michael's second career victory and my fifth since I joined the team.

Because of a glitch with the software settings on his race car's active suspension – a problem caused by 'finger trouble' when the electrician was keying information into the car's controller – Michael drove the spare car in the race. The major significance of this win by the spare car went largely unnoticed by the rest of the world. One of our test team mechanics, Carlos Nunes, had temporarily joined the race team, just for this race, standing in for Paul Howard, the car's Number One mechanic who had been unable to attend. Carlos had been in Formula One for years, working with the struggling March team, and had only joined Benetton after March had finally ceased their Formula One programme.

Here was Carlos, a Portuguese, a man who had never won a single race, running the Benetton spare car in Portugal. Now, a Portuguese Formula One mechanic is an extreme rarity and the local press were already demanding interviews and photographs of him working in the Benetton garage. After all, just to be a part of Grand Prix racing had made him a minor celebrity, but now, to be working with a leading team, a genuine contender for the race, had made him extremely newsworthy. However, immediately before the start of the Grand Prix, when word broke out that Schumacher was to be racing the spare car – with Carlos in charge of it – the local media became very excited. This had now become a guaranteed sports page headline. But when Michael crossed the line to win the race, the Portuguese media went wild! 'Hold the front page! Carlos has won! Carlos Nunes has won the Grand Prix!'

Local Boy Makes Good
Schumacher and Nunes Storm Estoril
King Carlos – The Hero of the Portuguese Grand Prix
...

Joan Villadelprat and the very top of the Benetton management were thrilled too. Before long Carlos found himself promoted to chief mechanic, and before much longer he was promoted again, this time to become the test team manager. He is a steady, easy-going chap, a man who enjoys the work of Grand Prix racing, but one who will always look after the people under him. When Joan asks him to work he will willingly do so, but when there is a chance to get back home to his wife, his kids and his prize-winning Koi carp, he will make sure that everybody gets home as soon as possible. Simple man-management skills and common courtesy, some people have got them, some people haven't. Carlos has these qualities in abundance and I'm sure he'll continue to prosper. He still enjoys the job and that makes an enormous difference to his outlook, his staff's perception of him and Benetton's appreciation of him.

The Estoril Grand Prix was also the race which saw Alain Prost secure his fourth Drivers' World Championship, making him the second most successful driver in Formula One history, just one championship behind the legendary Juan Manuel Fangio. It's a fair bet that if Prost had stayed with Williams in 1994 he could have equalled that record too. He should have stayed in order to defend his title, and it would certainly have made for an exciting season, but he didn't. Perhaps Mansell quit at the end of 1992 because he didn't want to race against Prost in equal equipment? Perhaps Prost quit at the end of 1993 because he didn't want to face Senna on the same terms? We will never know but if that is the case, it's a great shame on both accounts.

Once again Benetton decided not to retain the services of Michael Schumacher's team-mate, and after a total of 256 Grand Prix starts (a massive figure and another world record which looks set to stand for many years) Riccardo Patrese decided to call it a day and retired from Formula One. Like the years I spent with Nelson Piquet and Martin Brundle before him, I really enjoyed my time working with Riccardo. Benetton didn't win any Championships that year; with 72 points we finished the year in third place. Williams continued to dominate the sport, winning ten races and another Constructors' Championship. With 168 points in the bag they scored exactly double that of second-place McLaren; and all bar eleven of those 84 points were scored by Ayrton Senna. As it turned out, 1993 was Ayrton's last season with McLaren and he managed to win five races throughout the course of the year. In Adelaide, on 7 November, he won his last race for them. It was a fine finish to the season and an admirable way for two such great names to part company.

The win in Australia was also destined to be Ayrton's very last Grand Prix victory; in Imola just six months later, he would be killed. What more is there to say?

Chapter seven

1994

The end of sophistication…A single-make formula?…
The genius of Wolfgang, Michael and Salvador…Writing
books on Grand Prix teams…Formula One press-officers…
Life's three keys…1994: a brief summary…A dog's life, but…

I firmly believe that continuous advancement in technical engineering is what Formula One is all about. At one time the sport took great pride in being at the very cutting edge of vehicle technology, with many of its engineering principles taken straight from the world of aeronautics: the extensive use of exotic, composite materials; the preference for measuring fuel consumption by weight as opposed to volume; the detailed application of aerodynamics; even the electrical harnesses constructed by using aircraft specification, ultra-lightweight cable. The harness's multi-pin connections are also to special order, built to military aircraft specification and arrive from the supplier painted in drab olive green (truly!).

To me, speaking purely in my role as a mechanic, Formula One's appeal is the challenge to produce and constantly improve the fastest, most reliable Grand Prix car in the world. My interest has always been in the engineering, never the actual racing. But don't misunderstand me, the skill and the competition between the drivers is all very exciting: the thrill of the chase, the ducking, the diving, the derring-do, but to an extent the drivers' involvement is only a by-product of what we, the manufacturers, do. In reality, of course, the team/driver relationship is mutually beneficial for both parties: the teams need to compete, so the teams need drivers; the drivers wish to compete, so the drivers need teams. Fair exchange, no robbery.

Nevertheless, despite this current cosy situation of reciprocal back-scratching I would be quite happy to see the level of science and technology increase to the point where the cars could be entirely controlled by an intricate network of sensors and processors, negating any further need for driver input. A competition of pure mechanical performance and reliability, played out against other constructors and the omnipotent laws of physics. No more whinging that the seat needs extra padding, or that the rear-view mirrors have moved again; no more last-minute driver changes before the cars leave for the grid. No more need to put our drivers' safety at risk; no more need for drivers at all, in fact! The idea is not without certain merits, I think.

As far as mechanical interest is concerned, 1993 was Formula One's zenith. By the conclusion of that year we had reached our ultimate stage of technical progress. With active suspension, semi-auto transmissions, traction-control, start-control, antilock brakes and four-wheel steering, the sport was at full stretch. We had expanded to the maximum, and from 1994 we were forced to contract. Formula One will never again see that level of sophistication. As far as I was concerned, one stroke of the rule-maker's pen took away much of Formula One's reason for being.

We didn't need to stop, we could have continued to learn and to research and to advance the technology of our Grand Prix machinery forever – but the FIA didn't want us to. The position of superiority enjoyed by the top four teams was considered unfair. The argument was that it had become impossible for the smaller teams such as Minardi, to compete with the likes of Williams, McLaren, Ferrari and now Benetton, because they could never raise sufficient funds to build a car of similar finesse. They had a point, and, to a degree, I agreed with them. I don't know exactly how much the other teams had invested in their cars, but I remember a figure of $30 million being bandied around as Benetton's active car budget. $30 million! Quite obviously a ludicrous amount of money to have to spend merely to remain competitive. If we assume that Williams, McLaren and Ferrari were subject to similar costs, that makes an expenditure of $120 million just for the first eight cars on the grid; there are another eighteen lining up behind them.

The vast bulk of that money was spent in the teams' original research and development programmes and initial manufacturing costs of producing the system components; so although it's true to say that the teams wouldn't incur such huge costs every year, it's still very difficult to justify. Let's suppose that the teams could reduce their active budgets by 50 percent in the second year and by 75 percent in their third year, that still means an outlay of $52,500,000 per team over a mere thirty-six months. And that's just one element of the car, there's still everything else to take into account: the chassis, brakes, transmission, etc.

Personally, I'm of two minds about this. I wholeheartedly agree that the amount of money being spent was quite loopy, and it was perfectly true that people like Minardi and Larrousse and Scuderia Italia could never hope to build similar competitive systems. But, did anybody, for a split second, really think that if all the high-tech systems were banned from the cars and we all used manual transmissions and passive suspensions that Larrousse would be dicing with Williams or McLaren for the lead of a Grand Prix? Of course not; that particular justification for banning active technology is daft and should instantly be dismissed.

...

It makes little sense to my way of thinking, but from what I understand, the general consensus within the governing body is that Formula One should be portrayed as a drivers' championship, a demonstration of talent behind the wheel. This is another reason why such driver aids as traction control and ABS were banned at the end of 1993. According to some, the leading cars had become too driver-friendly; winning races was just a matter of pressing the throttle and occasionally turning the steering wheel in order to avoid the back-markers as the top cars sailed along, lapping the field within minutes of the start. Winning had become effortless. More equal machinery was desired, a levelling of the playing field.

Conversation overheard in a pub: 'Let's face it, when they were working for Ron Dennis, Prost and Senna won six Drivers' World Championships, because of the McLaren-Honda, the car was quite unbeatable! Look at Mansell in '92, the Championship was his because he was driving a Williams, what did you expect! Exactly the same thing happened when Prost returned in '93. Reduce the teams' technology, bring them all to the same level, then we can have real racing.' Piffle perhaps, but that was the sort of mumbling I was hearing; presumably the sport picked up on similar noises and reduce the teams' technology is exactly what the FIA did. And this is apparently how they want to keep it.

Look at McLaren in 1998: they pioneered the use of tractor-brakes in Formula One, making it possible to apply more pressure to one rear wheel than the other, thus helping reduce unladen wheel slip on corner exit. The two McLarens were blisteringly quick at the start of the season and their tractor-brakes were seen as being an 'unfair advantage'. The system was quickly banned. But what some people are forgetting is that the teams are constructors, they design and build their own cars. Since 1950, when the Formula One championship began, vehicle manufacturers have been producing and entering their cars into competition against each other. Alfa-Romeo; Ferrari; Honda; Lotus; Maserati; Mercedes – in the field of automotive engineering these are colossal names, all individual motor companies who compete with one another. Their race cars were all built to a given set of rules or formula – Formula One – and off to race they would go. And, providing that the teams remained within the rules of the formula, if any team then produced a technical advantage over their competition then good luck to them.

In 1958 this team rivalry – albeit polite and gentlemanly – was so recognized that a trophy was awarded to the sport's most successful team: the Formula One Constructors' Championship was born. In 1988, when McLaren International claimed its magnificent fifteen out of sixteen races, it did so because it had the best, most reliable car in the pit-lane, driven by two of the best drivers in history. I doubt that Prost and Senna would ever have been able to win the same number of races in any other car. And I agree, when Mansell finally won his Championship crown he was helped (enormously) by the quality of the Williams, but producing the best car in the world is what constructors try to do and have always tried to do.

However, if the world really wants to see Formula One played out as a drivers' championship – removing any significant team input – then a possible solution would be to convert Grand Prix racing into a single-make formula. For example: at the start of the year the teams would all be issued with a number of cars, produced by ABC Chassis-U-Like, with engines built by XYZ Motors-N-Go, with the FIA then declaring it against the regulations to alter the car in any way. If this idea was not acceptable because the governing body still wanted the teams to remain 'constructors' and the engine manufacturers still wished to compete, then each year the teams and engine builders could be issued with identical sets of drawings from which they could independently produce a clone chassis and engine. After production, the engines and cars could be inspected for regulation compliance and fitted with identification markers (as they are now, in fact, after passing the FIA crash test). In this way each team would still be able to manufacture their own cars, and each team's cars would be identical. Equal equipment for all.

If the equipment we had at the start of the year was what we were forced to use for the duration of the season – with any modifications only introduced by the FIA on the grounds of reliability and driver safety – the teams could have the cars ready to run and the mechanics back at their hotel by six o'clock every night. Unable to alter the fixed design, there would be no need for the teams to organize individual research programmes; for example, the introduction and development of a new aero-package (such as the small X wings which began to appear on the cars at the start of 1998) which the other teams are forced to copy and which the FIA then decided to ban. Having no beneficial reason to develop the cars, the teams' production and yearly running costs would plummet. Jordan Grand Prix claimed to have spent tens of thousands of pounds developing and producing their version of the X wing, and was miffed when the device was subsequently banned. Masses of money spent for nothing. Taking all the teams' design budgets into consideration, not allowing the constructors to develop their cars would potentially save millions of pounds each year.

Some people may argue this idea, pointing out that Formula One's design regulations decree that the cars are already identical, with each built to the same recipe; after all, every car on the grid is a Formula One car. True, but only to a limited degree. Yes, they are all built to the same guidelines but they are most definitely not all identical. When Aldo Costa designed the Minardi M192 he was subject to exactly the same technical restrictions that were imposed on Patrick Head when he penned the FW14B, but the performance and reliability of the '92 Williams was leagues ahead of the Minardi – and everything else for that matter.

I'm afraid I had to look up the Minardi designer's name in *Autocourse* as I had no idea whatsoever who drew their car. It strikes me as the sort of third question you'd get asked before being allowed to cross the Bridge of Doom in Python's Holy Grail:

'What is your name?'

'What is your favourite colour?'

'What is the name of the man who oversaw the initial design, first-build and further development of the 1992 Minardi M192 Formula One Grand Prix car?'

The current situation is that innovative design is first researched, then built, then developed and only then banned. If the world would rather see the drivers in equal equipment then it would be an awful lot less effort (and infinitely cheaper) if the teams didn't have to go through the laborious process of pioneering and building these advantages in the first place, only to have them outlawed later on. For example: rather than have the regulations merely specifying an area of the car where a wing can or cannot be, why not take the pen out of the designer's hand and simply issue his team's composite department with a drawing of the only allowable wing?

Such a policy would certainly make the mechanics' lives easier: no more constant messing about on the flat-patch with the new MK15 suspension geometry; no new diffuser designs fronting up that haven't any intention of fitting anywhere near anything; no new gearbox selector mechanism being flown out on the Friday night, which if all goes well should arrive at about two in the morning. All you need to do is slip the box off the engine for a bit of a rebuild and a couple of mods, then quickly slide it back on so we can fire the engine and look at the data to see if we want to run the new mechanism during tomorrow's practice. If the data doesn't look good, then we'll just whip the box off again, remove the new selector and all its gubbins and put everything back as it was.

The bottom line is that there is no easy solution to Formula One's problem. Banning technical advancement takes away the constructors' competitive spirit, as would converting the sport into a single-make formula. Giving the teams free rein to do as they wish would result in the top four teams developing the most incredibly advanced and ferociously expensive cars, while the rest of the field plodded along behind, fifteen or more seconds a lap slower than the leaders. Yet the current situation is clearly not working either. Perhaps what the sport needs is a freezing of the technical regulations, what the teams have now is what the teams have in five years time. I really don't know what the answer is, but I do know that the reduction of technology has severely dimmed the limelight in which state-of-the-art Grand Prix racing used to bask. There was a time when people used to say that Formula One technology fed the road car industry, that the innovative designs included on a Grand Prix car one year would be utilized by the mass-market vehicle manufacturers within the next few years. I don't hear people saying that anymore. Formula One has been left behind. It is now the road cars which have complex traction-control and ABS assemblies; it is the road cars which have four-wheel steering and hydraulically adjustable suspension. Of course they also have refinements which wouldn't be of use to a race car, such as ingenious climate-control systems, perfect-fidelity sound and satellite-assisted guidance, but even without these little luxuries, the current flag ship BMW or Mercedes sports saloons are making post-technology-ban Grand Prix cars, limited to using their four clonky springs and dampers, look pretty dowdy by comparison.

...

I've always thought that good music means one is never really alone and in times of greatest need my favourite albums have become firm and faithful friends. Years ago I remember listening to a late-night phone-in on the radio, with people discussing the various merits of different composers. One chap, based in the studio and apparently an authority on such matters, dismissed Mozart's work as 'frivolous, a man who is capable of amusing but nevertheless a man who failed to take his work seriously; he entertains in the same way as a circus clown. He makes music yet never understood how'. Didn't understand how? Wolfgang Amadeus Mozart! A man whose every written note bulges with talent, didn't understand how? Well, without doubt, the voice on the radio was on some hideous ego trip, and although I would never describe myself as being expert in anything, I'm certain that this particular 'authority' had utterly confused the real point he was trying to make. What Mozart did was to make it look easy, too easy. It was all just pure effortless fun, that was the difference. He could scribble down a masterpiece for the clarinet in the afternoon, get drunk as a lord in the evening and the next morning – still nursing a delicate head – he would compose a series of elaborate choral works for inclusion in a grand Mass. And later that night he would be out on the tiles again.

Schumacher is an example of a man who shares a similar genius to Mozart. Recently I watched a video of the 1998 Canadian Grand Prix, which Michael won (partly helped, of course, by the swift demise of both McLarens). After the race Michael climbed from his Ferrari and removed his helmet looking as bright and fresh as if he had driven but a single lap. There wasn't a hair out of place or a bead of sweat in sight, just a big beaming smile of success – but no visible signs of the skill, the determination or the complex talents that were required to win the race. It was all effortless fun.

Salvador Dali was the same. His sense of light and shade and depth is fabulous. His ability to conjure up more than one image from within a single work and to allow the alternative picture to rise through the colours of the first – for example, the painting of Gala looking out to sea, which changes into a portrait of Abraham Lincoln's head – is nothing short of magnificent. Yet, when some people observed Dali at play, simply gluing a plaster lobster atop an old telephone and declaring the work finished, they instantly dismissed him as talentless, a frivolous fool. He was making it look too easy. Mind you, it's also worth bearing in mind that Dali tried to kill himself through a slow process of self-dehydration. He thought that if he lay preserved in this utterly dry state, future generations could one day sprinkle him with water and his celebrated talents would be reborn like the budding of a springtime flower. Obviously, this made it patently clear that the great man was also barking mad. The fact remains, either you've got a God-given gift or you haven't. But the man on the radio couldn't see that; he thought that stern meant skilful, that grumpy meant dedicated. He was wrong.

...

Each year there is a plethora of books written about motor-racing, the majority of which are devoted to Formula One. I would suggest that about ninety-five percent of those books are driver biographies, the remaining five percent split between end-of-season reviews and the occasional book taking an inside look at this or that particular team. The reason that there is such an array of driver-dedicated books, I suppose, is that on the whole, they are a much easier topic to research. Most are written by Grand Prix journalists, people who are interviewing drivers as a matter of course, and the drivers will (fairly) willingly give the journalists much of the information they need to write their books.

However, on the flip-side of Formula One's coin, being granted sufficient freedom of information to be able to write a worthwhile account of a constructor's operation is an infinitely more difficult prospect. The very nature of the sport means that the teams tend to be most furtive and secretive when dealing with the press.

At Benetton we were under instructions not to so much as speak to the press; if anyone wanted any team information we were to politely direct them and their enquiries to the press-officer. At the conclusion of every running session, be it a test, a practice, qualifying or the race itself, the teams' press-officers write and distribute a press release. This is the official party line; what is printed on that sheet is all they really want the world to hear about the team's operations. Each team produces its own press releases: Benetton, Ferrari, Jordan, McLaren, Minardi, the tyre manufactures, the engine manufactures, the entire pit-lane in fact; but on the whole, other than the bare facts and figures – grid positions, lap-times, chassis numbers – these press releases are about as much use as a chocolate fire-guard. However, it's important to stress that this lack of substance isn't the fault of the press-officers. Their job is to deal with the media, and one of their tasks in dealing with the media is to produce a press release; but much of the time their hands are tied, and they can only reveal to the world what the team managers and their technical directors allow. Their job is made even more difficult by the fact that they are constantly trying to convey that a calm and serene atmosphere surrounds their team.

'Everything's fine, no problems that can't be fixed (nice smile), both drivers are suffering from a little understeer but the team will be working on that during the evening and we should be able to produce much quicker lap-times tomorrow (nice smile). Peter Perfect lost a little time with a small gearbox problem, but we confidently predict that both our cars will be in the top six on the grid, and all being well, a podium finish is not out of the question (nice smile).'

What this actually means is that the car is totally undrivable and regardless of the fact that the mechanics have been throwing springs and roll bars at it all morning, no amount of set-up change is making the slightest bit of difference to a chassis which has proved completely useless at every circuit since it was originally bashed together at midnight in the first-builds of January. The gearbox has utterly destroyed itself because of a bearing failure which was reported as being a latent problem over four races ago – yet nothing whatsoever has been done to solve it – and now the gearbox mechanics are threatening to burn their race-shirts, drive back to the hotel, get unfeasibly drunk and fly home two days early. The drivers and their engineers have spent the entire morning's session squaring up to each other over the radio, one accusing the other of being clearly far too talentless to drive a Formula One race car, the other retorting that his colleague is blatantly unable to engineer anything more complex than a lawnmower entered in the local village Run-What-You-Brung Open Challenge; and the team's major sponsors are sick and tired of the total lack of results and are on the verge of pulling out.

A journalist who is intent on trying to produce a written record of how a Grand Prix team functions is subjecting himself to all kinds of problems. The first obstacle to overcome is obtaining the initial credentials required to breach the team's ambitious security gates. The next difficulty is receiving a receptive response from the staff and being treated as a work colleague – not merely ignored by the mechanics and looked upon as just another prying 'journo' – and then, once comfortably able to mingle amongst the employees, the final problem (and the biggest) is being able to write an inside account of life spent working there without the press-officer wanting to check and approve every written paragraph. Indeed, the very word 'inside' would have both the press-officer and the team's entire marketing department squirming with unease; used in the right context its very existence implies skulduggery, embarrassing disclosure, a kiss-and-tell scandal.

'Inside story! What are you trying to imply? All above board in this team, nothing underhand would ever go on here, oh no, no, no, no, no.'

Like every other position in the pit-lane, there are good press-officers and there are bad ones – perhaps this means that they are either boring or not boring – and although I don't know many of them (as a mechanic I only occasionally came into contact with rival teams' press-officers) I think that Jordan's Giselle Davies must rank as being one of the best. Her press releases are always informative and quite frank, and possibly helped by her boss's relaxed attitude, she seems able to give more than some. If Eddie tells her that he has had a thoroughly dismal weekend and everything's been a complete disaster, then she will report exactly that. Giselle used to work with Benetton, which is where I first met her, but she left us to join Eddie Jordan when his previous press-officer, Louise Goodman, parted from them to work for Mach 1, the TV company currently producing the ITV Formula One coverage.

Even with all the potential pitfalls, there have still been some good books published on the subject of teams; *Race Without End* by Maurice Hamilton is a fine example of the genre (although after what I've just said about Eddie Jordan's approach to the job it's perhaps not a complete coincidence that Hamilton's book covers a racing season with Jordan Grand Prix). Nevertheless, the fact still remains that, by comparison, the writer's task is far more daunting when he attempts to explore a Grand Prix team, compared with the ease of researching and writing an account of a driver's career.

In December 1993 I decided that I would like to write a book on Formula One, but something a little different with a new approach. I was nurturing the vague notion of writing an account of my professional life, my time spent working as a race mechanic with what by this stage had become an established and reasonably successful Formula One team. I remember reading a book by Peter Lewis, a journalist for the *Observer* newspaper. The book entitled *Alf Francis - Racing Mechanic*, told the story of Alf when he worked as a mechanic with Sterling Moss in the 1950s. It was a wonderful read and I thought I'd try to do something similar by writing an update to the story of a mechanic's lot more than forty years after Lewis had transcribed Alf's anecdotes. However, one thing would definitely be different; I was determined not to give the task of writing the book to anyone else. If I was going to undertake the project then I would do all the work myself. Other than a few letters and the annual bundle of Christmas cards I hadn't really written anything substantial before, certainly nothing of such magnitude as a book, but I thought I'd have a go all the same. After all, I'd never ridden a push-bike until I climbed on one as a kid and started to peddle; I'd never stripped and rebuilt a Ferrari Testarossa engine until I was asked to do so; and, likewise, I'd never worked on a Grand Prix car before Nigel Stepney offered me the chance. The three keys to undertaking any task in life are: desire, guidelines and common sense. Bear in mind those three factors and almost anything is achieveable. This philosophy, based on logic and optimism, will never be a substitute for thorough training in a particular discipline but providing one is sensible and feels confident enough to try, then all manner of things are possible. On 1 January 1994 I began *Just Another Day at the Office – The Working Life of a Formula One Mechanic.*

I didn't realize it at the time, of course, but the decision to write that book would alter my life as much as my decision to join Benetton had five years earlier.

…

On 13 January I received a letter from our commercial director, Flavio Briatore, in which he said:

> *Dear Team Member*
> *Your managers and I have reviewed the options for increasing your remuneration in 1994. We were very fortunate in successfully negotiating the Mild Seven sponsorship to replace Camel at such an early stage. However, as you are aware, the world is in recession and finding the additional sponsorship to do all the things we would like to do, both on and off the track, is not easy. I look forward to 1994 being our most successful season yet and wish you well with your particular endeavours in this respect.*

On 19 January, I received another letter, this time from our operations manager, Joan Villadelprat.

> *Dear Steve*
> *I am pleased to advise you that with effect from 1 January 1994, your salary will be increased to £24,061 per annum. Where relevant this review takes into account a number of factors including your performance during 1993.*

…

I enjoy reading George Orwell: his works such as *Down and Out in Paris* and *London, The Road to Wigan Pier, Animal Farm* and *Nineteen Eighty-four* are among my best loved books, the latter, despite its unrelenting pessimism, has been a long-term favourite since reading it as part of my English exams at school. I always find Orwell's detailed descriptions, both imaginary and of everyday events, to be incredibly vivid. From time to time completely abstract situations make me think of scenes from *Nineteen Eighty-four,* and Flavio's circular letter provided another instance of just that. It didn't make his correspondence appear very personal, but I thought his 'Dear Team Member' was great fun; the odd form of address and the letter's news content made it seem like the start of a Party bulletin crackling out from Winston Smith's telescreen. I could easily imagine a series of similar telescreens dotted around the Enstone factory, the clipped, steely voice of the female announcer giving out a constant stream of tedious production figures before being interrupted and handed the latest news.

'Team Members, the world is in recession, yet we are able and pleased to announce that as from today we have increased the range of soft drinks in the canteen vending machine to three, instead of just two ("but I seem to remember we had five varieties in there only yesterday"). The Team wishes you well with your own particular endeavours in securing a resounding victory against the opposition. Oh, and here is a message for operative Matchett: put that carburettor away and get on with something useful!'

...

The year 1994 brought Michael Schumacher his first Formula One crown and it very nearly concluded with Benetton securing their maiden Constructors' World Championship too, but it wasn't to be. Williams finally held onto it by a margin of fifteen points. But we were close, at one point during the year we were thirty-six points clear of Williams. Not that it mattered much, since the actual racing took a very low priority throughout the course of the season.

That year turned out to be one of the most turbulent and tragic years in the history of the sport. At Imola, both Roland Ratzenberger and Ayrton Senna were killed in separate accidents, and several Ferrari and Lotus mechanics were injured by an out-of-control car and its detached, airborne rear wheel (Nigel Stepney was with Ferrari at this point and I remember seeing him hit by the erratic Minardi in the pit-lane); at Monaco – the very next race – another driver, Karl Wendlinger, was seriously injured too. His life hung in the balance for a long while, but he finally pulled through although his Formula One career was finished. At Hockenheim a few weeks later, the Benetton pit crew, myself amongst them, was engulfed by fire when Verstappen's B194 exploded during a refuelling accident. This tragic incident saw six of my colleagues rushed to hospital by the circuit helicopter.

At the same time as these appalling deaths and serious injuries were happening, Michael Schumacher and Benetton seemed to be permanently embroiled in argument and accusation with both the FIA and the circuit officials. At Silverstone, Michael was given a time-penalty for some slight misdemeanour; then he was black-flagged; then the flag was rescinded and we were allowed to continue; then the team was fined $25,000; then Michael was disqualified from the results and we were given an enormous fine of $500,000; and then Michael was banned for two more races. All of this at just one Grand Prix!

At Spa, five hours after winning the race, we were once again disqualified from the race results. At various times during the year the team was also suspected of having illegal driver-aid software on the car. And then, to top it all, notwithstanding the fact we had been seriously burned, we were also accused of causing the Hockenheim fire ourselves and deliberately cheating by illegally tampering with the refuelling-rig. Disqualifications, fines, arguments, counter-arguments, on and on it went. It was truly a most bizarre year, and while the events of 1994 were slowly unfurling I was in the process of writing *Just Another Day at the Office*. I'd no sooner finished commenting on the unprecedented happenings at one race, before the next Grand Prix was upon us, bringing with it a fresh bout of accidents, disagreements and finger pointing.

Of course, the fact that I'd chosen the 1994 season in which to write my book was complete coincidence; in January, when I sat down in front of the fire and began to write page one, I had no idea that fate was about to give me such a story. At the conclusion of 1993 Michael had won only two races in his Formula One career; at that point who would ever have guessed that by the end of the following year he would be crowned World Champion? It was incredible compared with the rest of the team's victories before Michael joined us: 1991, one win; 1992, one win; 1993, one win; 1994, eight wins and the Driver's Championship.

In the middle of May, shortly after the Monaco Grand Prix, I contacted Hazleton Publishing, the company who produce *Autocourse*, to see if they were interested in publishing my book at the end of the year, or whether after swiftly scanning the first few pages, they'd advise me that I was, most assuredly, writing it purely for my own amusement. I'd thought carefully about the timing of my enquiry. I wanted to leave it sufficiently late in the season to have written something substantial to show them and to convince them of my intent and commitment to finishing the book, but I also wanted to make contact at an early enough stage of writing, in case the publisher could suggest anything which might help me as I plodded along with it.

'Why don't you send us a sample of what you've written; we'd be delighted to take a look,' they said. A week or so later they rang me in Chipping Norton. They liked it. 'Would you mind sending us some more of what you've written?' I sent them another two chapters and by all accounts they liked those too. This pleased me greatly.

I found writing to be a lone, self-absorbing pastime. I often spent many hours entertaining the word-processor, sometimes until two or three in the morning. Eventually, over the course of an evening – and despite many gallant efforts to thwart it – my collection of random thoughts would slowly start to organize themselves into a series of purposeful ideas and finally grow and mature into a page of written text. When this happened the surprise of it would catch me unawares, requiring a stiff drink to settle things down again. I'd read the lines on the page, pause, then reread them, just to check they hadn't melted back into a garbled mess. Sometimes I was quite pleased with my efforts, but there was always a nagging doubt: I might have been happy with how it looked on the page and how it sounded when I read it aloud (actually just a quiet whisper), but would it make sense to anyone else? Was it generally coherent and in more simplistic terms, was it any good? So, to be told by Hazleton that they had liked what they had read was a great boost to morale. The next step was to get them interested enough to sign me up and publish the book.

As the season progressed and it became clear that we were genuinely in contention to win a major prize, I decided to change my book's title. I'd never really liked *Just Another Day at the Office*, it was a stupid name and I have no idea why I chose it in the first place. It became *The Mechanics of a Championship – the Work of a Grand Prix Mechanic*. I thought that looked much better; a nice little play on words, a touch of ambiguity, perfect.

By September *The Mechanics of a Championship* was 75 percent finished. It had consumed all my free time. In fact, other than when working late at the factory and travelling away to the races, I'd only been out of the house for two nights all year. Not that I minded; far from it, I was loving it. At last I'd discovered a hobby which didn't require me to stroll home from the Chequers afterwards – Josh thought I'd skipped the country. I was enjoying this new challenge like nothing else, and now that the book's structure was really taking shape I was longing to see my work in print. All of which made the call from the publishers telling me they couldn't find sufficient in-house budget to take my project any further all the more utterly crushing. The girl I had been dealing with for the last five months was most apologetic (and most sympathetic too), but the bottom line was that they had to say 'thanks but no thanks'.

To say that I was terribly disappointed by Hazleton's decision would be a masterstroke of understatement but I hold not the slightest grudge against them. I don't think they rejected me out of hand; they wanted to help, I'm convinced of that, but if they didn't have the available budget to produce my book, what could they do? Looking back now, perhaps I was naive not getting them to commit to signing a contract with me much sooner, but the gift of hindsight is always accompanied by perfect twenty-twenty vision. The problem was that I was walking blindfold in completely foreign territory (like being a first-day apprentice again); all I could do was to watch, listen and learn the ropes as I went along.

Of course, I could and would look for another publisher, but it was now September, I knew little of the book business but I did know I was leaving it terribly late in the year to get anything sorted out. Because the plot of the book was set within a single year it would need to be published in 1995 if the content was still to be current when it went on sale. It was now or never. I couldn't imagine anyone being prepared to publish the first book of a totally unknown author more than a year after its intended sell-by date. Well, that's not strictly true, there are always the 'vanity publishers', the you-pay-we-print operators, but they weren't for

Martin Brundle at the Montreal 1992 race that he so nearly won.

The author helping Brundle out of the car at Spa in what turned into another wet weekend in 1992.

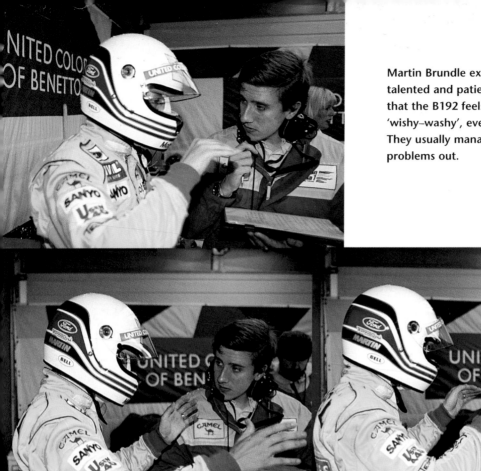

Martin Brundle explains to his bright, talented and patient engineer, Pat Fry, that the B192 feels 'a bit pointy' or 'wishy–washy', even 'a bit speedboaty'. They usually managed to sort the problems out.

Exactly one year after his Grand Prix debut, Michael Schumacher
took his maiden victory at Spa, 1992.

Martin Brundle was replaced by Riccardo Patrese at the
conclusion of the 1992 season. Both men have now retired
from Formula One.

Schumacher's expression says it all at Estoril, 1993, his second career win.

Nigel Stepney in the Ferrari pits talking to Gerhard
Berger at Estoril 1993. Nigel is the first English chief
mechanic to work for the legendary Italian team.

Jos Verstappen, a great bloke and a real star,
seen here during the 1994 Barcelona test.

J. J. Lehto's pre-season Silverstone shunt more or less finished his Formula One career (pictured here at Imola 1994).

One of the last photographs ever taken of Ayrton Senna, at Imola in 1994, seen here in his Williams ahead of Michael Schumacher's Benetton.

Steven Tee, standing alongside us, is the photographer responsible for many of the pictures in this book. He recorded the now legendary 1994 Hockenheim fuel-stop when Verstappen's B194 blew up.

The big screen, relaying live television coverage to the crowds in the stands at Silverstone 1995.

When Schumacher and Hill collided during the 1995 British Grand Prix, an incident which forced both of them out of the race, this surprising result became a possibility. However, it still required a lot of hard work by everyone in the team to secure the cup.

Michael Schumacher and Flavio couldn't believe what was
happening at Silverstone in 1995; indeed, none of us could.

Once again, with Schumacher and Hill out of the race at
Monza in 1995 the way was clear for the team's other
swift and reliable B195 to take the chequered flag.

Michael Schumacher's eighteenth Grand Prix victory at Aida in 1995
was the win that secured his second Drivers' World Championship.

The team celebrates its new success at Aida 1995 – the chap in the centre of these two photographs is Paul Seaby, the man inside the burning overalls of the jacket photograph.

It was all over bar the shouting. Michael Schumacher's victory in Aida secured his own Drivers' Championship and set the scene for us to clinch our Constructors' Championship in Suzuka in the very next race, where all that was required was for the two Williams' cars not to finish. They duly obliged. It was an important day for us – the big boss himself, Luciano Benetton, was also there – second from the left in the back row. He shook my hand, thanked me and even poured me a glass of champagne.

Gerhard Berger chats with Flavio at Aida 1995, soon after the announcement that Michael Schumacher was moving to Ferrari.

Ross Brawn tries to bring things back under control at Sao Paulo 1996.
Less than twelve months later he followed Michael Schumacher to Ferrari.

Two old Ferrari team-
mates, Gerhard Berger
and Joan Villadelprat,
try to figure out what
was going on at Sao
Paulo 1996.

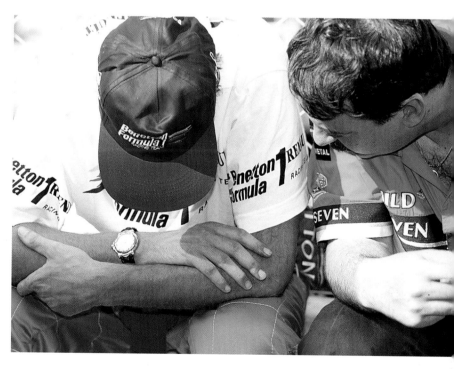

Sao Paulo 1996.

The last victory. Berger and I end our run of Grand Prix wins with this final one in Hockenheim, Germany, in 1997. He and I both experienced our first and last Formula One wins while working with Benetton.

Barcelona (test) 1998 – in the few months that I worked with Alex Wurz I saw the same qualities in him, the friendly relaxed attitude, the calm determination, that I had seen in Michael Schumacher some eight years before.

Throughout all of 1995 we worked to secure that number 1, and we then had to hand it straight to Ferrari. It is given as a reward to the World Champion driver, not the World Champion team.

Seen here at Buenos Aires in 1997, Michael is fully engrossed in his new challenge of helping to bring Ferrari back to the top again, while mine is merely to sit in the sun and write books in France. Formula One has been good to us both, although only one of us is a multi-millionaire.

My final task for Benetton was to install the lighting into their new garage equipment, seen here. I hope they're enjoying it. David Richards, standing along-side Giancarlo Fisichella, succeeded Flavio as chief executive in 1997 but lasted less than a year before he too was replaced. From being the 1995 World Champions Benetton finished in fifth position in 1998.

me, I wasn't writing for vanity. It's perfectly possible to star in your own Hollywood film if you're prepared to fund the project, but even with a hundred reels of film in the can it certainly doesn't mean that you can act. If an established and recognized publisher does not wish to take the financial risks involved with producing your work, then my advice is this: forget it and try something else.

…

Who should I contact now? I had no idea. Another approach then. Let's start from scratch: Who publishes books?

Ladybird? Puffin? Eye-spy? All household names I remember from childhood, but I doubted that they would be interested in books about Grand Prix racing. I picked a book at random from my shelf – *Hotel Pastis* by Peter Mayle – and looked to see who had produced it for him. Inside the back of the jacket revealed that Hamish Hamilton Ltd, 27 Wrights Lane, London, England was the publisher. I turned the book over in my hands, for the first time in my life studying its physical construction, its weight, its form. *Hotel Pastis* seemed a well-presented volume, clear print on good quality paper and an attractive jacket, rich colours within a lush sheen; all the signs (I guessed) of a serious publisher. Directory Enquiries furnished me with a number.

I dialled, but a voice claiming to work for Penguin answered my call, 'Oh, sorry,' I said, 'wrong number! I'm trying to get in touch with Hamish Hamilton, Directory Enquiries must have made a mistake'.

'I'll just put you through,' she said crisply.

Now that is impressive, I thought. I phone a wrong number and one publisher can transfer me directly to a rival company. I could never see McLaren redirecting calls to Ferrari, nice though the idea was. I wondered if all the publishing companies in London were in touch with each other by inter-connected switchboards.

'No,' another, though identical voice informed me, 'Hamish Hamilton is part of Penguin Books, that's all'.

'Oh.'

The conversation with Hamish Hamilton was brief and got me nowhere. Who did I wish to speak to, she asked. I didn't know, but I asked if I could talk to someone regarding an idea for a new book. Who was my agent? I didn't have an agent. It would be much easier for everyone if you approached the company through an agent. But I haven't got one, I said. Then you should get one, she advised. I knew nothing of Hamish Hamilton and only a fraction more about its parent company, the Penguin empire, but I got the distinct feeling that my conversation was utterly pointless, quite futile; the voice on the other end of the telephone was as polite as polite can be, yet I sensed, in no uncertain terms, great unspoken waves of PLEASE GO AWAY washing down the line at me. Presumably a similar response also awaited me from any of the other big publishing houses.

Clearly, my total lack of credibility in the profession was going to be a major stumbling block. I couldn't really blame Hamish Hamilton for its complete lack of interest, it must receive thousands of manuscripts every month from scores of earnest writers, masses of ardent unknowns scribbling precious first novels with stubs of bingo-hall pencil, filling reams of lined A4 jotter pads, all desperate to have their work published before the next Booker prize was short-listed. I could understand the publishers' dilemma, and Hamish Hamilton's suggestion that I should find myself an agent was sound advice – that way the onus would fall on the agents and not the publishers to thresh the few potentially fertile grains from the vast sheaves of chaff before any approach to a publisher was made, thus making life that little bit easier for the publisher.

It was a problem. I needed to be patient and think this through, there must be an answer, there is always an answer. I didn't have an agent – I still haven't. I suppose I could have tried to contact a literary agency, but I was very much up against the clock, and how long would it have taken to hear back from an agency: six weeks; six months? Sixty years? After reading Tom Sharp's *The Great Pursuit* I didn't hold out much hope of a reply before the coming of the second Ice Age. No, I decided firmly, there simply wasn't sufficient time to caper about trying to interest an agent in the merits of my work at this stage of the game, I would just have to take over that role myself.

I knew my book had worth. Hazleton Publishing had convinced me of that, even if they couldn't do any more for me. The facts were these: I was a current Grand Prix mechanic working with Benetton Formula and Michael Schumacher – the very team and driver currently leading the 1994 Formula One World Championships, one of the most controversial seasons in history, and I was actually working for the team at the centre of all the controversy – the team which had won the majority of races, been black-flagged, disqualified, stripped of points, burst into flames and accused of blatantly cheating. All of that and I'd written a race-by-race, on-the-spot, genuine 'inside' story of it. Who could resist that? (Well, Hazleton and Hamish Hamilton, obviously.)

It was time to go to Banbury. Moreover, it was time to go to Ottakar's in Banbury, the little town's leading bookshop, just a short stroll from their famous Cross. I thought I'd go to Ottakar's and look at their range of Grand Prix books, to see exactly who was currently keen on publishing such things. The book that immediately caught my eye had a large bright yellow cover: it was a tribute to Ayrton Senna published by a company called Weidenfeld & Nicolson. Like *Hotel Pastis*, I was immediately impressed with the quality of the book: the grade and weight of the paper, the layout and the clarity of the colour photography looked very professional. I scribbled the publisher's address on an old cinema ticket stub and headed back home. Well, home via the Chequers for a quick sandwich and a beer with Josh, to be more correct. I'd call Weidenfeld & Nicolson a little later, after they'd returned from lunch; they might be feeling more receptive after a pie and a pint.

...

'Orion Publishing.'

'Is that Weidenfeld & Nicolson?'

'Who is it exactly you wish to speak to?'

'Err, well, I'm not sure really. Look, the thing is, I don't know. I haven't a clue to be honest but I want to talk to someone about a new book. I work for Benetton, one of the Grand Prix teams and I've written a book about Formula One and I haven't got an agent and I haven't got time to go and find an agent and please don't hang up on me and could you please just put me through to someone who I could just talk to, please?'

There was a long pause while the receptionist held my life in her hands; it was as if she was toying with me, she could just cut my line dead and answer the next call. She could do that, or ...

'And will your book contain illustrations,' she asked. I could almost see one of her eyebrow raising in playful curiosity: a qualifying question, get this right and I advance to round two, get it wrong and it would be 'is the wrong answer but thank you for playing and good night!'

'Illustrations you say? Well, err, when you say illustrations do you mean like drawings or photographs?'

'Either, drawings or photographs, they're both illustrations. Will your book contain either of these?'

I hadn't envisaged any drawings or photographs but there was no reason why I shouldn't use photos to compliment the text, I just hadn't thought about the prospect before. Did she want to hear 'yes' or 'no'? If I said yes, would she say that Weidenfeld & Nicolson didn't publish illustrated books? If I said no, would she then say that they only publish illustrated books? I knew that their Senna tribute had contained photos, but was that book a unique case, a rare concession made for a very exceptional case? Perhaps, perhaps not. I plumped for yes.

'Yes?' I said, my answer sounding more like a question than a statement.

'Good, in which case I'll connect you with Michael Dover's office; he publishes all the illustrated books at Weidenfeld & Nicolson.'

God bless her!

Chapter eight

1995

*Life in the Fast Lane...Herbert arrives...An appreciation of
Jos Verstappen...Corradini arrives...Schumacher wins
the Brazilian Grand Prix...Benetton disqualified from the
Brazilian Grand Prix...The Barcelona pit-stop...
The Championship at last*

In Germany at the end of every September, the book business has a trade fair in the Frankfurt conference centre. More correctly, it has *the* book business trade fair. It is the busiest, most important time of the year for the industry, with more international business being organized during the five days of the fair than is achieved throughout the rest of the year. Wine is drunk and translation rights are negotiated; books are sold from publisher to publisher; book-club buyers are entertained; freelance writers and illustrators tout for more work; the latest computerized equipment is demonstrated. Parties, liaisons, affairs, break–ups, breakdowns, it's quite a ball by all accounts. I've never been there myself, but on the very day of my phone call to Weidenfeld & Nicolson, that's exactly where Michael Dover was heading.

'I'm intrigued by what you've told me, Steve, your book sounds an interesting idea, but the thing is, if we like it, want to get involved and want it in the shops by March we're going to have to move very quickly. Look, I'm flying out to Frankfurt tonight, in fact I've been trying to leave the office for the last hour, and must do so as soon as we finish this call! Can you fax me a copy of everything you've written so far directly to Frankfurt? I can't give you a fax number for the hotel, but I'm staying at the Hotel Hoff. If you can find the number and have the manuscript waiting for me when I check-in I'll read it tonight and we'll go from there.'

Five hours and three ink cartridges later, and the little Canon Bubblejet printer I'd borrowed had finally chugged and coughed its way through 150 sheets of A4. I managed to get a fax number for the Hoff from International Enquiries, but trying to transmit such a quantity of pages had caused my clonky old fax/phone machine to finally nip-up. Probably a good thing too in the long run: it would have taken me another five hours to fax it page by page – and God alone knows what the phone bill would have been. If I was ever going to do this for a living I'd have to update my technology. Well, I'd have to anyway, the phone was dead. The next morning I wrapped the manuscript in plastic bags and brown paper to protect it from the rain and posted it Swiftair to Frankfurt. It was the best I could do.

On his return from Germany it was an enthusiastic Michael Dover who telephoned me; he'd read it, liked it and a contract was in the post – and on 23 March 1995, Weidenfeld & Nicolson published *Life in the Fast Lane – the Story of the Benetton Grand Prix Year*. Apparently *The Mechanics of a Championship* was a good title, it just wasn't a great title, 'Steve,' Michael explained, 'you'll just have to trust me on this one.'

...

Johnny Herbert had been given the biggest break of his career towards the end of 1994 and had joined Benetton to replace Jos Verstappen as our number-two driver, playing a supporting role to Michael in the last two Grand Prix of the year. However, he failed to score any points for us in those final races – in fact, despite driving in every round of the World Championship he failed to score any points all year: thirteen races with Lotus, one with Ligier and two with Benetton yielded nothing better than seventh place. Not very impressive perhaps, but it must be remembered that Lotus was in its dying throes at the time, and Johnny had retired his car from five of his thirteen races with Lotus. (When I was checking these figures in the 1994 *Autocourse* I was surprised to see that Herbert had placed no higher than 35th in the drivers' listings! Surely that can't be right, I thought; then I realized that the drivers without any points had been placed in alphabetical order – with people like Belmondo, Beretta and Dalmas being placed ahead of him. If his name had been Johnny Zerbert he would have been number 47th on the list, one line below Alex Zanardi, his Lotus team-mate).

I thought it was the wrong decision to replace Jos, but I suppose the decision was taken because of Herbert's many years of experience in relation to Verstappen's. Jos had been thrown in at the deep end at the start of the year, drafted in from the test team to replace our original signing, J.J. Lehto, who had seriously injured his neck in a pre-season testing accident. Lehto had tried to make a comeback in the middle of the year, but it was no good; he was really struggling to drive the car competitively and after four disappointing races the drive was given back to Verstappen. In my opinion Jos did a remarkable job, regardless of the fact that it was his first season, and that he'd driven in six fewer races than Herbert and still managed to rack up two podium places and finished the season in tenth position in the Drivers' Championship. Jos's third place in Hungary made him the most successful Dutch driver in the history of the sport. Just looking at the bare facts of the situation I'd have to say that Verstappen's maiden year was actually very impressive. However, I can still appreciate the reasons why Benetton's management decided to bring Herbert in for those final two races; after all, winning the Constructors Championship was a distinct possibility for us in 1994 and someone with a thorough racing knowledge of the remaining two circuits could (should?) have made a difference to the outcome. Certainly this was Williams' assessment of the situation too: like Benetton they had also replaced their own rookie driver, David Coulthard (promoted from test driver because of the Senna tragedy) in favour of Nigel Mansell's vast experience. Right down to the wire the Constructors' Championship could have gone either way, and in Adelaide as soon as Nigel got a sniff of a potential victory he shot off to take the final win of the year. In just four races Mansell picked up thirteen valuable points for Williams. (Surely that win in Australia must also be his last?) The thing about Mansell is that even after he has publicly announced his retirement from the sport and when you are firmly of the belief that there is not the slightest chance of him getting another F1 drive, when you next look back at the circuit Mansell is back in a Grand Prix car again, going for gold, eyes bulging, foot hard down, moustache ends fluttering in the wind.

In fact, at the 1998 Monaco Grand Prix, I saw a girl sitting on the palace banking waving a Union Jack with 'Nigel Mansell' embroidered in thick black letters across its middle. Presumably she was patiently waiting to see him screech round the exit of Rascasse – on full throttle and full opposite-lock – and then cheer him down the pit-straight as he blasted over the finish-line to set another devastatingly quick pole before disappearing into the distance again. The thing is, I was so wrong-footed by seeing her waving that flag that I completely lost my confidence and had no choice but to walk back to the press-room, just to check there hadn't been a last minute driver change.

· · ·

In Australia in 1994 we lost the Constructors' Championship. As a team we tried our best but our best just wasn't good enough to take the trophy away from Williams. Lesson learnt? Try harder next time! However, it must be said that winning the Drivers' Championship with Michael was a marvellous result, and if you can't win the Constructors' Championship, then certainly the next best thing is helping your drivers to secure the Drivers' Championship. As a mechanic, there is only one drawback to winning the Drivers' Championship, and that only arises when the World Champion driver decides to leave the team, for when he does so he takes his crown with him, leaving the team with nothing. It's obviously disappointing when that happens but it's just the way of the sport and another reason why there are two separate Championships.

In 1992 I said that I could never understand Benetton's decision to replace Martin Brundle, and in 1995 I could never understand their decision not to reinstate Jos Verstappen as Michael's team-mate. It just didn't add up. What Benetton needed was continuity, this constant chopping and changing of one driver for another, presumably on the grounds that they always failed to prove as quick as or quicker than Schumacher, was doing no one any good. The management needed to accept the fact that no one was going to be quicker than Michael and concentrate on consolidating the effectiveness of the second car (exactly as Ferrari has done with its continuous commitment to keep Eddie Irvine as Michael's team-mate since both drivers joined the team in 1996). Piquet retires, then it's Brundle in, out; Patrese in, out; Verstappen in, out; now it was Herbert's turn and just like the others, he would be in, out and gone too. What possible feelings of team commitment does that give a driver?

In Jos Verstappen the team had a driver who was liked, a driver who knew the team well and one who was prepared to work damn hard in the car. With the signing of Herbert all that was lost to us again, we would have to start from scratch again. The team's decision on its 1995 driver line-up must have been a devastating blow to Jos's confidence after all he'd done for us.

Anyway, that was what happened, and what was done was done; there is never anything to be gained from whinging, and the obvious contrasts in our drivers' achievements would certainly make for an interesting challenge. Michael Schumacher would commence the season as the reigning Formula One World Champion while Herbert would start the year with a career total of just eighteen points; he had never finished a Grand Prix sufficiently high enough to stand on even the lowest step of a Formula One podium. Their respective records could hardly be further apart! Never say die. Off we went to Brazil, Michael jumped into our new car, I strapped Johnny into the other, and the chase for the 1995 World Championships began.

...

The first race of the season concluded in pretty much the same fashion as most of 1994 had: Benetton won the Grand Prix and was promptly disqualified. Of course, we were getting quite used to this sort of thing by now, and I actually took the news that we'd been kicked out to be a good omen for the season's eventual outcome. However, when the official announcement came that both we and

Williams had been thrown out – allegedly for using illegal fuel – our new gearbox mechanic, Claudio Corradini, sank to the ground in total disbelief. There seemed no consoling him, his face was ashen and he stared at the floor with the same blank look as the man who'd just bet all his worldly possessions on red, only to see the ball clatter and finally fall to rest in the wrong hole.

Claudio had only recently joined us, leaving his beloved Italy in the winter to take up his new position at Benetton. It had been a difficult move for him, one fraught with all sorts of uncertainties. Not only had he packed his bags and left his home and his country behind, but after fourteen years of continuous service he had resigned from Scuderia Ferrari too. Claudio wanted to see England, wanted to live in England and wanted to improve his (already good) English, but the pressure on him to remain in Italy and to stay with Ferrari had been pretty intense.

We all know that Ferrari holds a unique position in automotive engineering, with their Formula One team looked upon and treated as a revered legend. That devotion is felt most strongly in Italy itself, of course; I'm English and when I worked for Ferrari I thought it was terrific fun, a special time; but to be Italian and work for the Ferrari road-car factory is far more than just fun, it's an honour and a privilege. However, to be Italian and work for the Ferrari Grand Prix team is to be bestowed with a duty and an accolade like no other. Your country expects. In the words of Phil Barnard (one of my old Ferrari service managers): 'You have, most definitely, arrived!'

Claudio had been a most loyal and dedicated employee, serving his country's national team with great honour, and was constantly volunteering for another arduous tour of duty. Now it was time for change, time to leave the Ferrari stable and explore a little. Is there life outside the gates of Maranello? He had finally bolted from the Ferrari stable, driving over the mountains, through Mont Blanc, across France and into England. 'Welcome to Benetton Formula Ltd. Please have your FOCA pass ready for revalidation.' He had joined up and travelled to Brazil with us; he had proudly pulled on his new blue and white race shirt and had won the first Grand Prix of the year. What a sense of relief he must have felt! His decision to uproot, move to England and join Benetton had proven to be the right decision after all. Then, within minutes of the podium celebrations, his new team was immediately disqualified for an infringement of the rules.

Our disqualification was caused by a technicality. The fuel we had used during the race, supplied to both Benetton and Williams by Elf, had been a perfectly legal concoction, conforming in every way with the Formula One technical regulations. So why had both teams been disqualified? Because the sample of fuel given by Elf to the FIA – to confirm its legality at the commencement of the season – didn't match the fuel samples taken from the cars by the FIA after the Brazilian Grand Prix. All three samples were perfectly acceptable, but the chemical fingerprint of the library fuel didn't match with the post-race fuel.

Unlike our disqualification from Spa 1994 – where I still firmly believe we won the Grand Prix fair and square – I think the FIA's decision on the Brazilian fuel issue was perfectly correct. It was a simple case of black and white: our fuel did not match the library sample as the rules of the game stipulated it should have done, therefore the rules had been broken, and the teams not conforming to the rules should be thrown out. I was behind the FIA's decision all the way (unlike that decision on Spa, as I've said). But let's not dwell on that any more, it's over, finished, done. We have to move on.

However, there was one part of the Brazilian ruling I couldn't agree with, and that came a little later when the decision was taken to reinstate the drivers with their points, but for the teams to remain stripped of theirs. The thinking was that as the drivers had no control over the fuel that was used, they couldn't be held responsible for any irregularity; hence their points were returned. Sorry, but I don't agree. As far as I'm concerned the drivers are part of the team. If the constructors were to lose their points so should the drivers. Consider this: should a driver be allowed to keep his victory if his team was discovered to have won the race with a car equipped with a six-litre engine fuelled by nitrous-oxide injection? I think not. Yet there would be no extra cockpit controls to operate, so, theoretically the driver would be as oblivious to such modifications as he would be to merely having a perfectly legal but non-registered fuel in the car's tank. Should the engine manufacturer have been allowed to keep their race win in Brazil? How about the brake disc manufacture? I seriously doubt they could have had any control over what type of fuel was used. Should it only have been Elf who suffered, with everyone else being reinstated?

'No' is the only true and just answer. 'No' because the fuel supplier, the engine manufacturer, the brake disc manufacturer, the car constructor and the driver are all one and the same thing: a team and if one element of that team transgresses the rules then the whole of the team should be penalized for it.

The good news was that when Claudio realized that our disqualification was for such a petty technicality and that we hadn't actually done anything underhand, he cheered up again, and later that night, back in the hotel bar of the Morrumbi Novotel – despite none of us having slept for two days – he persuaded me to join him in a couple of Caipirinhas to celebrate his first race with his new team. 'Here's to winning the Championship!' he toasted as we chinked glasses. 'Cheers, Claudio! Welcome to the wonderful world of Benetton!' I quickly drank the hideously strong mixture of vodka, sugar, mashed limes and prawn juice and woke up in the wrong bedroom, still fully clothed, nursing a ferocious headache.

…

On the Friday afternoon of the Argentine Grand Prix I received a fax from the BBC. It arrived during lunch and rather took me by surprise; I don't often receive correspondence from the British Broadcasting Corporation. I was fairly confident of owning a TV licence, or (as Dirk Gently might muse) at least I had no overriding memory of not owning one, so perhaps my fax was just a friendly check, South America being just a tad out of reach to expect a personal visit from a detector van. My fax was from Broadcasting House – home of BBC Radio – an invitation to join them as a guest on Radio 4's *Midweek*, a prestigious chat show, which goes out live every Wednesday morning at 9:05 sharp. I was truly flattered. For me, Radio 4 is radio, there's nothing else, and whenever work schedules allow I listen to *Midweek*. I have to say it's not my favourite programme, since that place in my heart is forever taken by *Just a Minute*, hosted by Nicholas Parsons (oh, how I'd love to be invited on it, though, as the producer doesn't know me from Adam I think it's destined to remain one of life's unrequited desires, quite frankly).

I quickly phoned the *Midweek* researcher, Celia Quantrill, telling her I'd be delighted to come along.

'Good,' she said, 'just one slight problem, we'd like you to join us next Wednesday, the twelfth of April, the week straight after your Grand Prix. Will you still be able to make it?'

'Yes, well, I hope so anyway; let's see, the flight to England leaves Buenos Aires the day after the race, Monday afternoon, and gets into Heathrow sometime on Tuesday evening, the eleventh, about sixish I think. You'll have to excuse me if I'm feeling a little jet-lagged but barring any delays I should be okay.'

'Thanks Steve, that's great,' she enthused. 'We'll book you into a hotel for Tuesday night, St George's, Langham Place, right next door to the studios. Ingrid Muir, the programme's production assistant will fax you all the details in the next day or so. See you on Wednesday morning. Bye. Oh, and good luck in the race!'

I'd never been to Broadcasting House – somewhere I would willingly have paid to visit – and now I had been invited as a guest of the BBC, a hotel for the night, dinner, travel costs. What a treat!

While in Argentina Benetton stayed in the luxurious Buenos Aires Sheraton, a beautiful hotel with an enormous, marble-clad penthouse bar overlooking the city's many night lights, all very nice, as indeed was the city itself. Before I visited Argentina I had many preconceptions of what the life and the culture would be like – all of which proved to be fantastically wrong. Ever since the Falklands war of 1982 I had been under the impression that Argentina was a poor, tatty country, a land inhabited by an oppressed people who had little say in the actions of their government. I had expected the city of Buenos Aires to be similar to Sao Paulo: sweltering, humid weather, pollution, decaying skyscrapers, slums, shanty towns, poor roads and terrible conditions. But what I saw of Argentina was a stark contrast to all that. The people seemed substantially salaried, calm and chic: the men dressed in sharp designer suits, while the women – all of whom were a minimum of six feet tall and oozed Latin beauty – slinked through tree-lined avenues carrying

Gucci bags and model pouts. And far from stacks of crumbling concrete, the architecture was a subtle combination of Paris, Madrid and Barcelona: lavish neo-classical stonework, broad roads and smart street cafés.

Surely these weren't the downtrodden people my country had been to war with? Where had that preconceived image been born? From my own imagination or was it a more acceptable and greatly encouraged British portrayal of Argentina at the time? I understand that during the Anglo-Argentine conflict they had been under the rule of Galtieri and his junta, but a government – be it good or bad – can't change the entire infrastructure of a country to such a degree that a city looking like Paris can be transformed into Sao Paulo and then change back into Paris again just in the space of a few brief years, can it? Certainly not without a Blitz-style bombing campaign, followed by some remarkably nifty renovation work by several million eager stonemasons. Some things may change, for better or worse, but not everything. The rich architecture had obviously been standing for a hundred years or so! I'm making no political comment in these observations, I'm just curious as to why my pre-visit impressions of Argentina and her people were so terribly wrong.

Just outside the front doors of the Sheraton hotel is a carefully manicured park: lawns, flower beds, trees, all looking their pristine best. In front of the park is a grand memorial where two ceremonial guards and an eternal flame stand watch over the carved names of every Argentine sailor, soldier and pilot killed in the war with Britain. Soon after we had checked into our hotel I stood and admired the view from my bedroom window. In the growing gloom of early evening I could just make out the shape of the memorial, the yellow flame illuminating some of the facade around it, but from the eighth floor my vantage point was too high for me to make out what it had been built to commemorate.

The next morning, just before driving to the circuit, I walked over to the park to see exactly who or what the memorial had been dedicated to. Standing there, dressed in my Benetton team clothes, my legs turned to stone and I froze to the spot when I realized the memorial's significance. My skin prickled with goose-bumps, 'Oh God,' I whispered to myself, 'what am I doing? I shouldn't be here, I have no right to be here.' I'd taken no part in the conflict, yet just being English was enough to make me feel a responsibility for what had happened between our two countries. An over-reaction? Well, in a detached, clinical evaluation then perhaps it was; nevertheless, standing there, in the centre of Buenos Aires, surrounded by the inscribed names of their dead countrymen, I most certainly still felt the emotion.

However, as I looked around I could sense no hostility toward me: the two ceremonial guards continued to stare impassively ahead, looking straight through me as if I simply didn't exist, while in front of the memorial three women, dressed from head to foot in black, carefully laid bunches of flowers and wept silently. That day in April 1995, before I turned and walked away, I saw the women's tears fall, and, undoubtedly, the women continue to weep today for the loss of their children, their brothers, their husbands; they will continue to mourn their loss in exactly the same way as we continue to mourn our own. I climbed in the minibus and drove to the circuit, where we would unwrap our toys and play racing cars, in a nursery built for us by a people we had been at war with thirteen years before.

...

I was in the reception of Broadcasting House at 8:30, Wednesday morning, just as Celia had requested. Sitting next to me was another of the *Midweek* guests, Brian Glover, an actor who made his living from just being himself. I remember him most of all from when he played the demonstrative games master in *Kes*. The scene where he insisted that his class play football in the freezing cold and sludge, with the film's young star forced to wear those enormous baggy shorts, will always stand out in my mind as being Glover's finest hour. A few years later I remember him cropping up in *Porridge* and later he went on to make quite a decent living doing voice-overs for Homepride and Tetley tea adverts. The last thing I saw him in was one of the *Alien* follow-ups, without doubt an odd twist of setting compared to *Kes*, but he was still just playing himself, nothing had changed: same bald/shaved hairdo, same Yorkshire accent. And he was no different on that day in Broadcasting House either, just Brian Glover, a normal bloke, earning his living being Brian Glover, a normal bloke. I'm sad to say he's since died so I'm really pleased to have had the chance to meet him when I did.

Broadcasting House is a seemingly endless labyrinth of corridors and stairs. When Ingrid Muir, the charming *Midweek* production assistant, collected us from reception we walked up a steep flight of stairs, then down, then down again, then down again, with several left and right turns on the way. There were studios everywhere, and the surprising thing was how small they were. At the time the *Midweek* studio was B13, which if you're a Ned Sherrin fan you'll know as being the famous *Loose Ends* studio too. In the middle of the room was a large rectangular table, big enough to sit at least eight people, with a selection of microphones, cables and ancillary wiring disappearing into the small anteroom where the engineers and production staff corrected recording levels and prompted each other through headphones. 'The secret to consistently good sound quality,' we were told, 'is achieved through practising an exercise known as "lucky elbows". If you keep your elbows on the table it will subconsciously prevent you from moving your head around, taking it in and out of the mic's range. Also, we like to try and create an atmosphere of after-dinner conversation, so feel free to comment and butt in with questions for each other during the show.' Great, I thought, an atmosphere of after-dinner conversation eh? Perhaps the secret of consistently good conversation quality will be achieved through practising an exercise known as 'lucky cognac-laced coffee, with a nice bit of cheese and a sesame cracker'. Sadly it wasn't. I thoroughly enjoyed myself throughout the broadcasting of the programme; my only regret was that the show's usual presenter, Libby Purves, hadn't been there. I think she may have been on a publicity tour of her own recently published book. Instead, a chap called Pat Kane had been drafted in from Radio Scotland to cover for her. I had a vague recollection of the name and when I asked where I might know him from I was told he was a member of Hue & Cry, a band who achieved a certain notoriety several years ago. I had vague recollections of that name too. After the show, just as we were leaving B13 he turned to me, saying he thought I'd been fairly quiet and reserved after my own particular slot, 'I can't remember you asking too many questions of the other guests. Are you feeling tired or something, or are you one of life's observers, just happy to watch people from the edge of the floor without having any desire to dance yourself?'

'Yes, I'm a keen observer, I enjoy gauging peoples' reactions to their circumstance, whether they're being natural or if their poise is just a pretence,' I told him, 'but I must admit to being a little tired this morning'. I apologized.

'You're tired! What about me, I've had to come down from Scotland for this show, where have you had to come from?'

'Argentina.'

...

If you recount a story by writing it down on paper, who are you telling it to? When I write I do so by sitting in front of my screen and I watch it slowly fill up with different reminiscences, stories and general complaints, but who is it that I have written them for? Well, for you, of course, the reader. I write my pages which, all being well, provide you with a brief distraction from the rest of the world and in return, my pleasure is knowing that I've managed to entertain a few people I've never met. However, shortly after the publication of *Life in the Fast Lane*, a couple of letters arrived for me at the Benetton factory from people telling me they'd read and enjoyed the book, and they just wanted to say so. I was flattered: these are the people I wrote it for. Then more letters arrived, one from a family who said they kept my book in the loo and read it in instalments; another from a chap who wanted to know what the front-wing settings were on David Coulthard's Williams during the British Grand Prix; several asking for advice in how to become Grand Prix mechanics; another arrived from a girl who claimed to know the exact location of the rat-infested restaurant I'd described and wondered if she should inform the Japanese health inspectors.

Throughout the summer letters arrived almost daily, eventually trailing off around November only to start again in January when Weidenfeld & Nicolson published the paperback edition in time for Christmas. Could I recommend a hotel in Estoril? Would I pass the enclosed (heavily scented) letter on to Michael?

(Schumacher, not Dover) The best letter of all came from someone who had read my book, said he hadn't really enjoyed it and wondered if the publishers would give him a credit note for something else – I duly passed the letter on to Michael (Dover, not Schumacher). It's fascinating to know what kind of people read your work. On the whole, 1995 was a remarkably good year for me. And to top off my good fortune, the management awarded me a small pay rise too; in 1995 my salary was increased by £725.00 per year, which was nice.

However, despite having a moderately successful book on my hands, a little extra salary in the bank and a reasonable shot at winning the World Championship, the year's recipe certainly wasn't missing that unique blend of highs and lows which Fate carefully adds to her ingredients in order to keep our feet planted firmly on the ground (or firmly off the ground in the case of the Spanish Grand Prix).

…

In Barcelona, during one of our routine pit-stops, an accident happened which can only be described as being nothing short of bizarre. Johnny Herbert pitted, fresh tyres and fuel were supplied, but then he proceeded to drive off with both me and the rear jack still attached to the back of the car. I was taken completely by surprise by what happened and it took me several minutes to recover from the shock of it. The initial stages of the pit-stop had gone smoothly enough, but as Kenny and I tried to remove the quick-release jacks, mine – the rear one – jammed shut and wouldn't release from the car's jacking hooks. I looked underneath to see what had happened to the mechanism and attempted to force the thing to break free but before I could do anything, Mick Cowlishaw, the chief mechanic, had lifted his car-control board clear of the driver, giving Herbert the all-clear to drive off. The driver's vision is fairly limited through his mirrors and Herbert was obviously unaware of the problem at the back of the car. I didn't see Mick lifting the board as I was concentrating on unhooking the jack, and despite wearing safety glasses my vision was quickly blurring from the blast of the exhaust gases. The next thing I remember was a terrifically violent lunge from the jack handles as Herbert released the full might of the 800 horsepower engine. Within the space of just one second the car was doing over 40 miles an hour. Fortunately I managed to get free, but the jack travelled the entire length of the pit-lane before finally disengaging itself from the car. I felt both my arms stretch, snap and pop back again; nothing broken, thank God, but the two sharp spears of pain hurt like nothing I'd ever felt before; it was a relief when they finally went numb.

> *Beware the Jabberwock, my son!*
> *The jaws that bite, the claws that catch!'*

…

Harry, Schumacher's physio, rushed to see what had happened and carefully massaged some sense of feeling back into my fingers. It wasn't until I'd returned home and watched a video of the pit-stop that I finally realized what had happened to cause the driver to bolt off while I was still working on the car. My arms were sore for several days afterwards, but what hurt me far more was that the only person who apologized to me for what happened was Ross Brawn, our technical director, a man who played no direct role in the pit-stop. He was sitting on the pit-wall watching the timing monitors. That Ross took the trouble to quietly discuss with me what had happened and himself apologize for the accident greatly increased my estimation of him (and as a technical director I already rated him very highly). It was the action of a true team leader and I was very impressed; it was just a bit sad that someone else could never bring himself to say a simple sorry. Anyway, that's all in the past now, done and dusted. The upside of the day was that Benetton went on to score a one-two finish in the Spanish Grand Prix, the first such result for us since Nelson and Roberto did the same in Japan, nearly five years previously. Five years! How time flashes by.

Within minutes of the race finishing Murray Walker, sporting a huge grin, had left his commentary box and joined me in the Benetton garage.

'Steve, I'm amazed! I've never seen such an intriguing and wonderfully executed publicity stunt to launch a new book in my entire life! You authors will do anything to increase sales!'

'Murray,' I countered, 'if there was ever one pit-stop I wish you and the cameras had missed, believe me when I tell you it would definitely be that one.'

'I bet the story of that pit-stop makes it into your next book.'

'Well, you never know, Murray, it just might – if I live long enough to write another!'

In the following week's edition of *Autosport*, Jim Bamber, the motor-sport cartoonist who supplies a weekly lampoon of recent events, used that Barcelona pit-stop as the subject of his latest sketch. The cartoon showed Herbert driving along, with me grimly holding the jack handle, feet trailing in the wind behind, the caption read: 'Give the lads a wave next time round, Steve!' The week after it appeared in *Autosport*, Jim signed and posted me the original artwork for his cartoon. 'I hope you find a quiet spot in your house to hang it,' he said. 'From what I gather, most of my work usually finds its way onto the back of a bog door.' I was flattered that Jim should send me his work; it really cheered me up and I immediately had it framed. I tried to return the compliment by sending him a copy of *Life in the Fast Lane*. His drawing will always serve as a pleasant souvenir of what was otherwise a painful and somewhat bewildering incident.

Actually, that episode in Spain had genuinely scared me; it was another reminder of just how vulnerable the mechanics are during the pit-stops. Imola 1994 had been bad, watching the Minardi and its errant wheel ploughing through the

Ferrari and Lotus mechanics; then came the Hockenheim fire, in the very same year, where I had to roll on the ground and try to extinguish my burning overalls; and now 1995 and I'm nearly dragged onto the circuit like that poor stunt-man killed during the filming of Ben Hur. I'd never liked the pit-stops, but since the reintroduction of refuelling I had come to loathe them with a passion.

It was time for me to think about stopping, I'd had enough. I just hoped that damn Championship would come soon. I was living a charmed life in the pit-lane, I'd escaped serious injury three times now, and didn't want to push my luck much further. I had a real fight to regain my confidence during the pit-stops after that last accident. I decided that the best policy was simply to blot it out and not allow it to play on my mind; instead I trained myself to relish the pit-stops, I'd long for the radio call from Ross, telling us that Michael or Johnny were due in on the next lap. Time to get stuck in!

One circuit after another; race after race; stop after stop: let the car come in; lift the jacks; watch the fuel hose and the tyres go on; watch the hose come off; a quick glance at Kenny on the front jack to check he's okay; drop the car - and pray there's no fuel leak and that the jack releases; watch for the car-control board to move away. Monaco: thirteen points; Canada: two more; France: ten more.

Silverstone saw another ten points added to the pot, these scored by car number two, Paul Howard's car, driven by Johnny Herbert, the result was Paul and Johnny's first trip to the top step of the podium. Hill and Schumacher had collided while fighting for the lead, each blamed the other for the accident but the net result of their altercation was that both Benetton and Williams had lost their primary cars. The race lead was passed to David Coulthard in the second Williams, but he fell victim to a stop/go penalty in the very closing stages of the race. It was a fraught last few laps for everyone at Benetton, with Herbert's engineer talking his driver through every corner. When Herbert and Coulthard began fighting for position his engineer was constantly shouting down the radio: 'Yield to Coulthard, Johnny! Yield to Coulthard! You do not need to fight for position! Coulthard has to serve a stop/go penalty!' but Herbert was so excited by his good fortune he wasn't concentrating on listening and continued to duck and dive with the Williams, I could hardly bare to watch the monitors for fear of seeing Herbert gracefully sliding into the gravel. In the end I think Ross took control of the radio and finally the message sank in, the Benetton pulling wide to let Coulthard sprint through.

It was a tremendous win for us under the circumstances, made even more rewarding by the fact it was achieved in Paul's car – at last, all those years of dedication and thousands of hours of meticulous car preparation work had paid off – he was lifted shoulder high and carried around the garage to rapturous applause, Joan and Ross showering him with champagne.

We were on a roll now, with each successful pit-stop the points kept growing, and every chequered flag brought the season closer to its end. Hockenheim saw another Schumacher win; Spa, another – this time Michael won the race from a disastrous sixteenth place on the grid. I was holding the Benetton on the rear jack during a Spa pit-stop when Irvine's Jordan burst into flame just a few garages away from our own. From my vantage point at the back of the car I could see what the rest of the Benetton crew couldn't. 'The Jordan's gone up!' I shouted, I don't know why, no one at Benetton could have helped, just an instinctive reaction, I suppose. My eyes took the image of the fire in: the white flash of the initial explosion, the plume of black smoke lingering in the steady drizzle long after the flames had been extinguished; I remember thinking how terrified their mechanics must have been. I wondered if there had been any injuries, but I refused to be unnerved by what had happened. My warning cry must have been a bellow, for even over the wail of our Renault engine, Joan heard me call out from where he sat on the pit-wall.

The Italian Grand Prix, Monza: another victory, another ten points. The B195 was running superbly and was now a beautifully reliable car (it didn't have a completely unblemished record but it wasn't far off). Monza saw another racing collision between Damon Hill and Michael but, nevertheless, even with our reigning World Champion out of contention for the race win, the performance of the Benetton/Renault partnership was now in a class of its own; all Herbert had to do was stay on the track, stay out of trouble and tour home to collect the points. Just as in Britain, the Italian race result was a superb team effort, with our second driver doing a commendable job of picking up the pieces. More races and more pit-stops followed. In with the jacks, pray, tyres, fuel, out. Again. Again. Again. It must be now, surely it must come this year!

It did. In the two races of the Japanese double-header, with only the Adelaide Grand Prix to follow, our place in the record books was sealed. In Aida, Michael won his second Drivers' Championship, while in Suzuka, with a grand total of eleven race victories and a now unsurpassable score, we finally took possession of international motor-sport's most coveted and prestigious trophy. Benetton Formula was crowned and became the 1995 FIA Formula One Constructors' World Champions. The scores looked like this:

Benetton:	137
Williams:	112
Ferrari:	73
McLaren:	30
Ligier:	24
Jordan:	21
Sauber:	18
Footwork:	5
Tyrrell:	5
Minardi:	1

...

One, two! One, two! And through and through
The vorpal blade went snicker-snack!
He left it dead, and with its head
He went galumphing back.

'And hast thou slain the Jabberwock?
Come to my arms my beamish boy!
O frabjous day! Callooh! Callay!'
He chortled in his joy.

Chapter nine

1996

*Going bananas…I write my first article…The Melbourne
Grand Prix…Excessive hours in Estoril…'Turn out
the lights, the party's over…Time to go home…A flash of
inspiration…A meeting with Tony Dodgins…A clear decision*

The bar was only marginally better lit than the restaurant, which save for the meagre glow of flickering candles and a collection of near meaningless lamps, was itself in almost total darkness. Standing in the doorway of the entrance it was impossible to make out where the back of the restaurant was; small, huddled groups of people seemed to extend one after another until they eventually disappeared into total blackness, I guessed on about twenty tables, a mixture of round and square, most large enough to seat about six people – but there could easily have been double that number – all were full; the low, constant noise of table conversation was just audible above the sound of Mozart's *Requiem Mass*, a somewhat unexpected choice for restaurant background music.

While Bat and Kenny confirmed our booking with the pretty girl sitting behind the reception desk, I looked around and took in the rich fragrance drifting from the kitchen. It was a good smell, and a glance through the menu helped to identify some of the aromas: honeydew melons and fresh coconuts; roast duck; grilled fish and giant prawns; thick-cut steaks; spiced lamb cooked with garlic, coriander, cumin and garam masala. I wasn't feeling particularly hungry ten minutes ago, now I was ravenous. The menu also included the chance to meet the 'bugs' of Moreton

Bay. These are a local speciality, a crustacean unique to north-eastern Australia and a creature which must rate as one of God's most revolting-looking creations. Little bigger than a child's hand, the thing resembles the body of a deformed crab grafted onto a lobster's tail. Purely from an aesthetic point of view, it's a terribly unfortunate mixture, a real slip of evolution, but thankfully looks aren't everything, for when cooked the flesh of the Moreton Bay bug becomes soft, succulent and gorgeous. Of course, looking at life through a bug's two black and beady eyes, it's a crying shame it has to be hunted, caught, plunged into boiling water, ripped to pieces and eaten, before the world can truly appreciate its real beauty.

We ambled along the front tables and settled ourselves at the bar, the table was booked for nine o'clock, leaving us plenty of time for a cold beer or two before dinner. There was an ambience which immediately appealed, it felt relaxed and inviting, there was a make-yourself-comfortable-you're-in-good-company-here sort of feeling. The beers arrived dripping with condensation, the bottles pulled straight from a huge ice-bucket behind the bar, 'Here you go,' offered the barman, 'see how you get on with these!'

The end of another season, and for Benetton it had been the best year in the team's history – eleven race victories and both Championships – it doesn't get much better than that. To celebrate the occasion a few of us had decided to holiday, and a couple of days after the race we flew out of Adelaide, back once more to Port Douglas, Queensland. Because of the immense amount of nothing which makes up most of Australia, the majority of its people live on the coast. There's little point in going far inland – it's just sand and snakes and one very big rock. The huge distances which separate their coastal communities mean that Australians use planes as most of the world use buses, and Quantas has a series of daily shuttles flying between all the major cities; if you miss one you just wait and catch the next, no hassle. We jumped on the air-bus in the morning and hopped round the coast: Adelaide to Melbourne (morning coffee), Melbourne to Sydney (time for lunch), and Sydney to Cairns (afternoon tea); thousands of miles of polite, efficient service and all with far less trouble than trying to drive the seventy miles from Oxford to London.

I love Port Douglas, I love everything about Port Douglas: the remoteness, the sun, the brilliantly clear nights where the stars are so big you can reach out and touch them; the Great Barrier Reef with its miles of vivid coral, crystal waters and paintbox fish; Four Mile Beach with its acres of white, burning sand and a trillion burrowing crabs; the rain forest; the overwhelming sense of calm. Everything about this tiny corner of the world is perfect (well, except for the monsoons and the mosquitoes; killer spiders, snakes, jellyfish and sharks, of course).

While in Port Douglas we stayed in the tranquil, opulent Sheraton Mirage, which must be one of the most sumptuous hotels in the world. Slightly away from the main building we had rented one of their beautiful private villas, a self-

148

contained piece of paradise: exquisitely manicured lawns, pool, 18-hole golf course and staff who were both charming and discreet. It cost a fortune too, but it's not every day one wins the Formula One World Championship and I revelled in every minute of our time there. I knew I would never experience such unashamed luxury ever again.

...

It's a great art but I've never fully mastered the knack of switching off and doing nothing. I can sit for fifteen minutes, half an hour even, but longer than that and I become restless. I needed something to keep me occupied. Over the next few days while my friends were perfectly content to gently roast and recharge their batteries in the sun, I sat in the air-conditioned bliss of our villa and read, drank cold wine, listened to music, ate too many Pringles and generally pondered life. All of which was perfectly fine but I still felt that I should do something. I reflected on the season we had just finished, Michael's last with Benetton, and his parting gift was to leave us as the new reigning Formula One World Champions. Who could ask for a better momento than that?

So after four and a half seasons, our star driver had finally made another move. It had to happen some time, but it was a sad moment indeed when we shook hands for the last time as team-mates. I wished him every success with his new job and he the same with my writing. Then he was gone. I had been fortunate enough to see Michael develop and mature from a Grand Prix novice to become an outstanding champion during his career with us. What is it that makes one man shine out from all the rest and in such a dramatic style. What is it that produces a Fangio, a Prost, a Senna or a Schumacher?

I realized that something to do was staring straight at me, so I collected a few sheets of writing paper from the hotel's reception and began to jot down a few thoughts and observations...

With a total of 307 points, nineteen Grand Prix victories and two Drivers' World Championships, Michael's association with Benetton came to an end at 14:39, on 12 November 1995 when he flicked the ignition-kill switch and retired his car from the Australian Grand Prix. The premature finish was due to a collision with Alesi's Ferrari – a fairly minor shunt but still big enought to damage the Benetton's suspension. For some reason, the top-rear wishbones on the 1995 car seemed particularly susceptible to damage from extraordinary loads and as they were also enclosed within carbon aerodynamically shaped shrouds, it wasn't always apparent what the problem was until the shroud was removed. Such was the case with Schumacher's car in Adelaide. It was a great shame and a disappointing end to his relationship with us, but accidents happen. The very next morning Schumacher's marriage to Benetton was declared officially over and after exchanging his blue overalls for a pair of bright scarlet, he was free to enjoy his honeymoon and look to the future with his new racing partner, the highly distinguished motor-racing magnate, Scuderia Ferrari.

His future at Ferrari is secure for as long as he wishes to stay but it was at Benetton that he honed his great skills to such perfection. His great skills. Aside from the obvious talent one sees on TV when he is behind the wheel and his excellent health and fitness, what exactly are his great skills? What does the camera miss? Well, prior to any Grand Prix, when the team was busy testing and developing cars, Michael always wanted to be there whenever possible. During his time with us his commitment to constantly try to improve the car was so intense and his feedback so useful to any development work that the engineers were just as keen to have him there too. In fact his input was so beneficial that it finally became pointless for the team to offer a third driver a permanent testing contract.

Schumacher has the ability to memorize the handling of his chassis through the entry, the apex and the exit of each corner of every lap. He can recall each detail of the car's behaviour, however minute or insignificant it might have appeared at the time. He complemented this ability with a sound mechanical understanding of the car, and was aware of exactly what needed attention in order to cure any problems. In discussion with his engineers, when his comments on the handling of the chassis and any changes that have been made to the car were cross-referenced with the telemetry data, it was possible for the team to make very quick and accurate progress.

Schumacher possesses a deep, multi-layerd character and his abilities in a car are a result of an exotic compound of many different skills. The fact that his character is so complex makes it nigh on impossible to pinpoint one particular aspect and say 'that's it, that's it right there. That is what makes him so bloody good. Copy that trait and you can beat him'. Unfortunately, and all his Benetton partners will agree, his talent just isn't that straightforward or easily defined. Certainly a lot of his strength is drawn from his natural confidence (some say arrogance, but they would be wrong) and his remarkable attention to detail. Attention to detail in all things. For example, many drivers are capable of delivering impressive lap times – Frentzen or Irvine for instance; some are gifted with exceptional speed – Alesi or Coultard; some have good race craft (the ability to look after their cars, take care of their tyres and pace their race – Martin Brundle is a master of this. Occasionaly a few drivers possess more than one of these essential attributes – Coultard, Hakkinen, Berger, Hill. A very, very few drivers display all of these attributes and many more. Providing they are fortunate enought to be in the right team at the right time (and enjoying a long passionate affair with Lady Luck) it is these chosen few who are destined to be crowned Formula One World Champion and enter the annals of history as a motor racing legend – Fangio, Lauda, Piquet, Prost, Senna and now Schumacher.

Michael's crusade isn't stimulated in the same way that Senna's was. Ayrton felt he was driven to win, that he must win, and that nothing else would suffice. He was, of course, absolutely thrilled when he did finish first, but as he waved to the crowd, one could sense in Ayrton's eyes that he thought the only possible true, honourable result had just occurred. Michael's motivation is slightly different, he has a deep, concentrated passion to win every motor race he enters, it's as simple as that. He recognizes that to consistently win is a very demanding challenge, but he loves to win; he lives to win and as a consequence he willingly gives 110 percent to ensure that he does so.

However, just like Ayrton, when the race is over and the work is done he is, quite visibly, delighted with the achievement of it all.

Michael has a unique driving style too; he likes the car to be built with a very stiff suspension, a set-up which reduces chassis roll to the absolute minimum. This is fine providing the driver is capable of handling the car in such a knife-edge condition; the problem is that reducing the roll produces a car which is constanly trying to break free and slide across the tarmac as the tyres lose adhesion with the track. Forever playing with the steering wheel to catch and correct the oversteer, and constantly feathering the throttle to persuade the near on eight hundred horsepower to relent for a split second and allow the tyres to grip the track again is physically very demanding and requires great strength of mind. Nevertheless, that is how Michael chose to drive and in his hands at least, the results of such a set-up speak for themselves.

Successful for Michael, perhaps but it is certainly not the case that all drivers like this ultra stiff, almost cart-like reaction of their car's suspension. Thoughout the 1995 season, Johnny Herbert frequently complained about the handling and general performance of the Benetton (and to be fair, so did several of his predecessors too). It is sad to say, that in 1995 there were even dark mutterings that the equipment Michael's partner was given just wasn't the same as the other man's and that the team's technical back-up was biased towards Michael. But such things I simply cannot believe. When you stop to consider what a race team is actually doing, then such an argument seems to defy logic or reason. As a Grand Prix team, Benetton Formula existed to win as many races and score as many Championship points as possible (as do all race teams, of course). It follows that it would prove quite illogical for the team to give inferior equipment to one driver or another. By doing so it would offer an instant and most welcome advantage to the opposition.

Throughout my career with Benetton I worked with Schumacher and with each of his subsequent team mates; I have also worked with every one of the Benetton mechanics and with all the team's engineers and it has been my experience that the quality of commitment and standard of workmanship that was available to one Benetton driver was available to the other. I'm sure that the problems that Johnny experienced in competing alongside Schumacher were caused by two things: first, driving a car which was designed around the preferences of the team's reigning World Champion, and second, the different levels of expertise and skill between the two drivers.

Johnny's comments and general disenchantment with Benetton make me feel both uncomfortable and a little confused, and more than a little sad too. True, he may not have had the perfect season, he certainly didn't win all seventeen races, nor did he win the Drivers' Championship, and perhaps there are a hundred reasons why he didn't achieve either of these feats, but it was certainly not through any lack of effort by Benetton Formula. Out of all the Grands Prix throughout 1995, we only had one reliability fault with Johnny's B195. Compare that record of dependability with Williams, Ferrari, or McLaren and the figures speak for themselves. Benetton gave Johnny the most outstanding and successful season of his entire Formula One career; two Grand Prix wins (of which his maiden victory was his home race), 45 points – a rather impressive 250 percent increase over his whole career total, fourth place in the Drivers' Championship and his team mate won both World Championships. Realistically, how much better could it have been. To me, Johnny's 1995 achievements describe a year of which to be very, very proud, and I am convinced that they illustrate a Grand Prix season which he will find quite impossible to surpass throughout the remainder of his time in the sport.

Michael and Johnny are two contrasting personalities, their mental approach to work is different, their achievements in a Grand Prix car are leagues apart. Michael has won two World Championships in less time than it has taken Johnny to win but two races. Perhaps it's more comfortable not to dwell on such comparisons but when put under the spotlight, those are the bare bones of the matter. Johnny, just like Jos, Riccardo and Martin before him, all had a fair crack at trying to outpace Michael and fight for recognition as the team's number one driver. Without a doubt, Benetton would have been delighted if someone had proved to be consistently quicker than Schumacher. If that had been the case we could have had a team stronger than the Senna/Prost partnership at McLaren in the late 1980s. However, the bottom line is that not just Johnny, but all of Michael's partners have failed to put him under any real pressure. Perhaps these facts of life are a bit depressing for some of the more sensitive souls who stand on the wrong side of the Great Divide, but that is the nature of the beast, I'm afraid; it is a fiercely competitive game.

Another facet of Michael's genius lies in his ability to understand the potential effects of differing set-up changes without having to waste valuable track-time in needing to physically try the car with the new configuration. Comparing Schumacher with Herbert again to illustrate this: when things were going well for Johnny he was both cheerful and buoyant, and a quick lap in the practice session would bring a plethora of positive and constructive feedback. However, in the reverse situation, a slow lap could lead to a rather glum and despondent change in mood, and Johnny would grow frustrated with the situation and become quiet, even a little withdrawn. Schumacher, on the other hand, always remains calm, confident and sure of progress, irrespective of whether the previous few laps were slower than he or we expected. (Now, I know I just said always remains calm and I am aware that he completely lost his composure following that shunt with Coultard during the 1998 Spa race, but we are talking about his application and his approach to methodical set-up work here.)

At Benetton, the conversations between Michael and Pat Symonds, his race engineer, were always, always constructive. As the race weekend progressed, Ross Brawn would try and assist both of his drivers, constantly talking with the two men and their engineers, bringing the separate sets of results together, and advising both drivers of the benefits or deficits of the various changes that each car had just tried. However, from what I could see it was always Michael who was more able to focus and make the most use of this continually updated library of information. Remember that during a Grand Prix weekend, track time is the most valuable thing there is, and regardless of how many multi-million dollars their budgets can boast, it is possibly the only commodity that is impossible to buy more of. When the chequered flag falls to end the practice and qualifying sessions, that's it, game over; where you are is where you are...

…

I borrowed Bat's computer and by making use of these thoughts and notes, which by now had been scribbled over a dozen sheets of paper, I started to write my first article. I wrote my views on Michael's career at Benetton and how he is capable of doing what he does. It was my first attempt at writing an article and when the *Sunday Times* printed an abridged edition of it in December 1995, it became my first published article. I was delighted. *Autosport* also printed a version of it the following January and I was really thrilled when they used the story as their front page headline.

…

'You like chilli?'
The big chap who had joined our barman standing on the opposite side of the thick wooden bar to us had lifted his gaze to look at me, leaning forward and fixing me with his two dark eyes before quietly speaking. It was the first time we had met, his brief question our first communication. There had been no introduction, no handshake, no good evening, how are you tonight? Nothing like that at all, just the three words: 'You like chilli.' He spoke English to me, yet I strongly suspected that English wasn't his mother tongue, even if he'd used nothing else for the last twenty years. His voice carried a heavy but unrecognizable accent, German perhaps? No, much further east, Russian? Impossible to tell. His hair was long,

tinged with grey and straggled both in front and behind his broad shoulders; he obviously liked to keep its style liberated and free of artificial influences. He was very much an individual – no one could ever be in the slightest doubt of that – in fact the dark orange and blue sarong he sported was his only concession to fashion (though to exactly which fashion it was that he was granting this concession remained unclear). When he spoke his three words to me, the solid, heavily lined face, half hidden beneath the dark hair, bore no expression; there was no half-raised eyebrow, no smile, there were just the three words, the dark, watchful eyes and nothing else.

My friends were busy chatting among themselves and I was only half listening, lost in my own thoughts (wondering if I should contact a paper in England to see what they thought of my Schumacher article) and the two seconds it took me to realize that the big man was talking to me and that he was waiting for an answer to his odd question were obviously too long. Before I'd had time to reply he'd gone again. Carrying two strawberries, which he'd just carefully hollowed and filled with liqueur from behind the bar, he walked back into the gloom of the restaurant, the ankle-length hem of his sarong flapping as he went. He stopped at the nearest table to talk to the two couples sitting at it and to pop a now strongly fortified strawberry into each girl's mouth. Then he returned to the bar and reclaimed the flashlight he'd been carrying when he first appeared, he stopped in his tracks for a moment and looked at me (this time saying nothing) then he was gone again, walking deep into the back of the restaurant, shining his torch onto the customers' plates as he went. Occasionally in life you meet someone who completely enthralls you; this big man, with his few words, bright sarong and careworn looks was just such chap; he seemed capable of being quite a lot of fun.

Bat and Kenny were laughing when I turned to them, they had been here before and knew who he was; in fact they were keen that I should meet him.

'That's Alex,' Kenny explained, 'the owner!'

'You'll like him, Steve, I guarantee it, he's right up your street!' added Bat.

A few minutes later Alex reappeared, this time carrying a sizeable stick in one hand and his torch in the other. Slowly he prowled among his guests, banging on their tables as he walked past, causing some to spring round in surprise, the torch was used to light up dinner plates, a check that his clientele had dined well and that what had been served had been eaten without complaint. From what I could make out they all appeared more than satisfied.

After our own dinner we too were equally satisfied, the food was quite superb. While we ate our way through two wonderful courses – Kenny had Moreton Bay bugs to start with, followed by a main course of Moreton Bay bugs – we watched Alex look after his guests as only Alex could. He had abandoned his torch and stick in favour of touring the tables with a three-foot jelly snake and a serious-looking pair of tailor's scissors, he constantly clipped at the air as he walked. The snake would be placed in a willing mouth and a length snipped off. Half an hour later he was back with a bag of chocolate drops, 'Give me your tongue,' came the short, nasal request and as a tongue appeared he would carefully place a little treat on it.

By one o'clock many of Alex's guests, full to bursting point with fine food, fine drink, jelly snakes and choc-drops, had gone home to sleep it off, but we were in no rush to go anywhere. We sat around our table content just to talk, occasionally ordering more wine. The big man walked over to us carrying a tray of small glasses, 'Earlier on I asked you if you liked chilli, why didn't you talk?' I apologized and told him I loved chilli. He placed a shot-glass full of some misty spirit in front of each of us, the contents so cold they caused the outside of the glass to ice over. 'If you like chilli then perhaps you should try this, but be careful,' he warned us, 'it's very hot!'

'What is it?' I asked.

'Chilli vodka from the freezer' he said.

Now, it is well understood that the fiery taste of a red hot chilli pepper is something that takes a little getting used to but many of the world's peoples use the unique pungency of this little seed pod to spice up their everyday cuisine as a matter of course. However, when chilli is added to alcohol something quite extraordinary (bordering on the surreal) seems to happen, and the resulting cocktail is nothing short of blisteringly hot, far in excess of any vindaloo or phall curry I've ever come across. The effects of that little glass of spirit was similar to an internal incendiary grenade explosion, my throat burned, my eyes dripped and my lips tingled for more than an hour afterward, it was quite staggering. 'Another?' offered Alex a little later; there were no takers but we were back at his restaurant the next night.

Throughout my time with Benetton I've visited many bars and pubs and restaurants, some good, some bad, a few memorable: I've chinked Singapore Sling glasses in the Long Bar of the Raffles Hotel, and stepped over people at the Mask in Sao Paulo; I've foolishly drunk far too much tequila in Mexico City's Fiesta Americana, and I've eaten the most perfectly prepared chicken wings at New York's Red Blazer Two. I've shared a can of warm beer in Rosie's Bar in Monte Carlo, and sampled some of the finest beers in England at the Falkland Arms in Great Tew, but I have never visited anywhere quite like Going Bananas in Port Douglas. The only near comparison I can draw on would be Rick's Café American in Casablanca, where the enigmatic personality of Bogart's character provided such a magnetic attraction to his bar. However, Alex and Rick are most certainly at opposite ends of the spectrum, I somehow can't envisage Bogey swapping his white jacket and bow tie for a flowered sarong and cutting up jelly snakes for his bemused customers.

In many respects Alex is a unique restaurateur, a real character, yet his idiosyncrasies are all genuine. If I was asked to nominate my personal favourite out of all the places I've visited throughout the world it would unquestionably be his, and should you ever be within a million mile radius of Port Douglas I thoroughly recommend taking a trip to see him. On the night before we flew home we all braved a final searing vodka and Alex gave me a cow's pelvic bone to take back to Chipping Norton. You can't get much fairer than that, can you?

…

With my salary now set at £26,025 per year, the first Grand Prix of 1996 saw us back in Australia again, but this time the venue for the race had shifted from Adelaide to Melbourne. It was also to be the last Grand Prix in which I took part in a race pit-stop. The team had arrived in Australia absolutely exhausted, with several of the mechanics, myself included, suffering from either bronchitis or serious flu, induced by the ludicrous number of hours we had put in over the winter. The work had been relentless, from the moment that we disembarked at Heathrow after our holiday in Queensland to the time we climbed off another 747 and found ourselves back in Australia. The only saving grace of the twenty-four hour flight was that while the plane was airborne it was impossible for us to work on the cars.

We had built the new B196, had then flown out to Sicily in order to publicly launch the new car – and our new drivers, Berger and Alesi – and then flown back to Heathrow, changed planes and flown directly to Estoril to carry out three weeks of intensive testing with the new chassis. Then it was straight back to the factory to rebuild the cars after the test, pack everything into boxes for the fly-away and jump on the next Jumbo bound for Melbourne.

The test team had been called out to help us in Estoril, the idea being that they would sleep during the day and rebuild the cars for us during the night, ready for the following day's testing session, but the system was only partially successful, there was such a large overlap period caused by one crew explaining to the other what work still had to be done that it inevitably meant that both sets of mechanics were working close to sixteen-hour shifts. I spent three days in bed after the Estoril test, forty-eight hours of which I have no waking memory of whatsoever. On the third day I woke, totally wrecked and three kilos lighter, the bed sheets soaked in the sweat of a heavy fever. I made it into work the next day, feeling weak, though guilty for my absence at such a frantic time – only to discover that nearly half the race mechanics were missing, experiencing a similar illness to my own.

No one, from any of the teams, should ever be expected to work like that, yet a solution to the problem doesn't seem difficult to organize. Let's say that $2 million per year would pay for an additional twenty-five men, in wages, accommodation, travelling costs etc. An awful lot of money without a doubt but it doesn't seem such a massive amount when compared to the rest of a team's budget (just remember what everyone was spending on their active cars). Perhaps just throwing more people at the job isn't the perfect solution, but it would certainly make an enormous difference, the whole travelling staff could be alternated: one race on, two races off.

The hours in Melbourne were little better, the only time I left the hotel was to drive to the circuit, I never saw anything of the town whatsoever. We landed at six in the morning, dropped our bags at the hotel, then it was circuit, hotel, circuit, hotel, circuit, hotel until the final drive back to the airport on the Monday afternoon. Another twenty-four-hour flight was followed by just enough time in England to wash our pants before we were on a fourteen-hour trip out to Brazil for round two. Utterly bloody miserable. I felt like curling up in a ball and crying. I had seriously considered resigning before the Melbourne race, feeling that I'd achieved what I had set out to do in Formula One and therefore had little reason to remain any longer, but I knew it would be improper not to stay and defend the crown we had just won. A stupid personal ethic perhaps but that was the only reason I stuck it out.

However, Fate was once again about to play her hand. In Brazil, on the Friday morning of round two of the World Championship, I hurt my back trying to lift the rear of the car during a pre-session pit-stop practice. I felt something give, right in the middle of my lower back. I didn't think too much of it at the time but five minutes later I could hardly move, my back muscles went into spasm and I was crippled with pain. As the morning session was flagged under way and the cars took to the circuit, all I could do was to lie perfectly still on one of our 'packhorse' boxes. I remember thinking that of all the places in the world for something like this to happen it should be Brazil! I could hardly be further from home. The circuit medical staff arrived, gently loaded me onto their roller-stretcher (which was agonizing), then they wheeled me down the pit-lane (which was agonizing and humiliating) and into the medical centre. The doctors prodded me, left me, prodded me again, tried to inject me (no thanks), rolled me over (excruciating), X-rayed me, rolled me over again (ditto), prodded me once more and told me (in broken English) that there was no serious spinal damage, just torn muscle and aggravated nerves. One chap did a little mime for me, which I took to be him wringing the water out of something, I couldn't understand what he was trying to say until a nurse laughed and told me in her best English that I looked completely washed out.

I was wheeled into a small, cool and darkened ward; still clothed I was gingerly helped onto a bed and told to lie still, just relax; their assurance was that once my back muscles had come out of spasm I should be able to get up and walk – albeit with some pretty major discomfort for a while. I was grateful for their help but pleased now just to be left alone. The only light in the room came from small spikes of sunshine stealing through gaps in the blinds, I lay in the gloom listening to the sound of the fan in the air-conditioning unit. The medical centre sits close to the garages, just behind the pit-lane entrance, and through the thickness of the breeze-block walls I could hear the muffled scream of the engines as the cars exited the last corner and thundered down the main straight. The room contained half-a-dozen beds, all covered with starched white sheets. Alongside each stood a tall, polished drip-stand, looking like six regimental guards on parade. Even though I was lying down my feet still ached with fatigue; they had started to complain before the end of the first week of the Estoril test and continued to nag at me now.

If there was a bad accident, this is where the injured would be brought, the operating theatre through the adjoining door could provide everything for any emergency work. Presumably, Professor Watkins, the eminent neurosurgeon who travels with us as the FIA's medical expert, could operate on a severe head injury and fight to save someone's life a mere six feet away from where I lay – either a marshal or a driver hurt on the circuit, or perhaps a mechanic, engulfed by flame, mown down and hit by flying debris in the pit-lane. It was an odd, chilling thought: sport and potential brain surgery. When dormant, medical centres are clean, calm, peaceful havens – that is how they should always be. I felt so tired. The instant noise and rush and mess that is created when a catastrophe happens alters that serenity out of all recognition. I was thankful that the place was perfectly still and quiet now; I closed my eyes and breathed deeply. I listened to the cars in the dark, how strange not to be in the garage watching the timing monitors, preparing another set of springs for the impending set-up change. What happens if I don't know how quick we're going? I folded my arms over my head, covering my ears and listened to myself breathing. Nothing, I just fell asleep. My days with the Benetton race team were over.

...

The nurse woke me about an hour later, asking how I was feeling and telling me that the practice session had finished. 'If you feel able to stand,' she said, 'then the best place for you is back at your hotel, better still go home!'

I walked back to the garage – very gently – each step bringing a fresh jar to my back. I sat on a 'packhorse' drinking strong espresso that Luigi, our Italian chef, had made for me. Greg Field (remember him from my Onyx interview), Benetton's race team co-ordinator asked how I was and on hearing me yelp when he prodded my back he quickly disappeared to try and find me a lift back to the hotel (surely Greg must have known that my back was sore before he squeezed it). As I sat there sipping coffee and feeling sorry for myself, Tony Dodgins walked past the front of the garage; Tony has been around the Formula One pit-lanes for aeons as a journalist who had worked with *Autosport* for years, both as a writer and as its Grand Prix editor. He had recently switched jobs, moving offices within the same building to help set up a new Formula One magazine for Haymarket (*Autosport's* parents) called *F1 Racing*. Before the publication of *Life in the Fast Lane* we had occasionally chatted, but after the book had been released we had discovered a common ground other than just motor-racing and had talked more frequently. Tony saw me sitting on the packhorse, 'Steve,' he exclaimed, with a wry smile, 'what happened to you this morning, what have you done?'

'Hello Tony; I've hurt my back in the pit-stop practice, first thing; I've been down the medical centre for most of the morning. I can hardly walk.' For a second or so Tony looked slightly puzzled by this news,

'No, no,' he corrected, 'I mean what's happened to your cars, they've been storming ahead! What have you changed that's made such a difference?' Typical! There I was injured and in need of a few sympathetic words, and all Dodgins wants to know is how come the bloody cars are so quick all of a sudden! Never let a mechanic's woes get in the way of a good story!

I got a lift back to the hotel with Murray Walker, Jonathan Palmer and one of the BBC production staff, who fortunately happened to be staying at the same place as me. The condition of the Sao Paulo road surfaces leaves a lot to be desired at the best of times but, suffering as I was, that car ride will always stay with me as being the most painful journey of my life. Not the fault of our driver, by any means; in fact we were chauffeured with the utmost care and caution, but no amount of diligent driving can compensate for half-a-million Brazilian motorists, all keen to get home on the Friday afternoon of a Grand Prix weekend. Scores of condemned trucks with canvas tyres would pitch and slew their way ahead of us, gracefully sliding along, all wheels locked, flitting from one lane to another. Children bolted across the road like newly released greyhounds; enormous potholes, blaring horns, stinking fumes, on and on it went. At one point I noticed a dining table sitting in the road, presumably waiting to be laid for supper, cars braked and swerved to avoid it, causing a melee of squealing tyres and blue smoke behind them, the problem eventually solved when a truck drove straight over it sending a sprawl of matchwood splinters cascading along the road. And all the while, both Jonathan and Murray seemed almost oblivious to these conditions, sitting in the back calmly discussing a TV programme featuring Rowan Atkinson and an account of the years Tim Birkin had spent as one of W.O. Bentley's drivers in the late 1920s.

It was a sight for sore eyes when the Morrumbi Novotel appeared over the crest and we finally turned off the road and into the underground car park. Jonathan dug into his bag and discovered some strong pain killers, 'Here Steve, take two of these,' he said 'and save a couple for the flight home, you'll need them!' Murray took charge of my briefcase and carried it up stairs for me; two simple acts of kindness I won't forget.

My back pain eased slightly overnight and Greg had changed my flight to allow me to leave for England on Saturday evening. The plane landed at Heathrow early on Sunday morning, 31 March, where I was met and chauffeured to Chipping

Norton. I bought a copy of the *Sunday Times* at the airport and was pleased to see that they'd printed another article I'd written in Port Douglas, this time discussing tyre changing, pit-stop procedures and how the quality of the work in the pit-lane affects the result of a race.

On reaching home I hobbled round and eventually managed to light a fire to warm the cottage, and gently lowered myself onto the carpet. Switching on the TV I was just in time to see the mechanics fussing over the cars as they gathered on the grid prior to the start of the Grand Prix I'd just left behind. It was an odd sensation listening to Murray and Jonathan talking about the impending race from their commentary box, they seemed a million miles away from me now, another world. It was as if our recent car ride together could never have happened, that the memory of it was merely a snippet of colour from an otherwise forgotten dream. It was pouring with rain in Sao Paulo, rivers of water ran across the track, drivers sheltered in cars, mechanics hid beneath anoraks and hoods (and all looked totally pissed off). Despite my present discomfort I was so relieved not to be there. I eased a little more wood onto the fire and settled back to watch the race on the telly.

...

The team was staying in South America after the Brazilian race since the next Grand Prix in Buenos Aires, was only seven days later. It was another frantic time for everyone. Clean, wrap and load everything into the 'packhorses', fly down to Argentina, unload, set the garage up, rebuild the cars, and get everything ready to run for the following Friday morning. Push, push, push.

With the team out of England I stayed at home resting; it was pointless to go to the factory since there would be nothing to do. I'd been to see a back injury specialist in Oxford – at the sports injury clinic in Headington – and he'd confirmed the Brazilian doctor's findings: no permanent damage, which was very welcome news. Over the next week I gently stretched and worked my muscles and bit by bit the stiffness subsided. Eventually I felt as strong as before, though I knew it would be foolish and/or impossible to try and lift the car in a pit-stop again (and to be honest I had no desire to do so either).

It was time to go, I knew that for sure now, and I took my back injury to be a gentle reminder not to change my mind. The question was: go where? This had been a big enough problem when I was working with Ferrari; then the only way forward had been to break into Formula One – and then to try to win the World Championship – but with both of those ambitions fulfilled, where to now? There was no great rush, and whatever I decided to try, I wouldn't leave Benetton until the end of the season, by which time the new World Champions would have won their crown.

A total change of direction. I liked the idea of writing for a living, but was it possible to earn a living from writing? Well, people do, of course; a few established authors make millions from their books, the problem was that I wasn't established, nor had I written a series of celebrated novels (nice idea, though). So far I'd written one book and two articles; okay, all three had been published (which was jolly good) but they didn't provide a living wage. The journalists who cover Formula One presumably must make a living out of their writing; perhaps I should talk to a few of them and make a few tentative enquiries.

What to write about, that was the next question. Grand Prix racing is something I know a little about but to try and compete with the scores of Formula One journos would be silly. There are more than enough people trying to make a living by reporting the races and interviewing drivers and team owners without my trying to take work away from them. There was plenty of food for thought and I'd have to mull things over. I liked writing, I could see the possibility, I just needed inspiration. That inspiration came halfway through watching the next race on TV. I began scribbling and before I knew I had the basis for another article...

...

On lap twenty-nine of the 1996 Argentine Grand Prix, car number 10, the Ligier of Pedro Diniz, screamed out of the pit-lane after being serviced by the team's race mechanics. On lap thirty the car began spraying its replenished cargo of volatile fuel out of the onboard valve which had failed to seal after the fuel-rig nozzle had been disengaged during the pit-stop. The gushing fuel drenched the rear tyres, removing the car's grip and causing it to spin out of control. A split second later the fuel discovered the intense heat of the exhaust system and the carbon brake discs, the resulting explosion of fire engulfed the Ligier, its driver lost from view when the car finally came to rest in the gravel trap. Thankfully, Diniz wasted no time in evacuating, and with his helmet and gloves still ablaze he sprinted to safety, leaving the fire marshals to their work. The world had just witnessed another terrifying accident, but I'm sure all the Formula One mechanics breathed a huge sigh of relief at its conclusion – there was only one casualty, Diniz, and he had escaped with only minor burns. Grand Prix racing had, once again, been very, very lucky.

What would have been the result if fuel had flooded out as the car sped down the pit-lane? What would have happened if the Ligier had lost grip as it passed another pit, slewing into the mechanics trying to refuel their own car? What would have been the outcome if the burning car, sliding on its own fuel and now quite out of control, had slammed into one of the garages, hitting the personnel inside and spraying the injured mechanics with burning fuel. How many severe injuries would there have been then? How many dead?

Every year since the unnecessary act of mid-race refuelling managed to worm its way back into the regulations we have seen a major accident caused as a direct result of it. Less than eight months before the Ligier accident a similar incident happened to Jordan during the 1995 Belgian Grand Prix when Irvine's car burst into flame during a pit-stop, caused by fuel blowing back from the valve before it had sealed. I saw the resulting fireball burst into the air as we refuelled Schumacher's Benetton further up the pit-lane. I remember holding the rear of the B195 as steady as was possible on the jack, so as not to disturb the refuelling process, but after witnessing the Jordan fire, and feeling my legs burning with the searing heat of the revving engine's exhaust gases, I'll freely admit to being both scared and very sad. I had been amongst the victims of the most documented fire since the reintroduction of this idiocy, when Verstappen's B194 had exploded in Hockenheim. After pulling my smouldering overalls off, and seeing six of my team-mates being flown to hospital by helicopter, I genuinely thought (obviously naively) that this would be the end of the matter. It wasn't, of course. In Hungary, the very next race, with media attention firmly focused on Benetton's alleged responsibility for the fire, Intertechnique – the fuel rig manufacturers – carried out modifications to all of the nozzles that had been issued to the Formula One teams and the FIA informed the press that the practice of mid-race refuelling would continue.

On the grounds of safety, the regulation which allows for refuelling had previously been banned ten years before and it should never have been pulled back out of Pandora's box. However, now that it has been, we should move to ensure its swift entrapment again, this time once and for all. The regulations could be altered tomorrow morning in time to banish it for the start of the 1997 season. I know of not one team who is in favour of its retention; Ferrari initially warmed to the idea due to the high thirst of their V12 engines but they too have now rejected any further interest. It is not an impossible task, all it takes is the right people to be brave, to stand tall and proudly say 'No'. And best to do it now before it's too late.

. . .

After the Argentine race, when everyone had returned to England, I called Tony Dodgins to see if I could meet him for a beer and to chat about his job as a writer. He proved to be a real star and we met soon afterwards at the Compleat Angler, a rather grand old hotel-restaurant on the banks of the Thames in Marlow. The quaint spelling of the hotel's name, borrowed from Izaak Walton's book: *The Compleat Angler or the Contemplative Man's Recreation*, which was first published in 1653 (presumably the hotel thought the full title was just a tad too long to roll off the tongue every time the phone rang). Tony also introduced me to Mike Heard, the then editor of *F1 Racing*. It was a very worthwhile evening (for me at least); they explained a little of their work, they liked the article I'd written and were quite happy to help me if and when I left Benetton. They were both incredibly supportive and our meeting really perked me up.

The next day I reworked my rough notes and showed a version of my refuelling article to our marketing manager, saying that *F1 Racing* was interested in using the finished piece in a future edition of the magazine. I told him that I'd just like him to approve what I'd written before anything was published – something I had done with everything I had written in the past. He read it and refused permission. I asked why. He said he didn't want Benetton to get into any more conflict with the FIA, that the piece was definitely a strongly worded anti-refuelling piece and that publication of such an article would reflect poorly on the team. I said it was strongly worded because it was an issue I felt strongly about (bursting into flames does that sort of thing for you). 'No,' he said. A stand off. I backed down and agreed to leave it at that, we parted amicably enough but underneath I was seething. All the trouble and conflict that Benetton had gone through with the FIA in order to prove our innocence in connection with the Hockenheim fire, and now the management wouldn't allow me to comment on the very aspect of the sport which had given us so much unnecessary pain.

I had no personal disagreement with the marketing manager and given his role within the company I could understand his decision, that of keeping the waters as calm as possible, but it was an opinion I could never agree with. However, our conversation was constructive in so much as it clearly defined the decision I now faced. If I wanted the freedom to write what I considered to be just and to be able to speak my own mind, then I had to leave Benetton, otherwise I would be in danger of compromising my own integrity and be capable of writing nothing more than a series of sanitized press releases. I felt like walking off there and then, but I had to be realistic, I simply couldn't afford to do that. I needed to think things out, and it was definitely time to formulate a plan of escape.

Chapter ten

1997

*Shooting stars…A tactical withdrawal…A test
of endurance…Ross Brawn and Rory Byrne
join Ferrari…Patrizia Spinelli leaves…Berger and Alesi
out, Wurz and Fisichella in…A rainy night in
Monza…Breakfast with Dirk Bogarde*

Benetton's brilliant run of success proved very short-lived; we were but a shooting star in the Formula One heavens: a bright and colourful display, destined to shine briefly then cough, splutter and fizzle out. Whoosh-whiz-bang-clonk. After winning eight races and the Drivers' Championship in 1994, eleven Grands Prix and both World Championships in 1995, we finished the 1996 season without so much as a single race victory, not a sausage – a new experience for me and the first time Benetton had failed to win at least one Grand Prix a year since 1988. Regardless of how it was dressed up – a rebuild year, a new start, a season of reassessment – call it what you will, 1996 could only be viewed as a total disaster. All that we had worked for, all that we had slowly built up over the previous years, was all gone in a matter of a few months. Eight races and one Championship. Eleven races and two Championships. No races and no Championships. It was dismal and it didn't bode at all well.

Once my back had healed I stopped working with the race team and swapped roles with one of the test team mechanics, and I was more than happy to do so. I'd tired of a life constantly pounding the globe; five o'clock alarm calls, a twenty-four-hour flight here, a fifteen-hour-flight there; quick! change chassis;

push, push, bloody push all the damn time. Enough! Let some other poor sod have a go in the trenches.

Testing work can be tedious and the hours at the circuit can be much longer than when actually racing the cars, but the pressure is less intense and the atmosphere is infinitely more relaxed; more constant plod than constant push. At one time the tests used to be fairly infrequent – one a month, sometimes less – but as with every other aspect of the sport (every other business), demand always increases and now there is usually a test immediately following every Grand Prix: race, test, race, test, all season long. If the test was out of England – normally Monza, Barcelona, Jerez, Magny Cours – we would fly out on the Sunday afternoon, about five-ish, which was far more sociable than five in the morning, and depending on what we were testing (and on track availability), we would normally fly home again on the following Thursday or Friday morning.

As far as the mechanics are concerned, the biggest frustration with testing is the increased hours it offers the engineers to run the car on the track. At a Grand Prix, the times when the cars are allowed onto the circuit are rigorously controlled: practice, qualifying, warm-up, race; that's it, not a single second longer. But at a test the cars can run as soon as the circuit opens for business: nine-thirty or ten in the morning and they can continue to run non-stop until the circuit closes in the evening. Good old Silverstone is one of the few circuits which insists on closing for an hour's lunch break, most others are more than happy to let the teams keep running (which is jolly team-spirited and unselfish of them). Then there is the dreaded 'extension'. If one of the teams needs to do a teeny-weeny bit more running at the end of the day – because ten solid hours of banging half a million laps in just hasn't been enough for the engineers to get themselves organized – the test team manager will approach the circuit officials and plead to be allowed just half an hour longer, please! Silverstone is the only circuit I know of where the answer to this question is always an emphatic 'No!'; everywhere else will normally say yes and if one team is granted an extension then all the other teams are at liberty to run as well.

Eventually, however, even the sun decides it's had enough and with the track now plunged into darkness the engineers have no choice but to call it a day. Well, as far as actually running the cars on the circuit is concerned that is, but there is still all the rebuild work to do before the day's work is really done. There is exactly the same amount of work to do (often more) on a test car as there is on a race car before it takes to the circuit the following morning: engine change, gearbox rebuild, new brakes, development components etc. etc.; the only difference is that at a Grand Prix the mechanics can start on their job-lists at two in the afternoon, straight after qualifying, but at a test the car doesn't stop running until, well, who knows when? To finish a day's testing and be back at the hotel before midnight is almost unheard of.

This can easily be the case at a Grand Prix as well, of course, but a test is booked to last for much longer than the duration of a race weekend. It is also quite possible for the test to be extended, not just by half an hour, but by an additional day, or two, or three – even a whole week if you're really lucky! There's never any reason to be bored when working in Formula One, there's always something happening to keep you occupied. Carlos Nunes (the hero of the Portuguese Grand Prix), was the chief mechanic at the time I worked with the test team, and I found him a pleasure to work for. We got on well as work-mates, and as my immediate boss I couldn't have wished for better; in our two years together we never had so much as a single cross word.

However, despite the relaxed atmosphere, my *entente cordiale* with Carlos and a little extra money from the company (£27,326), I was still looking for a way out. It soon became apparent that I wasn't the only member of staff who was contemplating a career move either; over the following months many key personnel took stock of the situation and decided that the best course of action was to call it a day. It turned into quite an exodus.

After umpteen years service, Flavio parted from the Benetton family and after spending a few contemplative months in the sun he began looking into a new project, forming his own company and marketing Renault's rebadged (Mecachrome) engines. Super Performance Competition Engineering he called his firm – and although I'm sure Flavio knows what's best for his business, Super Performance Competition Engineering always struck me as being quite unnecessarily long for a company name (I think it has now been reduced to just Supertec Sports).

My favourite memory of Flavio is of sitting next to him at the dinner table in Japan on the Sunday night that Michael won his second Championship. We were celebrating the win in the rather courtly restaurant of the Aida circuit hotel, with more champagne flowing than I'd ever seen before. There were people chasing one another up and down the dining room spraying bottle after bottle over each other; the girls from our press office were dancing on the tables, Jamiroquai's *Space Cowboy* booming from the CD, the girls revelling in the fun of it all, relieved to shirk their responsibilities for a while and forget about team image and having to pander to the needs of the media. While all this was happening Flavio drank and laughed and chatted. 'Steve, I've read your book,' he said turning to me, 'you write good books and you should write more of them, but remember this, remember what I tell you now, you write good books, but you are terrible at ordering champagne. I have never seen anyone worse! Quite terrible!' I took the hint (unsubtle as it was) and went to get him another bottle – kept firmly under lock and key in the manager's special reserve. While everyone else was busy spraying Moet & Chandon around the room, Flav was quietly sipping vintage Krug. You have to hand it to him, he might not understand how to strip and rebuild a Grand

Prix car, but Flavio Briatore has Formula One figured out to complete perfection. Actually, I seem to remember that by the time we left the restaurant, well after three in the morning, we had made such a mess of the restaurant's plush white carpet that Flavio agreed to buy the owner a new one.

Ross Brawn and Rory Byrne were among the others to go, both following Michael Schumacher to Ferrari. Willem Toet – a work-mate of Rory's and the team's other aerodynamics specialist – and Tad Czapski, one of our electronics specialists, had also moved to join Ferrari. Patrizia Spinelli, who had done such an excellent job of publicising and finding new sponsorship for the team in the early days, had gone to work at Prost Grand Prix, joining the former World Champion at his new factory in Paris. John Postlethwaite, who headed the marketing department, also left Benetton to start his own company.

Jean Alesi and Gerhard Berger, the two ex-Ferrari drivers drafted in to replace Schumacher and Herbert for 1996, were both out by the end of 1997 – with only one race win to the pair's credit (Berger winning the '97 Hockenheim Grand Prix). Tthey were replaced by Alex Wurz, Benetton's test driver, and Giancarlo Fisichella, the young Italian who had previously been with Jordan.

From the all-conquering Benetton Formula of 1995, the team had now lost its World Champion driver, the commercial director, the technical director, the chief designer, the chief aerodynamisist, the marketing manager and the PR manager. These people were all replaced, of course, but they certainly weren't the last members of staff to leave, and Benetton Formula was fast becoming a team I no longer recognized. The replacement staff all wore Benetton race shirts at the circuits, but other than sharing the same insignia as me, many of these people remained total strangers. Of course, in any business, people come and go all the time, that is the way of things, but the key changes that Benetton had undergone in such a brief spell were quite unprecedented in the team's history.

I suppose I was also witnessing the end of my own time with the team too, a major era of my life was rapidly drawing to a close and I was acutely aware of feeling the new tide gently lapping at my feet. Times they were a-changing at Benetton. Nearly time to set sail.

…

The penultimate flight of my Benetton career was in September 1997, a trip to Italy for the Monza test. We had booked the circuit for four days, all of which were hot and sunny; too hot, and we had been plagued with vicious mosquitoes every night. The humidity was intense and there was no air, the sweat began to drip at ten in the morning and was still pouring from us twelve hours later; midnight was as hot as midday. September in northern Italy is always unpredictable: beautiful late summer sunshine and gentle breezes or sweltering heat and torrid rain. The weather cycles can change every few days, and over the four days the atmosphere grew progressively thicker and heavier; a storm, a huge storm, was building. I longed for it to break; the fresh air a storm brings would be blissfully welcome. However, the rain held off until the very last day, the initial rumble of thunder arriving about six in the evening, and the first big, ripe drops of water followed an hour later. Then, with the sun lost behind thick, pitch-black clouds, the storm finally got going, before long whipping itself into a violent fury. I found the size and strength of the storm fascinating, and while most people stayed in the garages I preferred to shelter just outside and watch it lash uncontrollably at the pits and the track.

Sheets of rain raced down the pit-lane and main straight as wave after wave of torrential water slapped the tarmac and headed off in pursuit of the one before, showing complete contempt for the chicane in its rage and wildly slamming into the trees as it whirled amongst the them. Vast streaks of stroboscopic lightning arced across the sky, showing up flickering views of the deserted grandstand on the other side of the track; moments later the lightning forks were followed by great explosions of thunder, one chaotic salvo after another, the blasts of noise and light cannoned around the town. It was as if Monza were under siege by some powerful advancing army.

I remember a close friend of my dad's, Ron Tivey, telling me a story many years ago about the time he served in the Monza region during the closing stages of World War Two. The fighting, he said, was terribly fierce, with the retreating German army most reluctant to pull back any further, and when the allies finally gained entry to the town, he described seeing it in almost total ruin, with many of the buildings either completely gone or reduced to burning rubble. On my first visit, in 1990, I noticed that although much of Monza's original architecture had survived – at least in a state to allow it to be rebuilt – many of the buildings did look relatively new. With the ear-splitting noise of battle, the death, the carnage and the suffering of the aftermath, Monza must have been a terrible place to behold in the war.

Every time I've visited Monza I've thought of Ron's experiences there, and although the immense ferocity of the storm I was watching could be nothing in comparison to the noise of war, I felt I could imagine him and his fellow soldiers slowly moving into position around Monza; instead of lightning there would have been tracer bullets; instead of thunder, artillery shells; but the blackness and the sheets of rain, they would be the same. My own memories of time spent in Monza are of winning the Grand Prix there in 1995, an infinitely more pleasant memory, and one which would have been impossible for me to have if it weren't for Ron's bravery and that of hundreds of thousands just like him.

My final flight with the team was the British Airways morning run from Milan to Heathrow, the day after the great storm. It sticks in my mind not merely because it punctuates my career with Benetton, but because of an incident that occurred during the in-flight breakfast. The early morning flights are usually quiet and this one was no exception: just us and a few sharply dressed Italian businessmen on their way to London for the day's round of essential meetings; the girl at the check-in counter had been kind enough to dot us about the Club cabin so that we might have as much space as possible to stretch and relax. We normally travelled Club, simply because it made it easier for the tickets to be changed if the test was extended at the last minute.

On European flights there is little difference between Club and Economy seats, but the one little extra that I do enjoy is the complimentary champagne served with breakfast. The week before we left England I'd bought a copy of Dirk Bogarde's autobiography *A Short Walk from Harrods*. The book had really held me; it also came with the added appeal that much of it describes the years he lived in rural France in the hills of Provence. I was reading the closing pages over my breakfast, a glass of champagne held in one hand, as we soared high above the snow-capped Alps. In these final paragraphs Dirk had been talking about the making of his last film, shot in the south of France, and what a wonderful restorative the work had been in lifting him from his depression. Then he went on to talk of his early-morning flight back to England once the filming was finished, describing how he drank a glass of champagne with his breakfast as the plane cruised over the Alps above Grenoble. He was describing exactly the same time of day and place in the world and describing the very same glass of champagne that I was enjoying at that very moment! It was the first time I'd read his book so I had no idea what was coming and I have to admit that it gave me quite a shock. I wonder what the odds are of such a coincidence? I suppose an even more unlikely occurrence would be if someone found themselves reading the closing paragraphs of this book while drinking a glass of champagne on an early morning flight over the Alps.

I left Benetton at exactly 5:35pm on Friday, 13 February 1998.

Epilogue

Alice remarked thoughtfully: 'and what are "toves"?'

'Well, toves are something like badgers - they're something like lizards – and they're something like corkscrews.'

'They must be very curious-looking creatures.'

'That they are,' said Humpty Dumpty: 'also they make their nests under sun-dials – also they live on cheese.'

'And what's to "gyre" and to "gimble"?'

'To "gyre" is to go round and round like a gyroscope. To "gimble" is to make holes like a gimblet.

'And "the wabe" is the grass-plot round a sundial, I suppose,' said Alice, surprised at her own ingenuity.

'Of course it is. It's called "wabe" you know, because it goes a long way before it, and a long way behind it.'

'And a long way beyond it on each side,' Alice added.

•••

Formula One has been very good to me. I have visited more places, seen more sights and met more fascinating people than I could possibly have dreamed. Travelling with Benetton has taken me to more than twenty countries, including parts of Africa, America, Argentina, Australia, Brazil, Canada, Indonesia, Japan and Mexico. I have dived the waters of the Great Barrier Reef and flown the skies above Ayers Rock. I've driven across San Francisco's Golden Gate Bridge and climbed to the top of New York's Statue of Liberty. I've visited the Salvador Dali Museum in Florida and Salvador Dali's museum in Spain. I've ridden the Bullet train past the natural brilliance of Mount Fuji and through the neon brilliance of Tokyo. I worked with some truly fascinating people, and along the way we won the most coveted engineering trophy in the world. All in all I feel I have been incredibly lucky.

So, a year after setting sail across the channel, do I now regret my decision to leave Benetton and start a new life in France, with the puzzles of a new language, the problems of restoring a wreck of a farm house without any building experience and the nagging question of how to keep the wolf from the door? Not a bit of it; every problem has an answer, you just have to be patient and adaptable – ask Alice.

Index

Index